# The Americanization
# of Religious Minorities

# The Americanization
## of Religious Minorities

*Confronting the Constitutional Order*

Eric Michael Mazur

The Johns Hopkins University Press

BALTIMORE AND LONDON

The Johns Hopkins University Press
2715 North Charles Street
Baltimore, Maryland 21218-4363
www.press.jhu.edu

A catalog record for this book is available
from the British Library.


Library of Congress Cataloging-in-Publication Data
Mazur, Eric Michael.
The Americanization of religious minorities : confronting the
constitutional order / Eric Michael Mazur.
p.  cm.
Includes bibliographical references and index.
ISBN 0-8018-6220-5 (alk. paper)
1. Religious minorities—United States.   2. Religion and law—
United States.   3. Freedom of religion—United States.   4. Church
and state—United States.   I. Title
BL2525.M39   1999
305.6'0973—dc21

99-24616
CIP

*Dedicated to*

## Gussie and Morris Himmel

*and to*

## Bessie and Julius Mazur

*without whose struggles, religious freedom
would mean nothing to me*

# Contents

# Preface

It was in a class at the University of Virginia, taught by one of the great public philosophers, William Lee Miller, that I learned about the fundamental victory that had been won for religious freedom in the debate over the Virginia Declaration of Rights. Article 16, written by George Mason to grant to all "the fullest toleration in the exercise of religion," was amended by James Madison (with the help of Patrick Henry) to make all "equally entitled to the full and free exercise of religion." The distinction, taught Professor Miller, was the difference between granting someone permission to do something while reserving the right to later deny that permission, and recognizing a person's inherent right to do something whether you like it or not.

This was a profound idea, both for one of the handful of colonies that would only a month later declare their independence from Britain and for me, a nineteen-year-old college student who had grown up a Jew in the American South. I wanted to believe Professor Miller and James Madison: I wanted to believe that religious freedom, rather than toleration, was Virginia's greatest gift to the new nation and this nation's greatest gift to the world. But as a fifth-grade student, I had been sent to the library as the only Jewish child in my public school while the rest of the student body gathered to sing Christmas carols. In order to participate in religious observance that occurred on a school day, I had to get permission from—and sometimes incur the wrath of—public school teachers who not only knew nothing about religious traditions other than their own but seemed insulted that I would want to be absent from school on what appeared to them to be an ordinary day. I had to appeal to the student member of the Board of Visitors at the University of Virginia when I learned that the calendar committee had scheduled the coming Parents' Weekend for the same day as Yom Kippur. When she reported to me the response of the faculty chair of that committee ("How were we supposed to know? That holiday is always on a different day. And if we move it for the Jews, we'll have to move it for everyone."), I asked her to remind the faculty member that Yom Kippur was, in fact, always on the same day, the tenth day of Tishrei, and had been observed on that day for longer than the current calendar system had been in existence. Parents' Weekend was moved.

I began reading more about the nature of religious freedom in the United States; that led to graduate work with John Corrigan and Jeffrey Hadden, work that culminated with an analysis of the different definitions of religion used by members of the Supreme Court in First Amendment decisions. I came to realize, as many others have before me, that religious freedom in this country has always been defined against the backdrop of Protestant Christianity, and its expansion has always been determined by the limits to which that dominant culture was willing to go—or in other words, by how much it would tolerate. I read more and more analyses that offered various suggestions about what religious freedom should mean and how the two religion clauses of the First Amendment should be interpreted, but I found little that actually explored the impact of the confrontation between religious minorities and the dominant culture and none (that I was aware of) that compared these experiences in order to gain a better sense of trends and patterns.

In the Department of Religious Studies at the University of California, Santa Barbara, I was able to work with Phillip Hammond and Robert Michaelsen, two scholars of esteem in the area of religion and law. It was with their support, and the support of American religious historian Catherine Albanese, that I was able to explore what the experience of religious freedom litigation had meant empirically to those who had gone through it and what that might mean more generally to the rest of us as Americans proud of our heritage of religious freedom. After all of this work, I do believe that Madison's amendment to Mason's Article 16 represents the gift with the greatest potential to be given by the Commonwealth of Virginia to the United States of America and that the First Amendment represents the gift with the greatest potential to be given by this country to the world. But I also believe it is a promise that, like the messiah, is always coming but never here. We must understand what we have done to others who have faced the dilemma of being religious minorities in this culture so that we can better understand the limits, and the potential, of our hopes for greater religious freedom.

A great many people have contributed to this project, making it impossible to thank them all specifically. I have attempted to give credit in my notes where I recognize their contribution, and I offer general thanks now to those scholars I may have unintentionally omitted later in the text.

However, there are people for whom no notes will appear, who nonetheless deserve mention for their contributions—particularly teachers, friends, acquaintances, and family. It seems traditional to thank family members last, since one assumes that their contribution to the work in hand was the most tangential. Breaking with this tradition, I am compelled to acknowledge the significant contribution of my parents, Rhoda and Marvin Mazur, without whose support (financial, but more importantly, emotional) none of this would have been possible. My sisters and their respective husbands (Jody Mazur and David Banyai, Amy and Michael Feldstein, and Leslie and Randy Needham) provided subtle reassurances that my work was worthwhile and that there existed a world beyond the halls of the library and the chasms of the mind that, although possibly interested in my work as a scholar, was much more interested in my being as a human. Most appreciated of those least concerned with my work are my nieces and nephews—Gabriel, Emma Kate, Jesse, and Dana Rae—who, without knowing (or caring), supplied decoration to my offices and provided me with a sense of reality and joy in those moments of greatest frustration. I consider myself fortunate to have been able to share simple joys with them. Special thanks should also be given to William S. Mandel, friend, critic, scholar, and sounding board, who, like a big brother, corrected my mistaken notions about constitutional law, criticized my philosophizing about religion, listened and debated with me on issues where the two areas met, and guided me through the graduate experience and much of life. Also instrumental in all of this were the people and groups who have provided encouragement and support along the way through conversations and diversions: Lisle Dalton, Julie Ingersoll, Tara and Dwight Koda, Kathryn McClymond, Oren Stier, Jon Stone, Brian and Cybelle Wilson, Roy and Colleen Zyla, the Seminar on Applied Probability, the Santa Barbara Port and Cigar Club, the regular guests at Chez Maze, the "Meal Fairies," and all of my friends and colleagues in the Department of Religious Studies at the University of California, Santa Barbara.

As for more formal assistance, thanks goes to my dissertation committee, Phillip E. Hammond (Chair), Catherine L. Albanese, and Richard D. Hecht, who provided me with an environment to explore my own ideas and guidance to focus those ideas in a scholarly fashion. A special debt is owed to Phillip Hammond, whose contribution as an admired mentor, a valued teacher, and a most trusted friend serves as a debt passed on to me, one that I can best repay by serving future scholars with the same esteem, trust, and support that it has been my privilege to share with him. I also gratefully acknowledge the assistance of Robert S. Michaelsen, who provided much appreciated advice, encouragement, and guidance on some of the later research. Several others also helped with the research, and although I did not become personally familiar with all of them, their assistance was greatly appreciated, particularly the staffs at the Library of Congress; the Davidson Library at the University of California, Santa Barbara; the Meriam Library at California State University, Chico; and the Ventura County Law Library.

Early versions of three chapters were presented to various academic professional association meetings and colloquia, and an attempt has been made to incorporate the comments, criticisms, and suggestions from participants, fellow panelists, and members of the audience. Particularly, I would like to thank Larry Cameron, Tracy Mitrano, Marianne Perciaccante, James Richardson, Inés Talamantez, Gabrielle Tayac, Mitchell Tyner, and the participants in the American Religions Group at UCSB for assisting me in clarifying my ideas. In addition, in part because of the exposure the material had at the various meetings, earlier versions of two of the following chapters have appeared in print. A version of chapter 1 was published as "Constitutional Authority and Prospects for Social Justice for High-Tension Religious Communities" in *Social Justice Research* 9, no. 3 (1996): 259–80, and a version of chapter 4 was published as "'The Supreme Law of the Land': Sources of Conflict between Native Americans and the Constitutional Order," in *American Indian Studies: An Interdisciplinary Approach to Contemporary Issues,* edited by Dane Morrison (Baltimore: Peter Lang Publishing, 1997). My thanks to Heidi Burns, Dane Morrison, and James Richardson (again), for their assistance with those endeavors.

Several institutions provided a safe haven by supplying both employment and intellectual stimulation. The Department of Religious Studies at the University of California, Santa Barbara, graciously gave me an opportunity to teach a summer school course on religion and law, a topic that intersected beautifully with a large segment of my dissertation research. The fine people in the Department of Religious Studies at California State University, Chico (particularly Bruce Grelle, Kate McCarthy, Sarah Pike, and Joel Zimbelman), shared with me ideas about my project specifically, or the relationship between religion, law, and culture more generally, and helped me understand more clearly the model of the teacher-scholar. My new colleagues in the Department of Religion at Bucknell University must also be thanked—their invitation to me to join their ranks provided the impetus to complete this work in a timely manner. For this fact alone I am forever in their debt.

Thanks must rightfully be expressed to those who helped feed the body while others fed the mind during the creation and development of this project. Generous support was received from the Interdisciplinary Humanities Center and from the Graduate Division, both at the University of California, Santa Barbara; as a result

I was able to work steadily for a year without prolonged interruption, and for that I am sincerely grateful.

Lastly, I owe a great deal of thanks to Henry Tom at the Johns Hopkins University Press, who saw promise in this work when it was only a proposal and a conference presentation and encouraged me along the process from dissertation to published manuscript, and to Lois Crum, who helped me clarify my writing.

Although none of those listed above bears any responsibility for errors that remain in the following work, they have all left their impression on me and my thinking, and this work is but a meager thanks for the precious gift of support they have provided me.

# Introduction

*Antigone:* You may do as you like, since
apparently the laws of the gods mean nothing
to you.
*Ismene:* They mean a great deal to me; but I
have no strength to break laws that were
made of the public good.

SOPHOCLES, *Antigone*

None of the facts presented here are newly revealed, and for the historians of the respective traditions much of the history I recount will appear both repetitive and possibly too simply stated. The value of the analysis does not lie in what it reveals about the particular constitutional litigation histories of the various religious communities considered, but rather in the pattern that emerges from the experiences these minority religious communities had when they encountered the authority of the dominant religious culture expressed through the instrumentalities of government. As citizens of a nation proud of its history of religious freedom, it serves us well to examine the extent to which that freedom has been tested and the limits to which it has subsequently been extended. It has long been accepted that no freedom is absolute, but we do not often examine the implicit boundaries set on religious freedom or think about the ramifications for religious communities that—for any number of reasons—do not consider themselves, or are not considered by others, to be part of the mainstream. Part of the value of this analysis rests in its exploration of how minority religious communities balance the desire to join the dominant culture, on the one hand, with the sometimes conflicting desire to maintain a particularistic community identity, on the other.

Before exploring this dilemma, let me be clear about my understanding and use of certain terms. I am not engaging in traditional legal analysis, and no such claim is made herein. Legal interpretations and the implications of the various decisions cited throughout the study are derived from analyses by those better qualified to provide them; my project is simply to interpret those analyses in light of their symbolic impact on cultural dominance and religious hegemony.

Indeed, it will become obvious that I use the categories of law, government, and authority as the symbols of interaction between competing religious communities. For example, in a response to an article about Mormon interaction with the U.S. government, Carol Weisbrod notes that it is best understood not as an encounter of a particular religious community with a disembodied polity, but rather as the competition between two religious communities acted out in the arena of the law. She suggests that by viewing the conflict in that way, one would have a more useful analytic lens through which to interpret the power of the conflict. Such a view would represent the Mormons not as outlaws against the state, but as a religious minority searching for "a rule broad enough to allow their particular institutions." It would also represent the dominant Protestant culture as a competing group that simply "wanted a rule making their institutions universal, with no exemptions allowed."[1] The confrontation can be seen less as a matter of alleged Mormon illegal behavior than as a result of competition between the Mormons and the mainstream Protestant Christian culture.

Remove the specific reference to the Mormons and replace it with any nonmainstream religious community in the United States, and you have encapsulated the debate explored in this work. In each of the communities examined, some particular behavioral distinction has worked in the same way that plural marriage did for the Mormons. Whatever actions have differentiated a minority religious community from the mainstream have served as the focal points of disputes that are not simply between the government and that community, but between that community and the mainstream Protestant culture that the government represents. One effort of the following analysis is to explore just whose interests are represented by the term *state* in the construction *church-state;* it has become common to overlook the fact that in a representative democracy the state purports to represent a majority of the people. Does it not make sense that, regardless of the language of the First Amendment religion clauses, it should also retain the religious sensibilities of that majority? If this is the case, then Weisbrod (and others) are correct, and we must investigate "church-state" disputes as conflicts between religious traditions, not simply as conflicts between one religious community and an allegedly neutral state.

In a democracy such as ours, it seems naive to suggest that with the adoption of the First Amendment, all religious presuppositions would be removed from the men (and eventually, women) elected or appointed to administer it; the battle over religious meaning continues in nearly every election over nearly every issue. As Marc Galanter has noted about India—but his statement is well applied to all democracies that promise government neutrality in matters of religion—"the State defines the boundaries within which neutrality must operate."[2] In America "the State" is made up of people with specific religious tendencies—the historically dominant one Protestant Christianity—and those outside that tradition or even on the edges have been at a severe cultural and political disadvantage in the contest over meaning in the American polity, regardless of the language of the First Amendment.

This use of law as the arena of cultural competition is not a new one, nor is its analysis. In his examination of the debates surrounding Prohibition, Joseph Gusfield suggested that this significant issue was not just a public policy debate but also an important power struggle over symbols waged by middle-class, native-born, conservative Protestants and immigrant, working-class Catholics and Lutherans. Gusfield concluded that the actions of the government in the debate (and enactment) of the Prohibition statutes could best be understood as "ceremonial and ritual performances, designating the content of public morality." Laws concerning the use of alcohol were not expressions of universal morality; they were merely expressions of different cultural ideals expressed through the political framework. The debate was one of "normative dominance, not of instrumental social control":[3] rather than simply desiring to reduce drinking per se, the conservative Protestants wanted to make the Catholics and the Lutherans act like conservative Protestants. Given such an interpretation, it is significant that the dispute resulted in the passage—and then the repeal—of Prohibition. Conservative Protestants were initially successful but ultimately ineffective against the changing power dynamic in American religious and social demographics. In like fashion, the following analysis focuses on minority religious communities' struggles to negotiate between their own sensibilities and those expected of them by the general Protestant dominant culture. This method of interpretation is vital when one examines any legal expression of religious ideals.

To assume that the backdrop is simply basic Protestantism, however, is to ignore the evolution of American constitutionalism. Although there are historic connections—and some have argued persuasively that constitutionalism would not be possible without Protestantism—over the last century and a half the form and content of American identity have changed with increasing speed. By the end of the nineteenth century, processes begun in the early Republic had resulted in significant cultural shifts that have continued through the present age. Political identity in "American" culture, once closely tied to Protestantism (particularly evangelical Protestantism), has now taken a form of its own and can no longer be assumed to parallel that one religious tradition. Historically the effects of Protestantism on the culture have been great, and reverberations continue to be felt, but with shifts within American Protestantism, the growth of non-Protestant communities in America, and more importantly, the increasing willingness of the non-Protestant communities to express themselves politically, the political hegemony of evangelical Protestantism has significantly diminished.

The vacuum created by the waning of this one religious tradition has not been filled by another single denomination, but has instead been occupied by the very institution designed to integrate the emerging pluralism required by the First Amendment: American constitutionalism. Although Thomas Jefferson's prediction that every American would become a Unitarian a generation after the adoption of the Bill of Rights was no doubt based on his own religious sensibilities, there is embedded in his statement the notion that, eventually, all constituents would approach the American polity as equals, with theological differences playing a distinctly diminished role in the operation of the federal government. James Madison expressed the same idea in a slightly different way when he noted in *The Federalist* that a free government depends on a "multiplicity of interests" and a "multiplicity of sects," each in competition and each able to minimize the accumulation of power by the other.[4] Over time, with the shifts in political dominance experienced by evangelical Protestantism, the federal government has in fact emerged as less interested in endorsing strictly Protestant ideals and goals and more concerned with clearly articulating its own interests and goals. That which is identified in this study as the American constitutional order represents the combination of bureaucratic and transcendent notions about the American polity: an entity that may have been, in early colonial times, a Protestant mission sanctioned by God but which has shifted its allegiance from the God of the Protestants and now seeks a god of the American people.

Although this discussion often leads to the notion of civil religion, it is probably in our best interest to avoid that debate altogether. Often used as a symbol of democratic unity, in its historical context the concept of civil religion actually suggests nondemocratic tendencies that would probably be uncomfortable for most contemporary Americans. One of the classical references for the term *civil religion*, Jean-Jacques Rousseau's *Social Contract*, addressed the notion of creating—even coercing—unity, and asked by what authority a majority can expect a minority to bend to its wishes. "[H]ow, unless the election [of a leader, for example] were unanimous, could there be any obligation on the minority to accept the decision of the majority? What right have the hundred who want to have a master to vote on behalf of the ten who do not?"[5] Rousseau answered the question by implying that at some mythic point of origin in the life of the polity, there must have been unanimity on the issue of authority, even if it manifested itself as a simple political agreement on the basic principle of majority rule. So important was this moment of primal unity to Rousseau that he suggested that communities joining the polity after such an agreement was made must themselves either consent to live by it or be forever considered noncitizens.

That might be exactly what majorities often assume to be the case, but it never occurs in reality. Rarely is consent so freely given, and quite often it is coerced. Although physical confrontation is not inevitable, it is frequently resorted to, and often only after some form of violence (either realized or threatened, physical or political) does a minority religious community succumb to the demands of the majority. In the case of a religious minority, where the stakes are ultimate, not merely temporal, the necessity to choose between agreeing to join the majority or remaining noncitizens is an extraordinary dilemma, particularly for those religious communities that believe their claim on American ideals is as valid as the dominant culture's, if not more so. The identification of Protestant Christianity with American culture historically has thus meant that minority communities have had to choose between succumbing to vaguely Protestant modes of expression or, to use Rousseau's formula, being forever considered noncitizens. My analysis explores the ways some minority religious communities have approached that dilemma.

Since the issue is often expressed in terms of political as well as cultural and religious dominance, we must turn to the political arena of contested constitutional meaning to better understand the confrontation between American religious minorities and the dominant culture. But just as the "state" reflects the interests of its constituents, so too the "law" provides the medium in which that reflection takes place. As Winnifred Sullivan has written in her analysis of religious rhetoric used in Supreme Court decisions, law is one of the specialized realms in which a society can discuss and enact ideas it considers to be important. In so doing, legislators writing the law and jurists interpreting it "participate in an intensely practical and multilayered discourse about what society should be like."[6]

It is a grave error, therefore, to assume that the areas of law and religion are naturally distinct and mutually exclusive. There is no doubt that in society they serve very different purposes, but we must be sensitive to how they serve society in parallel ways, and even how they are interdependent. As Sullivan notes, they are both "structurally related and they construct each other." Legal historian Harold Berman went further, suggesting that they are similar in that they both rely on ritual, tradition, authority, and universality to maintain their central role in society. Both law and religion have the ability to affect even the ways in which people see themselves and the world around them. According to Berman, "[a] society's beliefs in an ultimate transcendent purpose will certainly be manifested in its processes of social ordering, and its processes of social ordering will likewise be manifested in its sense of an ultimate purpose."[7]

Such a relationship between religion, law, and society can also be seen in the work of anthropologist Clifford Geertz, whose definition of religion could just as easily be used to define how law functions symbolically within society. Religion is "[a] system of symbols which acts to establish powerful, pervasive, and long-lasting moods and motivations in men by formulating conceptions of a general order of existence and clothing these conceptions with such an aura of factuality that the moods and motivations seem uniquely realistic." In the American context (and no doubt, in many other legal cultures) we could replace the word "religion" in Geertz's definition with the word "law" because of the strong parallels between religion and law in our society. Indeed, as Phillip Hammond has noted, in public rhetoric and interpretation the operation of the two spheres of society have completely overlapped; he argues that the courts are in fact working in the realm of the sacred.[8]

Sociologists of religion as well as legal theorists recognize that both religion and law, at their most powerful, function best when they are least questioned—when they can "establish moods and motivations . . . with such an aura of factuality that the moods and motivations seem uniquely realistic." It is when this process fails that conflict results. According to Sullivan, the inability of law (or, as we are now suggesting, the inability of the religious presuppositions behind that law) to communicate common cultural meaning can result in its "doing violence to the people and situations for whom and in which it practices and can contribute to contempt for the law."[9] Given the embedded nature of cultural presuppositions in the American legal system, it is no surprise that, on one hand, the dominant culture, so able to live freely under legal protections, can understand neither the claims of persecution made by religious minorities nor why they do not simply join the majority at the outset. On the other hand, religious minorities, unable to find themselves reflected in the cultural presuppositions of the legal system, can neither simply accept the system as it is nor live freely denying its applicability. In the system's hidden cultural assumptions lie the roots of the dilemma faced by religious minorities in the American constitutional order.

This study was motivated by a simple observation: the encounter between certain religious communities and the various branches of the federal government (most notably the Supreme Court) could best be described as confrontational. A cursory glance at Supreme Court litigation involving First Amendment claims (an easy marker of conflict with the constitutional order) indicates that certain religious communities have been engaged in confrontation with the government for very specific periods of American history. The greatest period of confrontation involving the Church of Jesus Christ of Latter-day Saints (the Mormons) lasted roughly from the 1850s until the late 1890s, whereas cases involving members of the Watchtower Bible and Tract Society (Jehovah's Witnesses) ran from the early 1930s until the 1950s. But there seems to be no similarly distinct periodization for confrontations involving Native Americans and the federal government. This periodization (or its absence) raises simple questions: why is it that certain groups engage in confrontation at distinct periods and then seemingly disappear with regard to religious disputes? And what is it about these groups that makes them different from those groups that never face serious, sustained periods of litigation or those that do so but in continuous, prolonged, and seemingly unending ways?

There are operational factors that must be recognized to provide at least some of the answers. The legal doctrine of *stare decisis et non quieta movere* (stand by past a decision and do not disturb things at rest) suggests that the expansion of rights, through the use of precedent, decreases the likelihood of a religious community's arguing for the same right twice, or of other groups litigating the same right. For example, there is no doubt that rights won by Jehovah's Witnesses have served other religious communities also, just as there is no doubt that rulings limiting the Utah Mormon community have been applied to other communities. Those communities may have won or lost in lower courts and simply never appeared on a more broadly focused radar screen. In addition, factors such as available resources (time, money, professionally trained personnel), group size, and particularly the arena in which the encounter takes place play a large part in the interpretation of the conflicts. Small groups without financial means may have much to say about their interactions with the constitutional order, but who would know?

Even with these operational factors in mind, it is worthwhile to pursue answers to these questions beyond simple operational bounds. Precedent is an important consideration, but since the Supreme Court is more likely to rule narrowly than broadly, it is unlikely that all issues of religious import have been addressed. The other two branches of the federal government have never felt limited by pressure not to repeat an issue if there was some political value in it. And because religious communities with the means to lobby or litigate will often (even unintentionally) represent interests of those without means, there is much to be gained in exploring the events related to different kinds of encounters of various communities with the constitutional order. Finally, a focus on encounters with the highest levels of the federal government (primarily the Supreme Court, Congress, and the White House) is justified not only because these institutions have a national jurisdiction, but because—with such an all-encompassing scope—the constructions and conceptions articulated by these institutions have a greater, more symbolic effect on national identity. Since one of the questions I will ask addresses the nature of religious inclusion in American society, it is important to maintain as wide a focus as possible.

As already stated, the symbolic level of meaning is my destination. This is not to dismiss the operational considerations from a study such as this one, but rather to recognize that, through actions and words, meaning can be found beyond the level of mere legal function. Since I am interested in how religious communities resolve conflicts over issues of cultural dominance, I examine how it is they approach, address, and (usually) resolve the dilemma of cultural encounter. And since, ultimately, my discussion pits federal against minority religious symbols and meanings, I focus on the leadership decisions of the federal and religious institutions rather than on the rank-and-file membership. This may seem to privilege one set of voices over another—and to be sure, it does—but the question I seek to answer concerns competing institutional authorities, the confrontations of social institutions. I am interested in how the institutions that represent believers negotiate conflicts over authority with the institutions that represent citizens, in the ordeal experienced by minority religious communities struggling to be true to their religious ideals while confronting often overwhelming forces of Americanization. How the rank and file resolve individual dilemmas of authority is the topic of a different study.

The dilemma can be simply restated. In a culture historically dominated by one broad (if general) religious tradition, religious communities not part of the mainstream have faced a difficult choice: maintain an identity based on particularistic notions of authority, or accept the sources of authority advanced by the dominant culture. In America, where these sources were derived from Protestant Christianity, this has meant a particular challenge to non-Protestant minority religious communities. They have often had their behaviors, beliefs, and symbols condemned, modified, or ignored by the dominant culture, which could not accept deviance. The history of religious persecution, physical as well as legal, in the colonial and early Republican periods provides ample evidence of this conflict.

In the case of religious liberty issues, believers and the institutions to which they belong must subordinate their distinct theological beliefs to the transcending principles of the majority articulated by the constitutional order, or they are forced to do so by the physical powers of the government. It is as if the particular religious community is expected to announce, "Our God tells us to do X, but we will do Y if you tell us to." Actually, given the nature of the conflicting authorities, religious communities may even rationalize their behavior in the following way: "God told us to do X, but now He has told us to do Y through His instrument, the federal government." Either expression represents a shift from the sole and ultimate authority of the community's particularistic theological realm to one of deference to the authority of the constitutional realm.

The situation has not necessarily improved with the wane of Protestant cultural hegemony. As the federal government has moved further from a specifically Protestant identity and has become increasingly pluralistic, acceptance of the notion of pluralism has become the price of admission to the mainstream; in other words, in the modern pluralistic society, religious communities agree to disagree, with civility and within the law. In that sense religious claims have diminished in their ability to command adherence from nonbelievers in direct proportion to the growth of belief in the individual right to express oneself. The government, once imbued with specific Protestant meanings and symbols, now expects all religious traditions to accept the state as the ultimate authority in society.

The power of this process is extraordinary. The very act of agreeing to submit religious practices to judicial scrutiny indicates a willingness to accept state authority over theologically mandated practices. Although some religious traditions are brought into the legal system unwillingly as defendants in a suit, the fact that they participate at all justifies the court's authority; those who truly reject the transcending authority of the legal structures would not even grace the court with their presence. There are examples of this strategy of refuting—or even ignoring—the judicial system in American religious history, and I will explore them briefly in my concluding discussion. My primary focus, however, is on the strategies through which minority religious communities do encounter the American constitutional order, and the first question I ponder is how a governmental complex can develop into an entity competing with religious communities over transcendent meaning and authority.

# The Americanization
# of Religious Minorities

# 1

# American Religions and the Authority of Law

Teach the [Constitution's] principles, teach
them to your children, speak of them when
sitting in your home, speak of them when
walking by the way, when lying down and when
rising up, write them upon the doorplate of your
home and upon your gates.

JOHN QUINCY ADAMS
from Deuteronomy 6:7–9

What is the relationship between religion and the authority of the
American legal system?

Several years ago, the city of Hialeah, Florida, found itself involved in a religious war. This conflict, known by some as the
Chicken War, was being waged over blood and land, and it was carried from the Miami suburb to the nation's highest courts. To hear
it from one side of the dispute, it pitted "the sensibilities of animal
lovers against a fringe order of poultricidal zealots."[1] On one side
of the battle were members of a Santeria community that wished
to bring its religious tradition into the public square of American
religious pluralism while at the same time protecting the integrity
and sanctity of its religious rituals; on the other side were members of the community at large who were attempting to protect the
integrity and sanctity of their neighborhoods by prohibiting the

seemingly dangerous Santerian rituals. In the resulting dispute the members of the Santerian community, encountering the powers at play in a democracy, had to choose between following the dictates of their gods and consciences on the one hand and the demands of their city and neighbors on the other, between being proper adherents and being proper citizens.

The city council of Hialeah, in an effort to restrict the practice of animal sacrifice, passed a series of ordinances that had the effect of prohibiting specifically Santerian ritual animal sacrifices. The city insisted that it was merely protecting the best interests of the entire community by restricting behavior that was deemed cruel to animals and dangerous to the public health and that posed a potential threat to minors; city officials maintained that "their law [was] not aimed at the Santeria faith." Responding to "widespread complaints that a local church was encouraging a 'regress into paganism'" and a growing concern over the number of carcasses littering Hialeah streets, the city council banned all animal sacrifice.[2] According to the district court record, the council was quite clear when it passed the ordinances; it was concerned with public health, animal cruelty, and the possible psychological ill effects on children who might witness animal sacrifice. However, as one Supreme Court watcher noted, "It was apparent that the city's real concern was the religious ritual itself, and not these other legitimate considerations." He expressed the hope that "the court would be able to get past the admittedly bizarre practice that's at issue in this case to the real principle that's at stake."[3]

But as another Supreme Court watcher noted, "The American public has a hard time seeing beyond the dead chickens." "[I]f their religion demands sacrifice," said Salvatore D'Angelo, city council president, "they're going to have to adjust for the 21st century." In fact, in one amicus brief filed in this case by a coalition of religious communities, the authors were careful to distance themselves from the practices of Santeria even while they advocated the rejection of the city's restrictions. "None of the *amici* espouses or endorses the doctrines of practices of petitioners," they wrote in the brief, "and many of the *amici* consider those practices repugnant for moral and religious reasons."[4] They were not interested in the future and well-being of the Santerian community, which had been described as "several tributaries off the mainstream." To be sure, as the Baptist Joint Committee noted in its newsletter, "[m]ost Americans would consider [ritual sacrifice of animals] a strange if not repugnant practice."[5]

Of course, to the Santerian community the practices were neither strange nor repugnant, and the "real" issue was not the larger ramifications of First Amendment jurisprudence but the very real prohibition the community faced when trying to practice its religion. Under the leadership of Ernesto Pichardo—who was described by community opposition leader Alden Tarte as "not the kind of guy you'd want next door"—the Santerians filed suit claiming that the ordinances passed by the city council specifically singled out their religious community. Pichardo's religious tradition had existed shrouded in secrecy for several hundred years in the Caribbean, and he was astounded by his neighbors' efforts to stifle his attempts to bring his religion into the public by erecting a religious and cultural center in Hialeah. "You can kill a turkey in your backyard, put it on the table, say a prayer and serve it for Thanksgiving," he said in one interview, "but if we pray over the turkey, kill it, then eat it, we violate the law."[6] Said one observer, "An animal can be killed for any reason in Hialeah, except for religious and ceremonial ones. You can boil lobsters alive; feed live rats to pet snakes; kill for food or for sport; slaughter unwanted pets in your front yard—as long as you do not perform a ritual while doing so."[7]

The singling out of religious sacrificial ritual, argued Pichardo, was an infringement of his community's constitutional right of free exercise of religion. Santeria, an Afro-Caribbean religion brought to this country primarily through immigration, had a clandestine history in Roman Catholic Cuba, where it developed from a blending of Yoruban and Catholic traditions. For their part, the members of the Church of Lukumi Babalu Aye made a conscious effort to obey city ordinances in order to "come out into the open," thereby removing some of the stigma attached to Santeria.[8] Church members just wanted to be treated like everyone else in the pluralism of American society.

In the end, both sides chose the path they felt would be most effective in adjudicating this highly charged, theological dispute. They may have called on their individual gods for action, they may have prayed for relief from a transcendent being, but in the end they still went to court.

## Constitutional Law and Theology

In the realm of constitutional litigation, the Santerian community's decision to sue for greater religious freedom is hardly extraordinary—the court has become the preferred arena for dispute resolution. However, if one examines the implications of this decision to pursue in the courts what cannot be secured in the neighborhood or guaranteed by cosmic forces, one encounters a shift in authority of theological proportions. The court has become not only the preferred arena for dispute resolution but also the arena for theological disputation, the forum of choice for religious communities to publicize their theological positions. In the United States many disputes of religious significance are arbitrated by the nine justices of the Supreme Court and prooftexted by appeal to the U.S. Constitution, a mechanism that is generally acceptable to the combatants in the dispute, even if the outcome may not be in their favor. Behaviors required by conscience and motivated by comprehensions of one ultimate cosmic transcendent power—a community's god, for example—are judged by an authority that rests in another transcendence—the nation's legal structure, which mandates pluralism and exacts limitations. "I will do what God tells me to do" is replaced by "I will do what the Court tells me to do." The authority of the Constitution as interpreted by the Court subordinates the theological authority of the losing party in the dispute; that party's willingness to abide by the decision only confirms the power of the American legal system.

This is not about a mere building ordinance or traffic violation.

The beliefs involved are deeply and sincerely held and represent a conflict in the ways people see the world, their fellow citizens, and themselves. In the American pluralistic society, in order to protect the constitutional order, specific theological disputes have been rendered secondary. Even in situations where religious communities, simply acting out their own beliefs, have become subject to legal action brought by an outside individual or governmental authority, once they agree to submit to a court's judgment rather than renounce the proceedings altogether, they have submitted themselves to the authority of the legal system. It would seem that the only way to maintain theological fidelity and primacy is to never submit to the potentially limiting dictates of the Supreme Court's interpretation of the Constitution, but instead to ignore them. The very reality of a law regarding religious practice, even though written in the negative (i.e., "Congress shall make no law"), requires the courts to determine when that law has been violated and when, even though a religious community says it has been violated, it has not. This inevitable judgment means that a religious community could be the "loser" in the dispute. In such a circumstance, where an aspect of religion is at issue, be it plural marriage, peyote use, or animal sacrifice, the losing religious community will have to either reconcile the authority of its theology with the authority of the Court's ruling, or flout it and risk becoming a target of the coercive powers sanctioned by the Constitution. This is powerful imagery indeed, and quite obviously it points to an issue of symbolic, if not substantive, legal concern.

## From Free Exercise to Toleration

Of course, not all religious communities living under the constitutional order in this country have been required to face to the same degree the dilemma of whether to invest authority in their own theological beliefs or in the Constitution, and some have actually been advantaged by historical or theological circumstances. From the beginning, though far from religiously homogeneous, the early Republic was politically dominated by a few Protestant denominations. By controlling the instruments of power and legislating based on parallel visions of law and religion, they could make laws that anticipated their religious sensibilities, creating for themselves a comfortable position with regard to the law while they were at it. In a piece exploring the relationship between the religion of delegates at the state ratification conventions and their support for the Constitution, historian Stephen Marini notes that because Congregationalism (in New England) and Anglicanism (in the South) represented the "legally established colonial religions," it controlled the overwhelming majority of the 1,420 total votes cast in those state conventions. The remainder of the votes were split among the politically less dominant Presbyterians and Baptists, with only a few scattered votes from Lutherans, Dutch Reformed, Huguenots, Moravians, Methodists, and Catholics. It is not surprising that the form of the national charter should reflect this establishmentarian versus nonestablishmentarian polarity. Marini concludes that the change in tone from the main body of the Constitution to that of the Bill of Rights is also a reflection of this polarity. Establishmentarian majority traditions favored "powerful instrumentalities of law and government that would produce the greatest good for all by preventing any disordered minority from taking power." The nonestablishmentarian minority traditions, in contrast, favored a Bill of Rights to permit greater freedom from the centralized (and by implication, establishmentarian) government.[9]

The die thus cast, religious communities who were not part of the establishment constantly faced the difficulty of being accepted sociopolitically into the "instrumentalities of law and government" and therefore were required to pursue equality through legal confrontations. With religion serving as one of the fundamental factors in determining political rights from the very beginning, the polity has reflected a dynamic in which group membership has been defined by the dominant Protestant culture and minority traditions have been forced to pursue their particularistic needs through the political and legal arena. As Edwin Gaustad wrote about nineteenth-century America, "Religious non-conformity found its path to pub-

lic acceptance paved with legal obstacles and illegal harassment,"
and groups that desired to be accepted had to fight for that right.[10]

That pattern exists to this day. In an article entitled "Religious
Marginality and the Free Exercise Clause," Frank Way and Barbara
Burt discuss the different effects the free exercise clause of the First
Amendment has had on mainstream and nonmainstream religious
communities in this country. They observe that those communities traditionally understood as mainstream rarely participate in free
exercise cases as litigants and that when they do, the topic of the
case (for example, tax issues) reflects their status as established
members of the community. Those religious communities traditionally understood as nonmainstream are involved more regularly in
free exercise cases as the actual litigants, and that litigation more
often involves an element of religious practice, such as public
preaching, that is "consequential" in the propagation of the community's religious beliefs. The nonestablishmentarian religious
communities are required to litigate over basic religious activities
more often than are establishmentarian religious communities, who
presumably have been involved in the creation of the public standards and have undoubtedly written them to take their own behaviors into account.[11] Evidence of this establishment of a dominant
religious culture is reflected in several of the Supreme Court's First
Amendment decisions from the past three decades—permitting
mandatory Sunday closing laws and religious displays on public
property—which are expressions of only one part of a pluralistic
culture.[12] The dependence of some of these decisions upon historical justification seems only to prove the point.

This preservation of the status quo can be discerned from the very
history of First Amendment jurisprudence. There has always been
an air of toleration in the guarantee of religious free exercise rights.
Although the sensationalistic example of human sacrifice is often
cited as a reasonable limitation of religious extremism, much more
subtle doctrinal justification—such as the perception of a "clear and
present danger" or a "compelling governmental interest"—has enabled the government to exercise control over specific forms of re-

ligious expression.[13] The existence of such standards suggests limits and thus implies a social mechanism necessary to establish those limits. When religious communities have been successful in free exercise litigation, therefore, the results have been an expansion of what the established legal structures of the United States were willing to accept as religious freedom. Harry Jones put it a bit more bluntly than Gaustad: "It is the nuts, *or those so regarded by the rest of us*, on whom government restraint or censorship are brought to bear. When they resolutely defend their constitutional liberties, the nuts are surrogates for the freedom of us all."[14]

## The Power of the Center and National Religious Self-Understanding

To understand the nature of this conflict, it is necessary to begin precisely with a focus on the interaction between the Constitution and those religious traditions not regularly considered establishmentarian with regard to the legal and political structures of this country. The fact that they suffer the limitations of law, and therefore litigate disproportionately, provides an important clue to their status in society. In his work *Religious Outsiders and the Making of Americans*, R. Laurence Moore argues that religious communities in this country are most "American" when they are involved in the business of fighting against the status quo and that it is the engine of sectarian splitting that drives the train of Americanism. "[T]he American religious system may be said to be 'working' only when it is creating cracks within denominations, when it is producing novelty, even when it is fueling antagonisms," says Moore.[15] The ability to fight against the center, the established power, has been—and continues to be—a powerful rhetorical tool in American religious life.

In one sense, of course, this is correct; denominational centrifugal force does seem to be the rule rather than the exception in American society. But legal structures demand centripetal rather than centrifugal force as a mainstay of authority; relative (if not absolute) consistency is the foundation of a common law system, which finds its basis in the doctrine of precedent. Thus, regardless of cultural and political forces that encourage fragmentation within and between religious denominations in this country, there is still a strong pressure in the legal arena to act in ways that conform to a socially accepted standard. As Alexis de Tocqueville observed more than 150 years ago while commenting on the American dominant religious culture's attitude toward law, "one can say that there is not a single religious doctrine in the United States hostile to democratic and republican institutions. All the clergy there speak the same language; opinions are in harmony with the laws, and there is, so to say, only one mental current."[16] Orthodoxy may not be an "American" standard of religious expression, but orthopraxy is, within reason, certainly a standard of legal expression—even, it seems, in the realm of law addressing religion.

In the discussion of religious participation, however, the difference between the two categories of belief (-doxy) and behavior (-praxy) may be more apparent than real. From the earliest expressions of religious deviance in American legal theory, belief and behavior have been treated as distinct and divisible. Nonetheless, though a debate about such a distinction is unnecessary in the dominant culture because of the integration of religious sensibilities and the mandates of the legal culture, there is certainly a connection in the life of the religious adherent between behavior and belief such that the two cannot be rendered logically separate.[17] The ability to limit the actions of the believers, in the realm of religious participation, is the ability to limit their religion in a very tangible way. An Orthodox Jew will find little comfort, for example, in being told she may believe in the dietary laws but that no kosher food is available. It is therefore the dilemma of cultural hegemony that establishes the agenda for nonestablishmentarian religious communities; those communities conflict with constitutional authority disproportionately not because they relish being different, but because they are struggling with pressures to be the same.

This process, which might in other circumstances be understood as the dilemma of particularism versus pluralism, may be endemic to the very nature of American citizenship. On the one hand, citizens are guaranteed the right to act on their religious beliefs under the full protection of the law (free exercise). On the other hand, government prohibitions against providing advantage to one religious community over another ("no establishment") pressure religious communities to get along rather than request special exemptions. And even though such exemptions are based on the free exercise rights of the religious adherent, they may be denied by the government based on "no establishment" jurisprudence and prohibitions. Constitutional scholars have noticed this seemingly inherent contradiction in the two religion clauses of the First Amendment, as have members of the Court.[18]

Ironically, such a tension between religious particularism and religious pluralism is rooted in strong and consistent currents in American religious history; it evolved as the national identity became integrated with a particular religious identity.[19] Citizenship has long been understood by many as more than a mere political coincidence—rather, as containing elements that take on religious overtones and transcend temporal politics. From Jonathan Winthrop's "City on a Hill" speech through the doctrine of Manifest Destiny, to continuing debates over foreign policy, Americans have regularly seen themselves as participants in a theological enterprise that transcended denominational attachments. They have felt that they were involved in what perhaps could even be called an "audacious attempt to conceive of the entire universe as being [nationally] significant."[20]

Sociologist Robert Bellah defines this phenomenon (usually known as American civil religion) as "a collection of beliefs, symbols and rituals with respect to sacred things and institutionalized in a collectivity [that] served as a genuine vehicle of national religious self-understanding."[21] However, if the term *civil religion* is traced to Jean-Jacques Rousseau, one of its early promoters in the modern period, we have to acknowledge its use in justifying the exertion of majority power over the minority. Rousseau counts on the fact that historically the creation of meaning for this "collection of beliefs, symbols and rituals" has been dominated by the majority culture and has rarely taken into account minority communities who may have understood their own (or in this case, American) destiny quite differently. Why else would Rousseau suggest that it is the responsibility of the minority to accept the authority of the majority or be forever resigned to outsider status? Less a force for unification than for division, debate over the meaning of what sociologist of religion Phillip Hammond calls a society's "legitimating myths" (or what some might argue is the "one true [American] faith") has produced a line separating those who live their lives within the definition of what the dominant culture means to be a "true" American from those who—whether by their own choice or not—do not. Indeed, by giving religious significance to social institutions, American society's legitimating myths regularly confirm the sensibilities of the religious majority and regularly marginalize the sensibilities of religious minorities who have their own understanding of those social myths. The religious meaning that the majority culture has given its governmental institutions, its objects, and its history, provides authority in the American polity. The dominant culture has woven its religious self-understandings into the very fabric of governmental institutions, which is why religious minorities face pressures not only from the majority religious community but also from the assumptions inherent in the social and governmental institutions.

There can be no question of this association between the federal legal structure and traditional religious cosmologies. In the early years of the Republic, a patina of sacrality developed surrounding events and items, creating a variety of myths and symbols. One of those sacred items in the religion of American nationalism was the Constitution. Comparing the Constitution to the Bible, Milton Klein asserts that "[r]eligion was invoked to demonstrate that the Constitution was as much a part of the divine plan as the Revolution, already sanctified in the public imagination." By the fiftieth anniversary of the Constitution's ratification, the document played a prominent and transcendent role in the American legitimating mythology. Writing on this process of mythologization, Klein says the public revered the document as if, deus ex machina, it had "rescued the nation from post-Revolutionary disaster. . . . It not only defined the past but shaped the present and ordained the future." The Constitution, according to legal scholar Thomas Grey, "has been, virtually from the moment of its ratification, a sacred symbol, the most potent emblem (along with the flag) of the nation itself." Furthermore, he adds, it is unique in such a treatment; neither state constitutions—even at the height of states' rights controversies—nor the constitutions of other countries are as important in the symbology of their constituencies.[22]

Of course, not all citizens shared a single meaning for any symbol. Furthermore, no meaning could remain unchanged over time. Quite to the contrary, the tapestry of American religious history, and American social history generally, is interwoven with competing notions of what it means to be an American. However, because of the predominantly Protestant nature and imagery of American legitimating myths, it is more reasonable to suggest that nonestablishmentarian religious communities might have difficulty feeling at home with the constructions of membership in the American sociopolitical world as articulated by establishmentarian religious communities. In the symbology of American legitimating mythology, *cujus regio, ejus religio* (whose the rule, his the religion) seems to be the order of the day—and since the establishmentarian religious communities have by and large controlled the rule (certainly in the political realm), they have controlled the official version of the nation's legitimating mythology and therefore the meaning and authority of the Constitution for the entirety of the nation. With no non-Protestant president until 1960 and no non-Protestant Supreme Court majority until 1996, it is not surprising that those in control would create a society representative of their religious sensibilities, making even the very instruments and institutions of power less sympathetic to religious difference, while still symbolically representative of the diversity of the citizenry. Writes Sidney Mead, "To ask if something is 'constitutional' is to ask if it is consistent with the fundamental principles of the nation. In this sense the court functions as the guardian of the character of the Republic."[23]

## The Cosmology of the Constitution

As consensual as Professor Mead's comment may sound, like many other interpretations of American constitutional theory it overlooks the fact that many religious communities have had little or no voice in the formation of the "fundamental principles of the nation" and might, in fact, articulate them differently given the chance. It is for this reason that in any discussion of American legitimating myths or civil religion, one should be wary of tendencies to unify, and instead focus on the processes of negotiation and political encounter. Anyone who has examined the drafting process of the Constitution knows that that exercise, like the drafting of all legislation, was the result of compromise and politicking—possibly enlightened, but no less elite.[24] If we can explore the political as well as the religious levels of meaning surrounding the American constitutional order—and religious minorities' encounters with it—we can better understand the nature of the struggle within the religious minority to maintain its own source of transcending authority while accepting another.

On the most basic, practical, and political level, the Constitution is a document, a written plan for the construction and maintenance of the legal structures of the national government; in the federal system the Constitution is the ultimate law. Even apart from the obvious religious metaphor, the Constitution is the highest law of the land, the "supreme and final jurisdiction" noted by Alexander Hamilton in *The Federalist*. In a very practical way, it retains (or has been given) the authority to limit actions of every citizen in the country—no one is exempt, and there is nowhere else to turn.[25] Recent events involving the investigations of the Clinton administration make this clear, as it was during the Nixon administration and in other situations in which presidential action has been limited or prohibited by constitutional interpretation.[26] Commenting on the ultimacy of the Constitution and the subsequent role of the Supreme Court to interpret it, one justice wrote, "We are not final because we are infallible, but we are infallible only because we are final," obviously and consciously playing on the Catholic doctrine of papal infallibility.[27] As the final word over the First Amendment (specifically the religion clauses), the Constitution is vested with the authority to control through the offices of the federal government the actions of those found in violation of the Constitution's mandates. Thus, though I asserted earlier the fallaciousness of splitting the religious adherent's world into behavior and belief, ironically it is just such a split that justifies the practical politics of the Constitution's authority. Behavior can be modified or limited, but belief is beyond monitoring and therefore beyond the state's ability to punish physically. For the Constitution's practical expression of political authority—the first level of meaning in the Constitution—such a split between behavior and belief is fundamental; people may be physically inconvenienced for violating its standards.

On the second, symbolic level, though, such a distinction between behavior and belief becomes unnecessary. As noted earlier, the ability to control behavior suggests the ability to coerce belief. To a great extent, the Court's ability to maintain the authority of the Constitution rests not on the fear of physical sanctioning provided by other branches of the government, but on the ability to convince people to do what they would not ordinarily be inclined to do. In the face of opposition from these other branches of government, this is often the Court's only power. According to Albert Beveridge, after the Supreme Court rendered its decision in *Worcester v. Georgia* (1832), a vehemently opposed President Jackson allegedly exclaimed, "John Marshall has made his decision:—*now let him enforce it!*"[28] This need to convince, though obviously sometimes precarious, is rooted in the authority of the Court to interpret the Constitution consistently with the general will of the majority or to ground its decisions in a manner that, to the legal community at least, seems consistent with society.[29] Not quite limited to the specific words of the Constitution, the Court's interpretations provide the second, symbolic—and possibly more powerful—meaning (the first being practical and political understanding) of constitutional authority that nonestablishmentarian religious communities encounter as they struggle with American society.

People are constantly bombarded with clues about how they are to behave and what they are to believe as proper Americans.

One way to make a connection between the written document—with its physical mechanisms of behavior modification—and its more symbolic manifestation is through an analysis of how people understand the Constitution. In *Constitutional Faith,* Sanford Levinson provides one such method by describing a two-tiered approach, the first tier an analysis of the textual meaning (literally or not), the second an analysis of interpretive authority (either of the average citizen or specifically of the judiciary).[30] He compares these approaches to religious outlooks, with the textually literal and interpretively universal positions identified as "protestant" (based on the Protestant notions of *sola scriptura* and the universal priesthood of all believers) and the textually nonliteral and interpretively limited positions identified as "catholic" (based on the Catholic nonliteral view of scriptural texts and hierarchical organization of authority). As applied to the Constitution, "protestants" of meaning would argue that the document means no more than is literally represented, and "protestants" of interpretive authority would say that every citizen (not just the judiciary) has the right to interpret the document. There is no need for one to be "protestant" on both tiers. Levinson spends some time describing the four different possibilities ("protestant" on meaning and "protestant" on interpretation, "protestant" on meaning and "catholic" on interpretation," and so on).

It does not appear to be coincidental that Levinson applies such denominational categories—the correlation seems almost natural. With such a schema in place, it is possible to investigate the Constitution's symbolic meaning, through what can now be identified as a "catholic"-by-"protestant" stance: "catholic" in the sense that the Constitution is understood to mean more than just the words on the page, and "protestant" in the sense that it is understood to be interpreted by a larger community than just the judiciary and is the result of a continued national conversation on its very meaning. Speculation on this open, seemingly citizenwide conversation on the larger (nonliteral) meaning of the Constitution is not new;

it has often centered on what has been called the "unwritten Constitution."[31]

## The Sacred Text of American Constitutionalism

Throughout American history the unwritten level of the Constitution's meaning has served as a reflection of the society that created it. It has expressed, writes Grey, "an arrangement vastly more complex than those underlying most legal documents: the web of society's basic institutions and ideals." This arrangement, based on the concept of a higher law only partly expressed by positive (or written) law, has contributed to the sense that the written document contains within it an element of the transcendent cosmos and that it is "not only an object of interpretation, but is also itself an interpretation of what *its* authors were trying to 'get in writing.'"[32] "Thus," Grey concludes, "in the framing of the original American constitutions it was widely accepted that there remained unwritten but still binding principles of higher law."[33]

The unwritten part, reflected in words of the Ninth and Tenth Amendments, suggests that there are other ("inalienable") rights that exceed the written document. Although it would be rather easy to suggest that the source of these other rights rested in the people's God, the evidence actually suggests that for many, such authority rests more in the people themselves. The Constitution expresses this sentiment in its preamble; "We the people . . . do ordain and establish this Constitution for the United States of America." The very citizens who have participated in the construction of the American society retain the right to form the transcending authority of the Constitution. They ordained it, they retain whatever rights are not enumerated within it, and they have the ability to reconfigure it, albeit only as a people acting in a manner by which they have agreed to abide, not by mere whim. The transcending authority of the written document is therefore posited in the very people who gave rise to its existence. Public philosopher and historian William Miller writes that "[t]he state is impartial about such ultimate beliefs . . . because it defers to the conscience of the people."

Putting it a bit differently, Thomas Grey provides the resounding conclusion that "Americans take the will of the people as sovereign . . . and the Constitution as the most authoritative legal expression of that popular will."[34]

The celebration of the American people as a nation (rather than merely as a modern state) strongly suggests a Durkheimian analysis of the American constitutional system, further strengthening the notion of parallelism between religion and law. As Sidney Mead declares, "A nation, in brief, is 'essentially a spiritual society,' its soul created in the compact of the people," reflecting in a very American way Durkheim's theory that a collectivity, sensing the transcendent power of its own existence, may express itself in a religious manner. "Men who feel themselves united, partially by bonds of blood, but still more by a community of interest and tradition," writes Durkheim, "assemble and become conscious of their moral unity."[35] This consciousness takes the form of action, and the group develops behavior that celebrates the unity.

Looking back on the earlier discussion of American civil religion, we can now distinguish between citizenship as ordained by God and the very powerful expression of the transcendent reality of the polity itself as experienced by some members of American society. Using such a method, it is no surprise that clear parallels exist between those communities traditionally understood as religious and those communities that express collective emotions of transcendence, such as in what I described earlier as American civil religion. For example, historian Jürgen Heideking notes the religiosity of the Constitution's ratification processions in various states. Similarly, legal theorists have expressed Durkheimian paradigms in exploring the transcendence of American constitutional law. Phillip Hammond focuses on the Supreme Court and constitutional disputes as the epitome of the Durkheimian expression of religion in the constitutional order, and Thomas Grey observes that "[f]rom Durkheim's conception of religion to a religion of the Constitution is an easy step. The Constitution is an explicit self-representation of society." Indeed, as proof of the religion of the Constitution, Grey points to the wording of the third clause of Article 6, which requires an "oath or affirmation to support this Constitution; but no religious test shall ever be required as qualification to any office or public trust under the United States." The "but," he writes, "suggests that the Framers considered the constitutional oath a *substitute* for the religious tests the colonists were familiar with under the English established church. To push the point a bit: America would have no national church, as the first amendment later made explicit, yet the worship of the Constitution would serve the unifying function of a national civil religion."[36] The nation, reflected in the documents it considers sacred, replaces traditional conceptions of religion with its ability to express its transcendence among the majority. Because those documents reflect the dominant culture, it is now understandable how attempts at "unifying" the "national civil religion" would pose serious challenges to religious minorities.

## The Theological Conflict Engaged

Through the concept of the Constitution as a collective expression of the citizens of this country, with its power resting squarely on the religious sentimentalization of national unity, the edifice of the Constitution's cosmological authority receives its final brick. A Durkheimian expression of social unity, the development of an unwritten Constitution and the placement of that Constitution as the final word of the people combine to make the cosmos created therein an awesome and powerful force of transcending authority. No wonder it is so often expressed in religious language. Furthermore, Thomas Grey identifies a causal relation between the doctrine of judicial review and the power of the dominant culture's definition of society in American jurisprudence. His syllogism is "(a) [J]udicial review requires that judges enforce the Constitution; (b) the Constitution stands for the American essence; therefore, (c) judicial review requires judges to discern and enforce the American essence."[37] This conceptualization provides the final link to understanding the enormity of the dilemma nonestablishmentarian religious communities face when encountering the conflict between their own theological dictates and the mandates of the American constitutional order. As noted earlier, only a very few religious communities (the majority communities) have been able to exercise enough political and social power to influence either the practical or the symbolic meanings of the Constitution. As the number of religious communities has grown over the nation's history, many have found themselves at the center of constitutional disputes involving the exercise of religion. They were not part of the debate that created the American social contract, and they have not been able to influence it significantly in its ongoing debate since.

This leads to the final question concerning the conflict over authority as experienced by religious communities facing the constitutional order. What of those members of society who do not share in the Durkheimian sense of unity? What about those communities that were not part of the construction of the social compact or who for some other reason do not share in it? How does the system preserve itself when nonestablishmentarian religious communities do not agree, even for the sake of national unity, on the implication of unanimity? Surely the answer is not as Rousseau himself implied; according to him the existence of dissent from the formation of the society "does not invalidate the contract; it merely excludes the dissenters; they are foreigners among the citizens. After the state is instituted, residence implies consent: to inhabit the territory is to submit to the sovereign."[38] Certainly there is a more subtle, though potentially no less brutal, battlefield for the conflict over particularistic, theological notions of transcendent unity versus Americanized, pluralistic notions of transcendent unity. Does a mechanism exist to incorporate those religious communities that do not share the social expression of unity, as manifested in the unwritten authority of the constitutional order?

Conflict with the constitutional cosmology is not necessarily a direct, overt assault on a particular religious community. It therefore need not be portrayed in such a bipolar image as represented by Moore. In fact, the issue is not merely whether religious communities split into denominations or join confederations, remain particularistic or Americanize, but rather how they exhibit different approaches to the pressure of Americanization and the over-whelming transcending authority of the constitutional order. It would appear that there are three distinct approaches religious communities use when negotiating the conflict between theological and constitutional authorities: they can receive an amount of recognition from the dominant culture that permits deviance, they can join the dominant culture in some way, or they can reject the dominant culture and refuse to acknowledge its authority. In other words, they can maintain their own sources of authority after establishing a separate peace with the dominant culture, they can adopt the dominant culture's sources of authority, or they can maintain their particularistic sources of authority, which—if no separate peace has been established—will lead to conflict with the dominant culture over the authority of those sources.

Although presented in the following pages as conscious decisions about viable options, these approaches should be understood as ideal types (thus never truly represented in their perfect form) and more circumstantial than optional. It is most likely that religious communities (through their leadership) do not consciously select an option from among the three, but rather pursue almost instinctually the strategy that makes the most sense spiritually, emotionally, and even economically and politically. The strategies described in this work, therefore, are best understood as classifications created for analysis.

## Potential Strategies for Minority Religious Communities

The opportunity to join the constitutional order is not always an attractive one, and some religious communities would rather abstain than pay the price of membership. In a sense, they meta-phorically expand the legal theory of being left alone, based on a personal privacy right, to a corporate right of seclusion and absten-tion from the constitutional order; they prefer their particularistic views to those of the majority and just want to be left alone. This abstention need not be problematic, and some communities may actually be permitted to pursue it vigorously. However, permission to abstain must still be granted by the constitutional order, which may do so only when it is convinced that no danger is presented by the abstention. In other words, the best that can be hoped for is that the authority structure of the religious community is either benign or congruent with the constitutional order, so that the behaviors of the group wishing to be left alone are to some degree compatible with the constitutional order. In such a manner it is possible for two different sources of authority to provide different—if not opposing—justifications for the same activity, giving the impression to an outside observer that there is agreement between the adherents of the two different sources merely because their actions coincide. For example, the Supreme Court provided a number of legal justifications for its decision in *Wisconsin v. Yoder*, which permitted Amish parents to remove their children from public school at an age younger than that established by the state legislature. The Amish community in Wisconsin justified its desire to withdraw its children from public school after the eighth grade by the belief that high school would have a corrupting influence on the religious ideals of the children. Community members were not interested in the Court's rationale; they knew their own position was justified, and they benefited from the decision regardless of the reason.

As noted earlier, the Constitution operates on two levels, the first physical and the second symbolic. As long as the minority religious community can withstand the social pressure of not sharing beliefs with the dominant culture, it can take advantage of the action-belief dichotomy inherent in legal institutions. In other words, by performing the correct actions, regardless of the underlying justifying beliefs, the community can avoid punishment from the state. From the state's point of view, this can be expressed by the statement "We don't care *why* they are doing the prescribed behavior, as long as they are doing it."[39] That is, the religious community could ignore the constitutional justification and live in peaceful coexistence as long as it behaved in the constitutionally mandated manner. In the early Republic this was the rationale behind the enforcement of Sunday "blue" laws and the like. Non-Christians would not be punished for not attending church (for the most part), so long as they did not act in a manner that insulted those who did by working or selling liquor.[40]

Such "constitutional congruence" of behavior permits the minoritarian community to maintain the integrity of its theological authority without succumbing to the pressures of the constitutional order. Independence, not interdependence, is the key characteristic of this strategy, and an ability to avoid participation in the constitutional order's political and legal systems is indicative of this strategy's adoption. Groups that have been involved in constitutional congruences are generally able to exist in some degree of separation from the sociopolitical order, since they are, in a very real sense, making the constitutional mountain come to Mohammed. Evidence of this congruence can be found in groups such as the Amish, ultra-Orthodox Jews, and Jehovah's Witnesses.[41]

It is true, though, that groups do concern themselves with the system of symbols and meanings held (at any given time) by the dominant culture, and many may come to adopt some or all of those symbols and meanings as their own. These communities can best be understood in terms of conversion to the constitutional order. Characterized by a shift within the religious community from seeing the theological dictates as ultimate to justifying the sociopolitical order, this strategy represents at most the subordination of theological authority to constitutional authority and at least the alteration of the theological authority to conform to the constitutional. It can be seen in religious communities that advocate constitutional adherence in conjunction with—or as opposed to—religious particularism, since they have the sense that their religious principles are now confirmed by the constitutional order. The process by which a community goes from without to within might best be understood as a "constitutional conversion": the religious community has been converted to a view that holds the Constitution as equal if not superior to particularistic theological mandates.

The most subtle of the strategies employed, the option of conversion has been a part of American history since the first disestablishment of religion. It is difficult to notice in the modern establishmentarian religious communities, in part because of the close identification, from the beginning of nation-building, between the desires of these religious communities and the dictates of the nation's legal structures. Religious communities that were in on the original disestablishment agreement implied that it would be better to get along with each other than to divide over competing revelations of God's will. Today, as Phillip Hammond writes, "[i]n the face of expanding religious pluralism, we uphold religious liberty as a value taking precedence over any of our particularistic creeds."[42] In that sense, the sensibilities of the framers' religious communities established the rules, the standards by which membership in the constitutional community would be judged. Religious communities that were not instrumental in the drafting of the Constitution or in the debate over disestablishment have agreed to the supremacy of pluralism, and therefore, in a sense, have been "converted." They have accepted what I labeled above as Rousseau's myth of primal unity, the notion that there are symbols and meanings that all groups must adopt to be accepted by the dominant culture. Although at first this method may be viewed as the most harmful of the strategies to the integrity of the religious community's ideology, it may actually be understood as integral to the process of "Americanization" and the peaceful expression of pluralism. Those communities that have utilized this strategy now live institutionally in the belief system of constitutional authority, which permits them to agree to disagree, and to do so in relative peace. The American Catholic and Jewish communities have gone through this process, as have the Mormons.[43]

If reflective of reality, no model of human behavior can be static; in any democratic order (even one constructed with cosmological references), change is a constant fact of life. Although constitutional law is based on precedent, it is not rigid. It maintains its flexibility through the mechanism of interpretation. Interpretations of constitutional law can therefore change noticeably over time, and it is possible that such change could be to the advantage of a religious community facing a conflict over authority.[44] One future chief justice stated, "We are under Constitution, but the Constitution is what the judges say it is." Nevertheless, it is still true that, as another chief justice said, "Judges are shaped in what's going on in the world around them."[45] If "what's going on in the world" for a time coincides with the authority structure of a minority religious community, harmony has been reached without coercion. This coincidence of justifications reflects a deeper level of parallelism than mere congruence of behaviors—for a moment in time, the authorities of both the minority religious community and the constitutional order are aligned.

However, the existence of an option permitting the peaceful coexistence of society (as reflected by the constitutional order) and the minority religious community suggests the converse possibility, namely a conflicted coexistence. Such discord can take two forms—eruptive and continuous. The result of shifts between a minority religious community and the constitutional order that are exactly the opposite of those noted in a "constitutional congruence," this conflicted coexistence is due to divergences in either the first (physical) or the second (symbolic) understanding of the Constitution's meaning. In the eruptive mode a religious community that has existed peacefully with society may adopt a new tenet, or the values of the dominant culture may shift, transforming what was once a coincidental parallelism of behaviors into an exposed conflict of justifications. Examples can be found in the histories of a number of religious communities, but the phenomenon may best be illustrated by the vocal encounters between the constitutional order and Christian Fundamentalism, the increasingly violent confrontations of the Christian Identity movement, and the disastrous clash of the government and the Branch Davidians.[46] In the other mode of conflicted coexistence (continuous conflict), basic terms and concepts are irreconcilable from the start, leaving little hope of peaceful coexistence on the epistemological level, and possibly on the physical level as well. Comparable systemic differences can be found, for example, in the Native American understandings of such concepts as land (sacred versus commodified) and personal rights and freedoms (communal versus individual) (see chapter 4).

In either of the conflictual modes, the inability to reconcile the conflicting authority of theology and the constitutional order can lead to philosophical, if not physical, violence. The strength of the constitutional order may be too overwhelming to permit differences in terminology, much less differences in practice, and an inability or an unwillingness to submit suggests an inevitable conflict. Such a test of wills is not limited to minority religious communities that find themselves in one of the two conflictual modes. As noted earlier, no group's response will exactly match any of the strategies I have described. Furthermore, it is likely that any minority religious community will go through several if not all of the strategies over time. Even in the strategies of conversion and congruence, minority religious communities are forced to decide between their religious particularism and the constitutional order.

## The Dilemma Revisited

The notion that the constitutional order has the power to coerce orthodoxy as well as orthopraxy conflicts with the traditional American ideal that the First Amendment guarantees freedom of religion. A more challenging assessment seems to be that it does guarantee religious freedom, but of a broadly theistic, possibly establishmentarian, Protestant variety. This suggests that those religious communities who find themselves outside of that description will face an extraordinarily complicated dilemma over conflicting authorities—their own particularistic ones and those derived from the general population as reflected in the written and unwritten constitutions. They will have to sacrifice their particularism to become part of the establishment, or they will have to sacrifice being part of the establishment for their particularism. In either case, minority religious communities are required to make a choice, and although there are always limits even in free society, grandiose rhetoric about religious free exercise seems hollow.

The Santerian community mentioned at the beginning of this chapter is an excellent example of this conflict. They were not here when the Constitution—the American social contract—was created. They have not been a part of the greater body politic in a significant enough way to alter its course. They are relatively recently arrived and relatively few in number, and they are perceived, at least by their neighbors in Hialeah, as "several tributaries off the mainstream." Yet by appealing to their constitutional rights to justify their ability to practice their religion, the Santerian community in Hialeah became like most religious communities in this country— it provided evidence of joining the congregation of constitutional authority. The community could have refuted pluralism, never desired to build a community center, and refused to share its religious tradition with its neighbors. It could have refuted the authority of the civil government when it passed restrictive ordinances, violated the mandates of the Hialeah city council, and lived its religious life as its ancestors had in Cuba—underground. Instead, by appealing (twice) to higher courts for relief, this community selected a strategy for the reconciliation of the two authorities, religious and legal. The municipal government representatives who took the community to court presumably were adherents of the authority of the Constitution long before the battle erupted and thus felt obliged to abide by the Supreme Court's ruling. They may not have liked the final decision, but they would be bound to live by it.[47] The Santerian community may have put its faith in a theological source of authority. It may have even spent much energy praying for the removal of the restrictive governmental measures. By appealing to the legal system, however, the Santerian community symbolically placed as secondary the theology of its specific community and permitted the transcending authority of the constitutional order to pass final judgment.

Of course, if the Santerian community successfully completes its plan to open a cultural and educational religious center in Hialeah (a desire that was the catalyst for the municipality's ordinances in the first place), it will undeniably have changed the face of Santeria.[48] When its leadership decided to take the city of Hialeah to court, the community began a constitutional conversion and symbolically subordinated its theological beliefs to constitutional cosmology. This is not a value judgment—there is no way of knowing whether that change is for better or for worse, and I have no interest in making that determination. But there can be no deny-ing that, not by receiving legal sanction *but merely by asking for it*, the Church of Lukumi Babalu Aye has created a very American, legally sanctified version of this once-underground religious tradi-tion. The power to provide such a sanctification has been taken from the realm of the gods and relocated in the U.S. Constitution.

Not all communities choose this option. The following case stud-ies provide examples of each of the strategies—congruence, conver-sion, and conflict—that are available when a minority community confronts the authority of the American constitutional order. The communities described here, and many others, have faced the over-whelming dominance of American Protestantism and its histori-cally close association with the American constitutional order, and they have reacted to that dominance in different ways. Many have integrated the different sources of authority successfully, whereas others have attempted to maintain their own particularistic sources of authority in defiance of the sensibilities of the American consti-tutional order. Many, like the Amish, the Orthodox Jews, and the Jehovah's Witnesses, have gone to court to seek the space in which to believe freely and the right to be left alone. They may not ever admit that transcending sources of authority in the constitutional order have any meaning at all for them. Instead, they use the court (and often only the court) as a means of creating breathing room in which their own sources of transcending authority can be ex-pressed—and the American constitutional order is left to make up its own mind. The first case study is an examination of such a strategy.

# 2

# Constitutional Congruence

*Jehovah's Witnesses and the
Constitutional Order*

It isn't that we aren't patriotic, but we will not
put God second and the country first.

WALTER GOBITAS

Only certain Protestant religious communities stood at the foot of
the proverbial mountain as God revealed the Word in the form of
the American constitutional order (see chapter 1). Over the course
of American religious history, many of the new Protestant—as well
as non-Protestant—communities that were not among the early
recipients or shapers of the constitutional order have been disdain-
ful of the compromise required for membership. There has been a
tendency not to seek membership into "mainstream" American
culture, but to exercise the theologically safer position of standing
outside the dominant culture in order to be critical of it. Religious
communities have found the means to criticize the American constitutional order while maintaining their own theological sources
of authority.[1] They are able to justify their actions based on their
own particularistic reasons, and the constitutional order is willing
to accept the difference so long as they behave. Of course, there need
not be a direct connection between the stance of a religious com-

munity toward the dominant culture and its attitude toward the American constitutional order generally, but if the constitutional order is as reflective of mainstream Protestant Christianity as I have suggested it is, there should be no surprise that those religious communities that seek not to join the former might also feel threatened by—and therefore be critical of—the latter.

For some religious communities, this stance must be negotiated, and what we might call "constitutional congruence" is achieved after a confrontation in which the legal culture is convinced that the claims of the religious minority, translated into majoritarian terms, coalesce with those of the dominant culture. Unlike the category of constitutional conflict (see chapter 4), constitutional congruence is the recognition of parallelism with the constitutional order, a strategy that acknowledges the behavioral standards of the dominant culture but not the sources of authority for those standards. A number of communities have achieved such constitutional congruence even while articulating serious condemnations of American society—most notably the Amish, but also Orthodox Jews and, increasingly, conservative Christians.

Strategies for the confrontation differ. Seventh-day Adventist scholar Malcolm Bull has noted that a key difference between Adventists and Jehovah's Witnesses is the way in which each has been perceived in the American culture: Unlike the Witnesses or the Mormons, "Adventists have never captured public attention through dramatic confrontations with the state. Having never become notorious, the church has not become familiar." He suggests that this is because Seventh-day Adventists have made use of social structures (schools, hospitals, and the like) and rhetorical expressions (Bull uses the phrase "civil religion") familiar to the American general culture and reinvested them with meanings peculiar to Adventists. Adventists are "heretics" of American civil religion because they have "inverted the institutionalized ideology of civil religion."[2] He concludes that the apparent emulation of American civil religion "has been based on rivalry rather than admiration. Paradoxically, this has meant that Adventists are rarely out-of-step with the mainstream of society." This accounts for the "curious" lack of conflict between Adventism and what we have been calling the American constitutional order.[3]

By this standard, the Jehovah's Witness community might not be considered heretical but an altogether different faith. It has met the American constitutional order head on and never hesitated to combat it. For the last century it has maintained its particularistic sources of theological authority while condemning the American government.[4] From 1938 to 1960, more than fifty cases involving members of the organization reached the U.S. Supreme Court, producing more than thirty separate decisions on issues from flag-saluting to colportage. The Jehovah's Witnesses were successful in the vast majority of these decisions, and the group established landmark precedents in free speech and the free exercise of religion. The membership suffered significant persecution in this country as well as around the globe, but throughout its most active period of confrontation with the American constitutional order, it was able both to maintain the integrity and centrality of its own sources of transcendent authority and to move the ethos of the American constitutional order dramatically. From 1929 until 1962, the Jehovah's Witness community defended its religious beliefs and practices regularly and consistently against the entirety of the constitutional order. And although the community lost cases as well as won them (but won more than it lost), during that thirty-three-year period it did not, even under the incredible social pressure, noticeably compromise its beliefs in order to prevail or even to be left alone. As Ronald Lawson observes, comparing the Witnesses to the Seventh-day Adventists, "the Witnesses' attitude toward society has remained so negative that when their expectations of persecution were confirmed, this encouraged them to stand firm in their convictions."[5] But over the same period, the ethos of the American constitutional order shifted significantly; and by the end of the great series of cases involving the Jehovah's Witnesses, the courts were accommodating their practices seemingly without question.

How was it possible for this small religious minority to do sustained battle with the majority consensus of the American constitutional order and emerge the apparent victor? One part of the answer lies in the nature of that community's challenge, and the other part lies in the reception the challenge received from its adversaries. In a combination of causes, the isolated effects of which it would be impossible to examine, the Jehovah's Witnesses were able to take advantage of timing that benefited their litigation, while at the same time they were able to benefit from the two most significant figures fighting for their cause: President Joseph Franklin Rutherford and legal counsel Hayden Cooper Covington. Rutherford, often referred to as "Judge" Rutherford, had been an attorney who had served as legal counsel for the Jehovah's Witnesses during the administration of the group's founder, Charles Taze Russell. He came to the organization having had a variety of experiences with the constitutional order.[6] Not least of those experiences were his own personal confrontations with the legal system—a prison term (for sedition) and litigation before the Supreme Court. Covington served as lead counsel for the Jehovah's Witnesses from 1940 until the 1960s and argued every case the organization took to the Supreme Court—more than fifty in all.[7] During that time he was able to translate particularistic claims into generalizable symbols and images that reverberated with the justices to such an extent that they were able to express sympathy for the claims; the result was overwhelming successes for the organization. This suggests that the legal achievements of the Jehovah's Witnesses were not solely due to the leadership but also owed much to the manner in which the Court heard the arguments the Witnesses were making. The community's ability to translate its theology into concepts accessible to nonmembers guaranteed that the mechanisms of government could be moderated and that the Witness community could achieve constitutional congruence with the American constitutional order.

In order to understand the manner in which the Jehovah's Witnesses were able to sustain the integrity of their own theological source of authority in the face of overwhelming power, one must begin with that community's attitude toward the system that would prove to be both its judicial adversary and ultimately its benefactor—namely, the American constitutional order.

## The Earliest Signs

Formally incorporated by Charles Taze Russell in 1884 as Zion's Watch Tower Tract Society, the Jehovah's Witnesses arose out of an adventist past that itself was the product of the premillennial dispensationalism emerging in this country and England. In addition, the organization built a theology based on conditionalism and Arianism that was an outgrowth of currents in American religious culture in the second half of the nineteenth century.[8] Of central import to their eschatology was the idea that 144,000 of the righteous would reign with Christ in heaven during and after the destruction of Armageddon.[9] Although this number was subject to some revision, there was always a clear notion that, whatever the exact number or the status of those beyond the 144,000, only a small righteous remnant would survive the final cosmic battle between good and evil and attain eternal life. Contrary to the dominant American triumphalism that was part of this country's history, Witness theology held that God would not distinguish along national boundaries: Americans were neither safer nor more righteous than anyone else. In the eyes of the Witnesses, writes historian R. Laurence Moore, "[t]he vast majority of [Russell's] countrymen were speeding, without hope of reversing direction, toward a miserable annihilation along with the rest of mankind."[10]

This position was not terribly popular in the United States. The community's eschatology predicted that the beginning of the end times would occur in 1914, a belief that seemed to be confirmed by the beginning of hostilities that would later erupt into World War I. The specific millennial expectation, coupled with the belief that all earthly governments (which were under the influence of Satan) would be overthrown by the forces of God and righteousness, enhanced the atmosphere of drama when World War I did break out in Europe. Although understanding the conflagration as vital to their eschatology, the Jehovah's Witnesses preached conscientious objection, since the battles in Europe were between earthly governments and had not yet become the full theological drama at Armageddon. In this country, that specific position was not considered particularly suspect until the United States entered the war in 1917. Then the organization came under increased scrutiny by the federal government; and as American religious historian Martin Marty notices, "[t]he Russellites stood alone for having violated consensus to the point that they antagonized the federal government over their religion."[11]

It is no surprise, then, that a watershed encounter between the Jehovah's Witnesses and the American constitutional order took place in 1918, nearly twenty years before the major period of Witness litigation in the Supreme Court began. Arrested on May 8, 1918, for violating the Espionage Act of 1917, Joseph Rutherford, who had succeeded Russell as president of the organization, and seven other members were found guilty of publishing and distributing materials that would "cause insubordination, disloyalty, and refusal of duty in the military forces of the United States." Of primary significance during the trial were two items, the first a work allegedly written by Russell and published posthumously, entitled *The Finished Mystery*, and the second a corporate letter written to members of the organization encouraging them to resist the draft even if it meant getting shot.[12] Attorneys for the government argued that the materials, including 850,000 copies of *The Finished Mystery*, were published and distributed to military installations between June 16, 1917, and May 6, 1918, and that these materials caused several inductees to violate command. During the trial Rutherford "admitted that as a 'consecrated Christian' he was opposed to war in any form,"[13] even though only two months earlier he had indicated that buying war bonds was "not a religious question, and that the association did not oppose the purchase of Liberty bonds by the members." When asked by presiding judge Harlan B. Howe, "What do you think would become of the country if we adopted your theories [of conscientious objection]?" one of the defendants answered, "If this people were wholly consecrated to the Lord the Lord would take care of them."[14]

On the day the verdict was announced, the *New York Times* ran an editorial powerfully articulating the American sense of the dominant culture's rights over those of the individual or the minority community. "Above all individual rights," declared the editorialist, "stands that of the Government to defend and perpetuate itself. The right of rebellion also exists, of course, and is inalienable, but the consequences of unsuccessful rebellion are always serious, and the rebel who whines or protests when he encounters them is a poor specimen of his class."[15] He seemed to suggest that Rutherford and the others were found guilty of being poor sports. Of greater significance, though, was the emphasis placed on the right of a government to pursue the course of war over the right of the individual citizen to protest against it. Thus, the editorial completely overlooked the vast disparity in numbers and physical power between the Jehovah's Witnesses and the federal government. The overwhelming authority of the government was more specifically articulated in the statement released by the U.S. Department of Justice: "The facts and documents presented to this Government by the Italian Government, together with the facts disclosed in the trial court, demonstrate clearly that Rutherford and his associates, while using what were ostensibly publications of a strictly religious character, were, in fact, using certain of those publications as a medium for circulating vicious propaganda solely intended to hamper the prosecution of the war by the United States."[16] Apparently no threat was too small when the authority of the constitutional order was at issue, and the government's need to prosecute the war could not be hindered by those who opposed it.

The trial seemed to have a profound physical and emotional impact on Rutherford. At the announcement of the verdict, one *New York Times* reporter described him as "completely dazed," and when the twenty-year sentence (per count, to run concurrently) was delivered the next day, although all eight men were described as visibly defeated, "Rutherford was the most affected of all. His body and hands twitched convulsively and his face grew red." Judge Howe refused to release the men pending their appeal, and they were sent to the federal penitentiary in Atlanta, Georgia, where they awaited its result.[17] The faithful in Brooklyn sold their real estate holdings on Hicks Street (also known as the Brooklyn Tabernacle) and considered moving to Atlanta to be closer to their leadership but ended up consolidating with the Pittsburgh offices. Finally, on March 26, 1919, six weeks before a circuit court would rule on appeals over bail restrictions, Rutherford and his associates were released on ten thousand dollars bond each. In May of that year the Federal Court of Appeals for the Second Circuit ruled two to one that the district court's behavior in pursuing the allegations of contempt against trial witness (and Jehovah's Witness) William F. Hudgings was "most prejudicial to the defendants." It therefore ruled that the accused "did not have the temperate and impartial trial to which they were entitled," and the judgment of the lower court was reversed.[18]

The experience of trial, defeat, and imprisonment irreparably altered Rutherford's position with regard to the American constitutional order. The Jehovah's Witnesses had advocated positions against all earthly governments before the trial, and indeed, this position is what had been the focus of the 1918 court confrontation. In the years immediately following the trial, however, the position of the Jehovah's Witnesses became more specific and increasingly antagonistic toward the American constitutional order. Ronald Lawson estimates, "This experience with the American system of justice strengthened Rutherford's insistence on maintaining political neutrality."[19] But in fact, with a very specific shift in biblical interpretation, the Witnesses positioned themselves not on a course of neutrality but on a course that would bring them into direct conflict with the American constitutional order.

## Jehovah's Witnesses and the "Higher Powers," Part 1

As early as 1886, Charles Taze Russell had articulated his theological position that, from the time of Adam's rebellion in the Garden of Eden, Satan had been given the earthly world to rule until that time when God would reestablish a divine kingdom on earth. Inherent in this view were two presuppositions: first, that man could rule himself in his imperfect manner until the reestablishment of that kingdom, and second, that God could intervene at any time to provide corrections to the progress of humanity on earth. That formula provided the authority for earthly governments and for the teaching that the faithful owed respect to them. It also explained how earthly governments (such as ancient Israel, the more modern early Zionist effort, and even the United States), which were assumed to be under Satan's domain, could do God's bidding. Even in the case of these governments, however, God had not chosen any government or citizenry as inherently righteous but only had guided their actions to further divine plans.[20]

A great portion of this theology was based on Russell's interpretation of the "Higher Powers" doctrine articulated in the Christian Scriptures (especially Romans 13:1–7). As he saw it, governments established by men were imperfect but created under the watchful eye of God and therefore due the respect of that supervision. Evil was to be opposed, but the regular operations of government were to be upheld. Russell did not advocate any refusals of civic duty beyond those that would indicate active participation in the earthly order—voting, running for office, and participating in the military. Nonetheless, Russell permitted the possibility of engagement even in these activities by suggesting that good Christians could participate if required by the government.

Even though it had been identified as a central moment in Witness theology, the advent of World War I saw Russell's resolve against war and against government participation therein strengthened. He became more vociferous in his opposition to military participation and was increasingly disappointed by the support the war effort received from clergy in Canada and the United States. His publications grew more outspoken, and at the time of his death in 1916, so noteworthy were his incriminations that he was prohibited entry into Canada and his organization was under increased scrutiny in the United States.[21]

The transfer of leadership after Russell's death was not simple and was not finally resolved in Rutherford's favor until early in 1918, just before the sedition trial. After his release from prison, Rutherford concentrated his efforts in rebuilding the organization; in March 1925, over the objections of the editorial committee, he published an article in the *Watchtower* that integrated recent events with Witness theology and urged members of the organization to press on with their evangelical agenda. Rutherford suggested that the trial and its verdict had been high points for the forces of Satan and that the release of the Witnesses on March 26, 1919, marked a turning point in Satan's rule on earth. On September 8, 1922—after the passing of 1,260 days, as prophesied in Revelation 12:6—Judge Rutherford had admonished the organization's membership assembled at a convention to "[a]dvertise, advertise, advertise the King and the kingdom." "Make no mistake," he reflected in 1925, "by treating this war [against Satan and Satan's forces] as a light or trivial thing. Satan will use ever [*sic*] conceivable method to destroy the remnant of Zion."[22]

At the 1928 annual convention in Detroit, the Jehovah's Witnesses unanimously passed a "Declaration against Satan and for Jehovah," pledging their energy to defeating the forces of Satan on earth.[23] In a speech read in support of the declaration, Rutherford made the connection between Satan and the earthly governments and charged the Witnesses to commit themselves to do battle here on earth. "I now submit the proof that there is an evil god that controls the world; that Jehovah the Almighty God of righteousness will shortly destroy the power of the evil god, and will establish on earth a righteous government that will relieve the people of their burdens and bring them everlasting blessings; that we are now at a crisis and the issue before the people is the greatest of all time." He condemned all governments that were under Satan's control, including the United States, where "millions are without employment and suffer in want for the necessities of life." He exposed corruption in government, in the school systems, among the clergy, and in the media, and attributed all of it to Satan. He encouraged the conventioneers to vote "not against the people," "the men in office," or "the blind preachers who have misled the people." Instead he asked every Witness to vote in favor of Jehovah, entreating "every one who desires to see evil eradicated and righteousness for ever established in the earth, and the people blessed with peace, happiness and life" to vote for the declaration.[24] They apparently all did so, and with the organization well motivated and instructed, the war on Satan was declared and the period of aggressive colportage was begun. So, too, was laid the foundation for the next great period of confrontation with the constitutional order.

## Jehovah's Witnesses and the "Higher Powers," Part 2

Rutherford provided the justification for the new phase of Witness activity with the announcement of a new interpretation of doctrine, which significantly shifted the Jehovah's Witnesses' understanding of the nature of authority and the obligations owed to temporal earthly powers. In 1929, in a two-part series of articles entitled "The Higher Powers," Rutherford explained his new interpretation of Romans 13:1–7 and parallel references in Hebrews 13:17 and 1 Peter 2:13–14.[25] He wrote that the "instruction of the thirteenth chapter of Romans has long been misapplied" and that it was wrongly used to justify such institutions as the divine right of kings. It had not been applied solely to the Christian community, as it was originally intended. He argued that the "Higher Powers" referred specifically to Jehovah and Jesus and that there were no greater authorities. All obligation was owed Jehovah, and any governmental authority in conflict with the "Higher Powers" was invalid and not worthy of loyalty. Respect for governmental authority was based on its laws' harmony with God's, and not on any inherent authority of the state. In other words, whereas Russell had interpreted governmental authority to be founded upon God's ultimate control over institutions that might be temporarily under Satan's influence, Rutherford understood all non–Jehovah's Witness institutions to be irreparably lost; they were owed respect only insofar as their laws coincided with God's law. This was a significant shift; Russell's position of respect for earthly government based on the Witnesses' part in God's plan became for Rutherford a position of condemnation of those earthly governments, which he interpreted as subordinate to Satan.

This new position freed the Jehovah's Witnesses from authority that was not in concert with that derived from Scripture, while it increased the importance of the members' loyalty to the central leadership. Wrote Rutherford, "The Christian obeys every law of the land that is in harmony with God's law. He does not obey merely because it is the law of the land, but because to obey is right," suggesting that those laws determined not to be in harmony could be disobeyed. The only proper position for the righteous Christian was complete disengagement from the affairs of nations and preparation for the final conflagration. "These anointed ones," he wrote, "have a warfare in which they must engage, but it is not a warfare with carnal weapons."[26] Truth came from following God and Jesus, and no earthly government could claim righteousness. Only God's kingdom, as established by faith and obedience to divine law, could claim the loyalty of true Christians.

In issues of the *Watchtower* following the new interpretation of the "Higher Powers" doctrine, it became clear that the interpretation of the role of the United States had shifted significantly. Though Russell had admitted years earlier that the United States, like all other nations, was under the control of Satan, there was also a sense that God's work was evident even in the ministrations of the U.S. government. With Rutherford's new interpretation of the "higher powers," the United States ceased to be a beacon of hope and instead became the proof of Satan's grip on earthly governments. Writing in 1931, Rutherford stated that "[t]he United States government is conducted by imperfect men who are under the influence and control of the invisible ruler, Satan the Devil. . . . If Satan is the invisible ruler of the United States government, which is claimed to be the most nearly ideal, then what can be said about the other governments of earth?"[27] Increasingly the U.S. government served as the target of attacks on the evil of earthly governments. Fraud, corruption, and greed marked the United States, reconstituting as a paragon of evil what had once been understood as the very model of freedom.

It is said that the government of the United States of America comes nearest of any on earth to being an ideal government. No honest man understanding the conditions in the United States can claim that it is a satisfactory government. True its founders declared that all men are endowed with the inalienable rights of life, liberty and the pursuit of happiness; but this ideal has never been realized by the people. True also that the founders of that government said that all just powers of government are derived from the consent of the people; but now the consent of the people is neither asked nor obtained. For some years after it was founded, there was an attempt to carry into effect the announced principles of government; but never has it succeeded. The fundamental laws of the land declare that the people shall have freedom of speech, the right of peaceable assembly, the liberty of conscience without coercion, and the privilege to worship God according to the dictates of each one's conscience. These rules of action are ideal, but they are denied daily by those who have and exercise the power of government. The officials of the United States government take a solemn oath to safeguard and protect the interests of the people; but such an oath is repeatedly violated by the officials, both high and low.[28]

Only one hope was left to the Jehovah's Witness who faithfully followed the word of God. With the removal of the United States from the pedestal of goodness (such as was possible for earthly governments), the Jehovah's Witnesses could trust God and Jesus as the only authorities for righteous living, and the community of faithful Christians (the Jehovah's Witnesses) as their earthly interpreters. No other sources of authority deserved loyalty, and no other sources deserved the devotion of a faithful Jehovah's Witness. Writing on the issue of loyalties divided between God and earthly governments, Rutherford noted that "God will permit no divided devotion between his kingdom and that of the enemy. He will permit no compromise with worldly organizations which at all times blaspheme God's holy name. The faithful anointed, therefore, must do as commanded, that is to say, be fully subject to God and Christ Jesus, who constitute 'the higher powers.'"[29]

The need to concentrate one's devotion on God only and to protect against divided loyalties for fear of violating God's will enabled the organization to set the stage for the next and final step before the greatest period of constitutional litigation was to begin. In a November 1939 issue of the *Watchtower*, Rutherford announced the existence of the "Theocracy," a theocratic government organized around the Jehovah's Witnesses' leadership and based on the model established during the biblical period.[30] As part of an ecclesiastic reorganization begun years earlier, congregational leadership had been altered to become more responsive to the organization's leadership, and responsibilities and geographic supervision were defined more specifically. The article made it clear that the result of this reorganization was a streamlining of authority from God through Jesus to the leadership of the Christian community (in the form of the organization) and then its membership. It marked the development of an articulated, well-defined, well-organized, and self-conscious polity, representative of God and an equal rival to Satan's governments on earth. The community was clearly gearing up for a concerted effort that would have to be well organized, and although that effort was assumed to be of biblical rather than political proportions, in the minds of the community's leadership there was little distinction.

With the announcement of what was called the "Theocratic Government," the forces of good and evil in the minds of the Jehovah's Witness community were clearly set against each other, and there was no doubt about the identity of the enemy. On at least two separate occasions, the *Watchtower* printed calls to action written and signed by Rutherford, calling the Jehovah's Witnesses community to carry the battle to the enemy. "The time of preliminary war is here," he wrote, proclaiming a concerted period of witness. "The Field Marshall of Jehovah, Christ Jesus, is in command of his forces."[31] The field marshal may have been Jesus, but the drill sergeant was Joseph Rutherford, and the Jehovah's Witnesses were ready to do battle.

## The Constitutional Confrontation Begins

Growing in numbers and in confidence, with a theology liberating them from damnable human governmental authority, the Jehovah's Witnesses began a more confrontational program of proselytism. Law professor William McAninch calculates that, beginning with the first Jehovah's Witness arrest in 1928 for preaching, arrests for "selling literature without a license, disturbing the peace, and violating sabbath blue-laws" ballooned, and in the three-year period from 1933 to 1936, the number of arrests increased over 400 percent (from 268 to 1,149). Beginning in the 1930s, the *Watchtower* began offering for sale transcription machines, sound cars, and portable phonographs, and by 1935 the rapid increase in arrests led to the reopening of the legal department at the national headquarters, an office that had been unstaffed since Rutherford became president nearly twenty years earlier. According to historian Merlin Newton, "The plan was that Witnesses would confront legal authorities with the First Amendment," which they were convinced would be applied to state action through the Fourteenth Amendment. This strategy was deployed not because of a deep, abiding faith in the Constitution of the United States, but rather because the leaders of the Jehovah's Witnesses recognized the mechanisms available to further their evangelical interests legally. Commenting on the Witnesses' publications for this period, McAninch observes that "[n]othing in [the Jehovah's Witnesses'] literature indicates an interest in these [First Amendment] rights as generally desirable goals except to the extent that their availability facilitates the Witnesses' own undertakings."[32]

Litigation goals notwithstanding, the earliest court confrontations were not particularly successful for the Witnesses. Beginning in 1937, cases involving the Jehovah's Witnesses began to appear regularly on the docket of the U.S. Supreme Court. But the earliest cases to be considered by the high court, and thus face a full confrontation with the transcending authority of constitutional order, were dismissed for a variety of reasons, including the perceived lack of a federal (i.e., constitutional) question. In 1938 only one of the two cases brought by the Jehovah's Witnesses was given a full hearing before the Supreme Court. In what must have been seen as a major victory for them, the Court ruled in *Lovell v. City of Griffin* that a "city ordinance forbidding as a nuisance the distribution . . . of literature of any kind without first obtaining written permission from the City Manager" was in violation of the Fourteenth Amendment.[33] The other case brought to the Supreme Court was dismissed for want of a federal question.

The Witnesses experienced only modest success in 1939. Of the three cases that reached the Supreme Court that year, one was denied certiorari, and the second was affirmed per curiam (that is, by unsigned and usually brief opinion) against them. Only the third case, *Schneider v. New Jersey* (another colportage case), was decided in favor of the Witnesses. By 1940 the Jehovah's Witnesses saw three cases produce full decisions from the high court's proceedings, and of the three, one ruled favorably to the organization's proselytizing interests, one resulted in a devastating decision permitting the expulsion of students who, for religiously conscientious reasons, refused to salute the flag of the United States, and the third permitted state restrictions on proselytizing activities as long as the restrictions were content-neutral and not arbitrarily applied.

The second of the three to be argued that year, *Minersville School District v. Gobitis*, was pivotal in the development of the Jehovah's Witnesses' participation in the constitutional order. Olin R. Moyle, the attorney for the Jehovah's Witnesses' national office, had been dismissed (and disfellowshipped) after a serious disagreement with Rutherford over the *Gobitis* brief. His replacement, Hayden C. Covington, did not participate in a significant manner in the preparation of the brief, and as Leonard Stevens chronicles, "the Gobitis effort was personally taken over by Judge Rutherford."[34] Though the apparent disagreement between Rutherford and Moyle had little to do with the pending litigation, it seems clear that the litigation strategy of the Jehovah's Witnesses shifted markedly. Stevens describes the Respondent's (Witnesses') Brief as written in the "colorful style of the pontifical religious leader" and comments that its words "seemed to have been chosen more for their oratorical effects on [his] flock than for their judicial impact upon the nation's highest judges."[35] This attitude followed Rutherford into the Court; Stevens describes the scene: "When the impressively tall Judge Rutherford, wearing an unusually colorful suit, stepped to the lectern, it might as well have been a pulpit. He sounded more the evangelical preacher than the lawyer addressing the Supreme Court of the United States. His flamboyant speech favored the Biblical reasons for the Witnesses' opposition to the flag salute and paid hardly any attention to the great constitutional issues at hand." Rutherford had agreed before oral arguments to split his allotted time with the legal representative from the American Civil Liberties Union, who had filed a brief on behalf of the Jehovah's Witnesses. Rutherford did not use all of his portion of the allotment, instead leaving time for the expected questions from the bench, but "as the final echo of his voice bounced from the marble columns, there was only silence that continued to the point of embarrassment. It signified the justices' desire for no more—and finally the disappointed religious leader sat down."[36] The Jehovah's Witnesses lost the case.

Much like Rutherford's imprisonment, this moment was determinative of how the Jehovah's Witnesses would interact with the constitutional order. It is arguable that this experience ensured Covington's position as the official legal spokesperson for the Jehovah's Witnesses and that it also cemented Rutherford's position toward governmental restrictions. According to legal scholar David Manwaring, by 1940 Rutherford was even more convinced of the righteousness of his position and increasingly advocated persistence to the Jehovah's Witnesses who faced legal opposition. The community he led, writes Manwaring, "readily became convinced that their divinely sanctioned work was properly subject to no restraints of time, place or propriety whatever; to make any concessions to public convenience and order would be an affront to Jehovah."[37]

Nevertheless, from this same point forward, Hayden Covington argued every case brought by the Jehovah's Witnesses before the U.S. Supreme Court, winning over 65 percent of them.[38] The briefs became much more legal and less religious and focused primarily on the constitutional issues.[39] Newton comments on the change of legal stewardship: "Hayden Covington, in directing the Witness campaign to 'defend and establish legally the good news,' encouraged fellow Witnesses to put their faith in the Bill of Rights. He stood firmly on the argument that the basic personal liberties protected by the first eight amendments to the U.S. Constitution were guaranteed at all levels of government in the nation through the due process clause of the Fourteenth Amendment. But he concentrated his fire particularly upon violations of the First Amendment guarantees of freedom of religious exercise, speech, and press."[40]

The change from Rutherford to Covington signaled not a change in position, but merely a change in strategy. The key had been found to translate the aims of the Jehovah's Witnesses into the language of the American constitutional order. Over the next ten years, the Jehovah's Witnesses (and Hayden Covington specifically) argued twenty cases before the Supreme Court, litigating such issues as flag-saluting, colportage, and conscientious objection. Throughout that period, the leadership of the Jehovah's Witnesses continued to identify the United States as corrupt while it maintained the integrity of the "Theocratic Government"—the difference was that now the *Watchtower* carried frequent reports about ongoing litigation as it was climbing the legal ladder to the Supreme Court. As early as 1940, commenting on recent legal losses, the *Watchtower* noted that the "dictator spirit" was "rapidly advancing and the liberties of the people are disappearing." In December of the same year, the publication printed an article articulating to its readers (particularly parents of children in public schools) the organization's theological and legal justifications for the battles being waged in the courts over flag-saluting. Over the next decade the readership was regularly encouraged to maintain their vigil; biblical references were provided for use against non–Jehovah's Witness judges and politicians, with the comment on one occasion that "politicians and judges who are wise will refuse to use their public office to serve religious interests against Jehovah's witnesses."[41]

By 1950 the Jehovah's Witnesses had submitted to the U.S. Supreme Court documents for more than fifty cases, resulting in twenty-four full decisions and twenty-nine victories for the organization and its membership. Based on its vast litigation experience, the organization published a how-to manual entitled *Defending and Legally Establishing the Good News,* in which Covington provided a step-by-step description of what could be expected if a member were arrested. The manual instructed its readers on how to interact with the police and the magistrates and how to behave in court; it provided sample copies of legal memoranda and questions to ask various officials, advised the members about what they should do in notifying the national office, and supplied a broad and detailed legal explanation of the Jehovah's Witnesses' rights as litigated to that point. Though most immediately intended for the membership, the manual was also written with an eye toward those officials the members would encounter in the field, for it also contained the traditional warning to those who opposed the work of the organization: "Equality in dealing with us, Jehovah's witnesses, and allowing us full freedom of worship granted by the fundamental law will avoid disturbances in the community or trouble for the state and for us. Granting such freedom, moreover, will bring blessings to the officials from Jehovah God." This was not a severe warning, to be sure, but a theological one, and there can be no doubt that by 1950, standing atop an enormous foundation of positive legal precedent, the organization was confident of God's presence in American legal history, fully aware of its members' legal rights, and not afraid to press those rights in court even at the risk of antagonizing elected officials. Reflecting the confidence borne of such success, in a law review article that appeared in 1946 (but which was probably written as early as 1944), Covington even argued for a less doctrinaire interpretation of stare decisis, using his own victories as specific examples of the benefit such a stance could produce from the Court.[42] The Jehovah's Witnesses, in large part because of Covington's stewardship of Rutherford's mandate and their startling success in court, were able to establish their prerogatives legally and to maintain the integrity of their own particularistic transcending source of authority.

## Jehovah's Witnesses and the "Higher Powers," Part 3

Joseph Rutherford had died in 1942. He was succeeded by Nathan Knorr, a man dedicated to leaving the legalities to his proven litigator, Hayden Covington. "By that time," declares Newton, "the society . . . had discontinued using the phonograph and asked the Witnesses to know their scripture, to dress modestly, and to remain courteous even in the face of rudeness."[43] Litigation was not discontinued, however, and many cases begun in the last of Rutherford's years continued to work their way through the system.

The Jehovah's Witnesses were successful to a remarkable degree.

In addition to its favorable Court record up through 1950, the organization by 1955 could claim another seven victories from eleven cases argued. In other words, out of fifty-one cases to produce a decision, the Jehovah's Witnesses were victorious in thirty-six (almost 71 percent) of them. As James Penton concludes, this level of success itself became a challenge for the leadership, who "came to feel that it was obvious that there was much good in human governments. Hence, it was unreasonable to hold strictly to their 1929 position." "If secular governments were entirely outside of God's favor," he asks, "how was it possible that at least some of them were coming to recognize and even protect Jehovah's Witnesses in their persons and activities?"[44]

In a series of articles published in the November and December 1962 issues of the *Watchtower*, the Jehovah's Witnesses' leadership announced a new interpretation of the "Higher Powers" doctrine that had been so instrumental in justifying the organization's confrontational stance toward the constitutional order for over thirty years. Since God had created the world, the leadership concluded, all of the political entities therein must also have been created by God. The political authority of the non-Christian (that is, non–Jehovah's Witness) world therefore must have derived its authority from God. "Certainly" wrote the author, "we [Jehovah's Witnesses] cannot close our eyes to the fact that there are authorities outside the Christian congregation." Furthermore, since "truly dedicated Christians like Jehovah's Witnesses do not meddle in politics or run for political office," there could be no avoiding non-Christian authority. And even though Satan still ruled the earthly governments, all were under the watchful eye of God, who had given even non-Christians consciences: "[A]ll nations and peoples descended from the one original man Adam and his wife Eve, in both of whom God implanted this sensing of right and wrong called 'conscience.' . . . Hence many of their laws show the effect of a God-given conscience still lingering to some extent." Because of this residuum of God's design in all humanity, and because of the supreme lordship of God over all, there was reason enough for members of the Jehovah's Witness community to give respect to governmental authority—their authority was understood to be relative rather than absolute. "Since the Christians' subjection to worldly 'superior authorities' is only relative, it does not obligate them to obey any worldly laws that go contrary to the laws of the Supreme Lawgiver, Jehovah God."[45] Even non–Jehovah's Witnesses were part of God's plan; therefore, good laws could be obeyed and the Witnesses could be cooperative with governmental authority.

The significance of the new interpretation became startlingly obvious in the examples chosen by the *Watchtower* to illuminate this position. "For not taking a stand against God's arrangement concerning the 'superior authorities' on earth, Jesus was rewarded. He was resurrected from death to heavenly life and was given a royal seat at God's own right hand in heaven." Suggesting that going along with earthly human authority, even if it meant death, was the preferred path for the Witness, the *Watchtower* offered a radically new way of interpreting the stance of the Jehovah's Witness community toward the constitutional order. Witnesses were admonished to behave well since "[s]tate rulers or officials may voluntarily praise members of the congregations of Jehovah's Witnesses, particularly if, *en masse* or as an assembly, they observe right conduct, morality, decency, and good order." Model (if disengaged) citizenship became the mode of behavior for Jehovah's Witnesses, and as Witness historian Penton observes, the members were now expected to "show deep respect for governmental officials and public order, to pay taxes as required by law, and to obey secular authority in every matter not specifically contrary to divine command."[46] The confrontational style begun under Rutherford's leadership was out of step with the organization's new interpretation of the Scripture.

Quite possibly as a result of this change, by the 1970s the Jehovah's Witnesses had ceased to be in regular, sustained conflict with the American constitutional order. The cases to reach the Supreme Court after 1962 involving members of the community were relatively few, irregular, and built on precedents developed in earlier Supreme Court decisions. Supporting documentation for a 1981 unemployment compensation case involving a Jehovah's Witness showed no evidence that the organization's legal office participated in the preparation of the legal briefs or oral arguments for the case. And although the organization continues to represent its members before courts in this country and around the world, sustained litigation before the U.S. Supreme Court has virtually ceased. Legal scholar William McAninch ponders with some curiosity why it was that the group, "previously the victims of harsh, if not discriminatory, treatment, should suddenly be dealt with more leniently." He suggests that the reason could be that Witness claims had stood the test of time, and that the Witnesses were "not the most shrill example of society's dissenters." In addition, as a result of the theological shift in 1962, the community was "acquiring a reputation as hard-working, responsible individuals." Finally, the issues originally raised by the organization were no longer of concern to the constitutional order, and thus their claims ceased to be a threat. As historian R. Laurence Moore notes, by the second half of the twentieth century, the American public made no distinction between Jehovah's Witness colporteurs and any other door-to-door salesmen.[47] Just as significantly, the organization had established a foothold in the constitutional order, had engineered enough of a change to provide itself with room to accomplish its mission effectively, and thus had found a separate peace for itself. In other words, by taking the fight to the Court and doing so in terms that the Court could translate for its own purposes and agendas, the Jehovah's Witnesses were able to redirect the limiting parameters of authority in the American constitutional order and still maintain the integrity of their own theological presuppositions.

## Constitutional "Higher Powers" and their Favored Arguments

It is suggestive that the experiences of Joseph Rutherford played a pivotal role in explaining the Jehovah's Witnesses' trajectory toward confrontation with the constitutional order and its stance thereto once the confrontation was engaged. However, on the other side of the debate were factors that argue that at least part of the Witnesses' success was due to the nature of their arguments or, at the very least, to how they were interpreted by the Supreme Court before whom they were brought. Indeed, a pattern emerges when one considers the extensive litigation argued by the Jehovah's Witnesses before the Supreme Court, particularly when their gains and losses before that bench are compared.[48]

Most of the decisions rendered by the justices rely on the role and significance of the First Amendment right to free speech alongside—but just as often *rather than*—the other First Amendment right to free exercise of religion. From the beginning, the religious free exercise argument was less persuasive than the free speech argument. All of the cases denied a full hearing by the Court from 1937 to 1940 relied solely on religious free exercise grounds, whereas three of the five that received a full hearing during that same period and that relied in part or wholly on free speech arguments were decided in favor of the Witnesses. Even the Court's decision in *Cantwell v. Connecticut*—which not only gave credence to the religious free exercise argument but expanded its application to state as well as federal action—took special note of the free speech arguments offered by the Witnesses, affirming their plausibility as significant in the decision. The decision in *Minersville School District v. Gobitis,* a significant loss for the Jehovah's Witnesses, is problematic in part because the Court sidestepped the issues of the First Amendment altogether and based its decision on the proper parameters of Court involvement in such an issue. It is clear that Justice Felix Frankfurter, writing for the Court, recognized the role and value of religious free exercise, although in the end he convinced enough of the Court to support his position in favor of judicial restraint, leaving to the democratic process the difficult issue of educational policy.[49]

The string of losses from 1940 to 1942 illustrates the power of the free speech argument. In a series of three decisions involving Jehovah's Witnesses, the Court permitted restrictions on public speech so long as the ordinances were content-neutral; it permitted restrictions on speech deemed to be "fighting words" that might provoke a breach of the peace; and it permitted licensing the distribution of Jehovah's Witness literature, an activity that was considered a commercial enterprise. It is worth noting that in this last, closely divided decision, *Jones v. Opelika,* the Court compared the license assessed to the Jehovah's Witnesses with other proper limitations on (secular) free speech. In each of these decisions, although the Court permitted limitations on the actions of the Jehovah's Witnesses, in the Court's view it was their free speech that was being limited, not their free exercise rights. Moreover, the restrictions were deemed permissible only because the ordinances remained neutral as to the content of the information being disseminated.

Beginning in 1943, the Jehovah's Witnesses finally seemed able to take advantage of the combination of the religious free exercise and the free speech arguments of the First Amendment. The Court's brief decision in *Jamison v. Texas* integrated defenses of both in a case involving the distribution of Jehovah's Witnesses' printed material. In the arguments concerning religious free exercise, however, the Court still used a content analysis of the distributed literature to distinguish it from "purely commercial leaflets" (whose distribution could be restricted), implying that there was something qualitatively different about religious speech that differentiated it from nonreligious speech. In *Murdock v. Pennsylvania* the synthesis of the two rights reached its jurisprudential zenith. Writing for the Court, Justice William Douglas recognized the religious significance of colportage, comparing it favorably to evangelism worthy of protection.[50]

Ironically, the *Murdock* decision was the last of the Jehovah's Witnesses' decisions to rest so strongly on religious free exercise grounds; subsequent decisions relied more heavily on arguments involving free speech. Even *West Virginia State Board of Education v. Barnette,* considered a landmark religious free exercise decision, rested almost completely on free speech grounds. Justice Robert Jackson, dismissing the religious status of the parties involved as less than controlling, wrote for the Court that "[t]o sustain the compulsory flag salute we are required to say that a Bill of Rights which guards the individual's right to speak his own mind, left it open to public authorities to compel him to utter what is not in his mind."[51] Powerfully underscoring the continued value of the free speech arguments—or the effects of their absence—the Supreme Court ruled in *Prince v. Massachusetts* that a state statute prohibiting minors from being engaged in the distribution of literature was not an infringement of the First Amendment guarantees of religious free exercise. No free speech claim was made.

The remainder of the decisions from the Jehovah's Witnesses' litigation docket rested primarily on free speech grounds. In two nearly parallel cases, the Court ruled that the ownership of a municipality (a company town and a housing area for civilian military employees) had no effect on the right of a Jehovah's Witness to distribute information. But the Court argued less on the right (religious or otherwise) to distribute the information and more on the right of the public to receive the information, noting in one of the decisions that "[t]o act as good citizens [the residents of these municipalities] must be informed. In order to enable them to be properly informed their information must be uncensored. There is no more reason for depriving these people of the liberties guaranteed by the First and Fourteenth Amendments than there is for curtailing these freedoms with respect to any other citizen."[52]

Underscoring the vital part free speech arguments played in the decision, in his concurring opinion in *Niemotko v. Maryland*, Justice Felix Frankfurter referred to the role of the Jehovah's Witnesses in the debate over free speech rights. He cited fourteen separate Supreme Court decisions involving that organization and the debate over free speech.[53] The power of the free speech component in Jehovah's Witness litigation made a lasting imprint on the judicial philosophy of the Court. In the 1977 decision of *Wooley v. Maynard*, the Court ruled that a Jehovah's Witness couple who objected to the presence of the New Hampshire motto, "Live Free or Die," on their license plates could not be compelled by the state to advertise an ideology they found objectionable.[54]

## An Extrapolation of the Free Speech Argument

Not all of the cases brought to the Supreme Court by the Jehovah's Witnesses involved flag-saluting, colportage, or public preaching. The significant struggles experienced over the country's military involvement in World War I left the organization better prepared to address the issues when the United States entered World War II. But when cases involving Jehovah's Witness conscientious objectors reached the Court, there was no overt effort to argue them on the grounds of free speech, and judging by the evidence alone, there were no First Amendment rights at issue.[55] Notwithstanding that point, it seems clear that the level of engagement and success enjoyed by the group rested in no small part on the Court's sensitivity to free speech concerns over religious free exercise concerns. In fact, the numerous cases involving Jehovah's Witness conscientious objector claims mirror the pattern of apparent success for free speech claims. Although all of the cases involving objection to military and alternative service rested on procedural grounds—as opposed to the mostly substantive, First Amendment decisions handed down by the Court in the other more traditional Jehovah's Witnesses cases—they, too, suggest a privileged position for free speech over free exercise. And while none of the decisions relied on First Amendment reasoning, but rested instead on the statutory construction of the federal legislation surrounding military conscription, there is still a pattern of differentiation between action and belief. It may be more obvious in the colportage and flag-salute decisions, but it is present here nonetheless.

The pattern does not seem intentional, but from 1944 to 1960 the Supreme Court rarely challenged the alleged misclassification of Jehovah's Witnesses as conscientious objectors rather than as ministers. According to the relevant statutes regarding conscription, those classified as conscientious objectors were required to serve in some form of alternative service, whereas ministers were exempt from all service.[56] All members of the Jehovah's Witnesses consider themselves ministers, but in case after case the Court commented only on the process of how the classification decision was made and specifically avoided the substance of the decisions. In each case the Witness involved was criminally charged with violating some aspect of the conscription statutes, was given some manner of hearing (court trial or administrative hearing), and raised appeals based on what he believed to be his misclassification as a conscientious objector rather than a minister. In each case the Court granted a new trial on the matter because of procedural improprieties and either reversed the lower court's decision because of violations of due process rights or affirmed the lower court's decision based on proper procedure.

The Court rarely questioned the conscientiousness of the claimant in these cases, and the fact that the parties involved were Jehovah's Witnesses seemed of minimal significance to the rulings. In *Falbo v. United States*, religious identity was not even mentioned until Justice Frank Murphy's dissent.[57] However, since the Court did not recognize the Jehovah's Witnesses' claim that all of its members were ministers, it differentiated between the right to hold conscientious beliefs and the capacity to act on those beliefs by ministering to others. This historic doctrine of distinguishing between action and belief, most strongly argued by the Court in a Mormon decision in 1879, was weakened in 1963 and evaporated in 1965 in two very different cases, neither of which involved a Jehovah's Witness.[58] Yet throughout the 1940s and 1950s, the Court continued to differentiate between a Jehovah's Witness's right to hold beliefs and his or her capacity to act religiously on them, seeming to give preference to the free speech right to speak or not speak about a belief, while leaving in a disadvantaged position the free exercise right to perform a religious function based on those beliefs.

## The Role of Free Speech

The evidence thus is overwhelming that free speech arguments were central to the successes of the Jehovah's Witnesses. In the few cases brought solely on religious free exercise grounds, the Witnesses were singularly unsuccessful.[59] The period of the Witnesses' greatest success (1943–46) saw the winning combination of free speech and religious free exercise rights. And though the organization did experience defeats in cases argued under the rhetoric of free speech, there is no doubt that such arguments were more likely than not to be the focus of the Court's decision, regardless of the ultimate outcome of the case.

The power of the free speech argument was not overlooked by the organization's leadership. After a period of significant success using that strategy before the U.S. Supreme Court, Covington and Canadian Witness attorney W. Glen How conducted a campaign to expand the rights of Jehovah's Witnesses beyond the northern U.S. border to Canada, where the organization had experienced continued legal trouble since World War I. At that time Canada had no written bill of rights and therefore no stated guarantee of religious freedom. Most of the charges brought against the Jehovah's Witnesses in Canada were prosecuted under laws regarding sedition, which made the public advocacy of Witness beliefs a crime. In two articles printed in consecutive issues of the *Canadian Bar Review* in 1948, Covington and How, appealing to a general audience, minimized the specific controversies in which the Jehovah's Witnesses found themselves and argued for a Canadian bill of rights that would protect free speech in addition to freedom of religion.[60]

Both articles emphasized the free speech element of their arguments. Covington discussed the "clear and present danger" doctrine that the U.S. Supreme Court had developed to protect free speech, as well as the successful cases he had argued before the Court for the right to disseminate information. He spent less than six pages of his thirty-three-page article on the issue of freedom of religion, and in the end he framed his argument as one for an increased "dignity of the individual." Quoting Supreme Court justice Jackson's decision in *Edwards v. California,* Covington noted the story in the Christian Scriptures in which Paul's Roman citizenship served as a shield to protect him: "Take heed what thou doest; for this man is a Roman."[61] Covington argued that all citizens would benefit from a Canadian bill of rights, much as their neighbors to the south had. He did not have to address the benefit to be reaped for the Jehovah's Witnesses specifically; his appeal was for all citizens of Canada.

Glen How similarly devoted a disproportionate amount of space to the protection of free speech in the British Commonwealth. He traced its development from the Magna Carta through the English Bill of Rights of 1689, pointing out that the document protected the speech only of members of Parliament. He also examined the history of the doctrine of habeas corpus and the citizen's right to challenge the government's authority to censor communications. Just over two pages of his thirty-eight-page article discussed freedom of religion, and like Covington, How argued that a Canadian bill of rights would be beneficial for all Canadians. "What can be done to one minority in Quebec," he wrote, referring to the particularly difficult situation of the Jehovah's Witnesses in that province, "can be done to other groups in other parts of the country, until there is unending discrimination and persecution."[62]

Both attorneys seemed to understand that the argument for free speech would be most persuasive to the Canadian audience, apparently hostile to the religious rights of Jehovah's Witnesses, much as it had been instrumental in their organization's victories in the United States. This understanding was based in part on an article in the *Minnesota Law Review*, written four years earlier by retired Minnesota state judge Edward Waite, which had given the Jehovah's Witnesses sole credit for the expansion of free speech rights in the United States. Discussing the stream of Witness litigation from 1938 until the article was written, he pointed to the role of speech as a central element of each case. "The cases involving the numerous activities of the Jehovah's Witnesses," wrote Waite, identifying the conjunction of freedom of speech and freedom of religion, "are points on the line that defines the scope of protection accorded these rights by the due process clause of the Fourteenth Amendment in the field where freedom of expression and disseminating ideas is employed as a means for propagating religion." He concluded that "present constitutional guarantees of personal liberty . . . are far broader than they were before the spring of 1938," owing in large part to the sixteen decisions returned in the thirty-one Jehovah's Witnesses cases.[63]

And indeed they were. By 1944 the Supreme Court had ruled that the truth claims of a particular religious belief were not subject to judicial scrutiny, and by 1963 it had established that, for the most part, there could be no acceptable way of distinguishing action from belief when the two were related in the religious life of the believer. But the greatest impact had been recorded in the realm of free speech. Declares constitutional scholar Philip Kurland, "Particularly in that area where freedom of religion blends into freedom of speech have the Witnesses been active, with resulting confusion of [Court] doctrine but expansion of the right of militant minority sects to the protection of the state in the virulent attacks on the views of others."[64]

## Free Speech versus Religious Freedom

It would seem to be more than coincidence that the Jehovah's Witnesses benefited from shifts in contemporary jurisprudence as they were bringing their own litigation to the Supreme Court. Some Court historians have suggested that their period of intense litigation brought about a shift in legal philosophy, resulting in an acknowledgment that the rights guaranteed in the Bill of Rights were beyond political consideration. Writing in the heyday of Jehovah's Witness litigation, U.S. Justice Department attorneys Victor Rotnem and F. G. Folsom observed that the value of the Court's decision in *Lovell v. City of Griffin* was "the tacit and not much disputed acknowledgment that free religious expression is protected by the Constitution's free speech and free press guarantees." More than fifty years later, reflecting on the busiest period of Jehovah's Witness litigation—the string of decisions from 1942 to 1946— Merlin Newton states that "*Jones* and *Marsh* were vital links in the chain of events and the legal philosophy that championed the cause of individual liberty. The decisions represented not only victories for the Jehovah's Witnesses but also turning points in the nation's constitutional commitment to individual rights and indexes of the increasingly activist role of the Court as the guardian of personal liberty."[65] Describing a slightly different period of Witness litigation and the reason for the Supreme Court's reversal from its position in *Gobitis* (1940) to its position in *Barnette* (1943), Joseph McKinney argues that

The legal realists' expansion of Constitutional [sic] interpretation from economic legislation to the first ten amendments, including civil liberties, seems to be the principal reason why the Court reversed itself within three years. Underlying the change in judicial philosophy regarding the role of the Supreme Court was the Court's view of the "temper of the times." The circumstances of the 1940s were such, as we have seen, that the Supreme Court would not rely on the political process to protect the Bill of Rights. Justice Jackson argued that the very purpose of the Bill of Rights was to withdraw certain subjects from the vicissitudes of political controversy and to place them beyond the reach of majorities and officials and to establish them as legal principles to be applied by the courts. Thus, an enlightened legal realist could not leave to the politicians the most important and fundamental values on which America was built.[66]

All of these scholars suggested that the fortunes of the Witnesses rested solely on the changes occurring in the Court's attitudes toward individual liberty. This is certainly true enough. Nonetheless, the very fact that the most successful arguments offered by the Witnesses were couched in free speech claims—whereas religious claims seemed less than compelling—implies that, regardless of the Court's shifting jurisprudence, there was still a significant difference between how it understood free exercise rights and how it understood free speech rights. First Amendment scholar William Van Alstyne proposes that, regardless of seemingly nostalgic claims to the contrary, free speech might actually be considered the "first freedom," because its foundation can be found prior to the First Amendment in such places as Article 1, section 6, of the Constitution, which protects the free speech rights of members of Congress when speaking on the House or Senate floor. This protection dates back to Parliament's assertion of it against the royal practice of imprisoning legislators in the Tower of London for what they had said in Parliament and explains much about the priority given by the government to speech over religion.[67]

It is a more plausible explanation that the Court was more comfortable with free speech claims specifically in contrast to religious free exercise claims *by their very nature*, not necessarily because of the shifting topography of constitutional jurisprudence. Given the Court's long history of preferring the protection of belief over action, as well as its role as the high priesthood of the American constitutional order, it is not surprising that speech would be less a perceived threat than would challenges to the transcending authority of the U.S. Constitution.[68] As long as the Jehovah's Witnesses continued to press their claims in terms of greater free speech rights, the Court could maintain its position as protector of the ultimate authority of the realm. But when the Jehovah's Witnesses relied on claims for greater religious free exercise rights—given Rutherford's well-publicized declarations of an alternative theocratic authority and concomitant motivations for massive unorthodox religious activity—the transcending authority of the Constitution was at stake and had to be protected. Granted, the Court never expressed the dilemma over conflicting transcending authorities as baldly as I have here—it never had to. By reference to the maintenance of order, keeping the peace, and protecting society, the Supreme Court was articulating its position as the guardian of the American constitutional order. By shifting the terms of the debate and thus removing the threat, the Jehovah's Witnesses' leadership was able to safeguard the integrity of its community's transcending authority and to establish for itself a position in the American polity congruent to, if not subordinate to, the transcending authority of the constitutional order.

According to survey researchers Barry Kosmin and Seymour Lachman, in 1990 Jehovah's Witnesses represented just under 1 percent of the American population over the age of eighteen, and of the "larger churches," were the only religious community to be populated by a "minority majority" (in other words, only 48 percent identified themselves as non-Hispanic white). However, as historian Mark Noll indicates, the Jehovah's Witnesses grew by 42 percent from 1980 to 1988, a growth rate surpassed only by the Presbyterian Church in America (45 percent) and the Assemblies of God (102 percent) and tied with the Church of Jesus Christ of Latter-day Saints.[69] And yet, amid this diversity and growth, the Jehovah's Witnesses still do not display social characteristics emblematic of the pluralism one would expect from such statistics. Instead, they remain in many ways a community detached from the surrounding culture. Among all of the religious communities analyzed in the Kosmin-Lachman survey, the Jehovah's Witness community ranked last overall in the "social-status ranking on 'Protestant Ethic' variables." Within that category, it was lowest in percentage of its membership to graduate from college (4.7 percent), second lowest in percentage working full-time (44.1 percent [only Christian Scientists ranked lower, with 40.1 percent working full-time]), sixth lowest in median annual income ($20,900), and seventh lowest in home ownership (59.1 percent). And as Kosmin and Lachman argue, one of the more unusual features of the Jehovah's Witnesses is their stance toward American political interaction; they "abhor politics in the same way they do blood transfusions and higher education. ... [O]nly 9 percent aligned themselves with either of the two main political parties [6 percent Democratic, 3 percent Republican] (16% refused even to answer the party-preference question)."[70]

Of course, none of this contradicts what has been found in the Witnesses' engagement with the American constitutional order. Discovering themselves at odds with American culture, they were able to maintain their particularistic source of authority while translating their arguments into terms understandable to the arbiters of the order, the U.S. Supreme Court. They refused to recognize the superiority of the Constitution over their religious fundamentals but were willing to use the legal institutions insofar as they could protect their right not to assimilate (as the socioeconomic and political findings of Kosmin and Lachman's survey indicate). Although there were significant changes in the theology of the community, the changes were the result of the community's successes; they were not caused by the external pressure from the constitutional order that the group regularly confronted. In fact, given what we can now see as a significant change in First Amendment religion and free speech conceptualizations, it seems more accurate to identify any shift in policy with the constitutional order itself, not with the Jehovah's Witnesses. By recasting their claims in free speech as well as (or instead of) religious justifications, the Witnesses were able to convert the constitutional order rather than vice versa.

This first study provides a view of the ground rules of engagement with the American constitutional order. First, confrontation of some sort is inevitable, and the results are thus the product of this confrontation. Second, in the case of constitutional congruence, the key is not complete separation. As can be seen from the case of the Jehovah's Witnesses, both the American constitutional order and the religious community are convinced they have been victorious. However, as the next study shows, victory is a relative concept in the struggle over authority, and different results may lead to the same declaration of victory. In the case of the Jehovah's Witnesses, the degree of sacrifice in community authority was minimal compared to the corresponding sacrifice of the constitutional order— the Supreme Court ruled regularly in their favor and against the governmental bodies named in the suits. In the case of the Church of Jesus Christ of Latter-day Saints, the sacrifice of authority asked of the community by the American constitutional order was great and the confrontation intense. The difference between constitutional congruence and constitutional conversion might be a subjective one of degree, but as we shall see, for the Mormons it had more than symbolic repercussions.

# Constitutional Conversion

### Latter-day Saints and the Constitutional Order

> Behold, this is a choice land, and whatsoever
> nation shall possess it shall be free from
> bondage, and from captivity, and from all other
> nations under heaven, if they will but serve the
> God of the land, who is Jesus Christ, who hath
> been manifested by the things which we have
> written.                          ETHER 2:12
> Book of Mormon

It might strike the reader as unusual—and certainly ahistorical—
to present the history of Mormon interaction with the American
constitutional order *after* a discussion of the Jehovah's Witnesses.
The latter account dates only from the middle decades of the twentieth century, whereas the former begins in the second half of the
nineteenth. Nevertheless, there are significant reasons for ordering
them this way. First, we move from a confrontation that was primarily with the Supreme Court—making the story relatively simple—to one in which Congress played the leading role and the other
two branches of the government had significant parts. Second, the
challenge of the Church of Jesus Christ of Latter-day Saints to the
American constitutional order included a physical, territorial claim

that was absent from the Jehovah's Witnesses' claims.[1] Although the Jehovah's Witnesses fully expected the destruction of all earthly realms (including the United States), their theocratic alternative never included an actual site-specific relocation or the creation of an alternative competing government to await the final cosmic battle between good and evil.[2] Speculation on the role of this factor will be left for general conclusions, but it should be noted here that the absence of a territorial feature does distinguish the Jehovah's Witnesses from the two remaining cases.

Even though the discussion in the first chapter implied that Mormons "converted" to a position of accepting the authority of the American constitutional order, it is also true that from its earliest articulations Mormon theology strongly supported many of the ideals of American society. The evidence suggests that progressively, over the course of forty years, Mormon confidence in those in positions of authority waned to the point of complete distrust in the system, eventuating in a perceived need to choose between particularistic and pluralistic sources of transcending authority. It would be more accurate, therefore, to categorize the Mormon position less as "converting" to a particular position than as accepting over time what the dominant culture envisioned (with great vigor) was the community's proper place in the American constitutional order. During the period before that moment of acceptance, the Mormons experienced an incremental increase in conflict with the instrumentalities of the order; and unlike the Jehovah's Witnesses, they were unable to translate their particularistic source of authority in terms familiar to the order. Thus, the Mormons could not convince society of their authority's general acceptability. Ultimately, significant concessions were required of the Mormon leadership, with very little conceded by the American constitutional order.[3] Because of this unequal power dynamic and because the LDS Church would eventually adopt the rationale behind the authority of the American constitutional order, the LDS Church's experiences can be understood as more conversionary than congruent.

Turning to the specifics of the Saints' encounter, it has become rather common to discuss their difficulties with the American constitutional order in terms of the debate surrounding plural marriage. There is no doubt that charges of polygamy were often the rallying cry of anti-Mormon forces in Ohio, Missouri, Illinois, and ultimately across the nation, causing a great many of the political and social difficulties experienced by the Mormon community from the 1840s until the early part of this century. And it is certainly apparent that a significant number of non-Mormons were sincerely offended by Mormon practice. However, as historian Lawrence Foster has argued, Mormon plural marriage was only one of several unorthodox family arrangements practiced in the middle nineteenth century by various groups. Yet politically the Mormons received the brunt of antipathy and attack.[4]

The threat to the American constitutional order, though often cloaked by the issue of polygamy, actually centered on the competition over authority between Mormon leadership and the federal government. It was over the issue of polygamy that this competition was expressed, but the heart of the matter lay in the claim of authority Mormon leadership attempted to establish through the policy of plural marriage (as well as other doctrines unorthodox in the constitutional order) in the first place. Whether it was plural marriage or nontraditional economic and political structures, the LDS Church wished to express itself as authoritative on issues affecting Mormons. It can now be seen that there was little hope such behaviors and expressions of authority challenging the American constitutional order would be acceptable, regardless of the issue. Though many, both Mormon and non-Mormon, may have understood the issue to revolve around the morality of plural marriage, there can be little doubt that so far as the American constitutional order was concerned, the issue was whether the Church had the right to deviate from traditional conceptualizations of that constitutional order. In this case it was a question of who controlled the authority to declare any policy—such as plural marriage—acceptable. Once the full weight of the American constitutional order was brought to bear on the LDS Church, and the issue of competing authority was finally resolved, Mormons entered the mainstream of American religion to become what Leo Tolstoy called "*the* American religion."[5] The conflict over plural marriage was only the outward manifestation of this struggle; once the confrontation over authority was resolved, so, too, was the confrontation over plural marriage.

We must therefore go beyond the issue of marital arrangements in order to understand the nature of the encounter between the Mormons and the federal government. In the earliest phase of Mormonism may be found the roots of the sense of authority—including physical and social as well as moral and spiritual realms—that brought it into open conflict with the American constitutional order.

## Joseph Smith and the Kingdom of God

One hundred years before H. Richard Niebuhr published his classic analysis of Protestant Christianity in the United States, Joseph Smith, Jr., was at work generating his own Mormon version of the Kingdom of God in America.[6] Smith, a product of the religious ferment spreading through upstate New York and New England, would develop in his religious teachings the notion of a totalistic society functioning under the religious ideology articulated in the Book of Mormon. Fully millennial in its expectations, the Mormon notion of the Kingdom expressed traditional Mormon notions of materiality—it was not to be a mysterious or spiritual configuration beyond the grasp or understanding of humanity. Instead it was to be a physical, experiential reality initiated by the elect, fulfilled by God, and ultimately governed by Jesus Christ. Based in part on traditional Protestant Christian eschatology and in part on American nationalism, the Mormon expectation saw God's hand in the concealment of the North American continent until a time when it could be revealed for specific cosmic purposes. Also included in this cosmic drama was the belief that the Constitution of the United States, as the instrument that would guarantee Mormons the ability to flourish in an atmosphere of religious freedom, had been inspired by God and created to serve divine purposes. Cited on several occasions in the Book of Mormon and in Joseph Smith's Doctrine and Covenants, the Constitution foreordained the establishment of the United States in order to permit true religious freedom and make possible the reestablishment of the teachings of Lehi and his descendants (the ancestors of the first Mormons). When the time was right, the Church of Jesus Christ of Latter-day Saints, with the help of righteous non-Mormons, would establish the Kingdom of God and begin the holy administration of the cosmos under divine order and sanction.[7] The LDS Church and the Kingdom of God were understood as two separate and distinct bodies, although in Mormon theology the former would certainly serve to guide the latter.

Given their understanding of the U.S. Constitution as a tool inspired by God to serve specific purposes, it is understandable that in addition to considering that document sacrosanct, the Mormons believed it to be beyond the corruption of human limitations. Thus, when assistance was needed to combat local anti-Mormonism, Smith and the LDS Church leadership turned to the federal government, fully expecting it to enforce the doctrines inspired by God and established in the federal charter. As early as 1834 the Mormon community sought federal intervention and relief from persecution suffered at the hands of anti-Mormon state governments. Petitions to Presidents Andrew Jackson and Martin Van Buren begged for relief from actions of states unwilling to safeguard the Mormons from unruly citizens.[8] The response to these requests was generally the same—the federal government had no authority over state actions. As Mormon experiences in Ohio, Missouri, and Illinois steadily worsened, Mormon leadership became more and more frustrated by this declared lack of federal jurisdiction.[9] The refusal of the federal government to intervene by applying the sacred freedoms guaranteed by God in the Constitution provided the Mormons with increasing evidence that, although the institutions of the federal government rested on a holy foundation, they were governed by evil men bent on the destruction of God's people. As Brigham Young, the second great Mormon leader, admitted after the Mormons were safely outside of any state jurisdiction, the problems experienced by this community could all be traced to "the damned rascals who administer the government."[10] With every rejection of the pleas for help, federal officials increased the cosmic tension experienced by the Mormons.

However, still firmly believing in the sanctity of the institutions established by the Constitution, the Mormon community was not ready to abandon the process. If the states could not be trusted to control their citizens and the federal executive branch considered itself helpless to get involved on behalf of the persecuted Mormons, the logical conclusion was to pursue positions of authority within the federal government. On January 29, 1844, after considering the responses of the various announced candidates to questions of specific Mormon interest and finding them unsatisfactory, Joseph Smith decided to run for president of the United States of America. As historian J. D. Williams notes, Smith justified the campaign on the belief that the Mormons could not get a fair hearing in the respective states and the fact that the federal government as it was presently administered had not come to their aid.[11] It is just as likely that Smith felt that, given his intensifying political and legal difficulties in both Missouri and Illinois, he was between a rock and a hard place and could not openly support either of the major political parties. Smith's candidacy for the presidency ended abruptly with his assassination on June 27, 1844.

Increasingly tense confrontations with local communities had encouraged the Mormons to consider the possibility of yet another relocation even before the assassination. Because the LDS Church leadership recognized that part of the problem was based in hostile local communities and their supportive state governments, Church leaders had begun formulating plans to remove to unsettled territory. Addressing Mormon attitudes after their experiences in Missouri, legal historians Edwin Firmage and Richard Mangrum accurately describe Mormon conclusions reached by 1844. They argue that, with each encounter with state and federal governments, the Mormons became more aware that "the political branches of the federal government . . . were incapable, incompetent, or at least disinclined to offer either protection or redress. If indeed the law was to be their protector and shield, it must somehow be structured to meet their particular needs and be interpreted and enforced by sympathetic individuals." Part of the strategy to structure the law as "their protector and shield" included the creation of the Council of Fifty, a governmental body established on March 11, 1844, and composed overwhelmingly (but not entirely) of Mormons. The council was designed primarily to resettle Mormons in an unincorporated territory and to administer the law as they understood it under the U.S. Constitution. As the architects of the Kingdom of God, the council would establish a polity in which all peoples were free and the principles of the Mormon priesthood under the direction of Jesus Christ governed society. Clear lines were to be drawn between the Kingdom of God (administered by the council) and the LDS Church, always under the jurisdiction of the First Presidency and its advisors, the Quorum of the Twelve. Historian Richard Poll suggests that the creation of the Council of Fifty was part of Smith's strategy for his presidential campaign and that it represented what would have become, if his campaign had been successful, a cabinet of sorts.[12]

The escalation of difficulties in Illinois that ultimately led to the assassination of Joseph Smith also ended the formative stage in the Mormon community's frustrated relationship with the federal government. In retrospect—and in light of this analysis of the authority of the American constitutional order—it seems inevitable that the Mormon community would encounter difficulties (even on the state level) as it stressed its differences with its neighbors. Observes Klaus Hansen: "[T]he Mormon prophet refused to honor the unwritten contract that the denominations had entered into with American society to mind their own business and not to question the social and political arrangements of the powers that be."[13]

As a result of the assassination, the Mormons were left with only one clear choice. If they were to gain some control over their own destinies and to live free of the persecution that had followed them, they would have to establish their own polity in which they controlled the state government. By doing so, they could guarantee the protection of their religious tenets. With the federal government unwilling to pursue First Amendment claims against state governments, however, the Mormons realized that current state configurations would be insufficient for their purposes. In 1846 Brigham Young began organizing a massive relocation of the Mormons to the Great Basin of Utah in territory that at that time was under Mexican control. However, within two years the territory would be ceded to the United States by treaty, and the property would come under direct federal control. These circumstances would give the Mormons an opportunity for a drive toward statehood; instead they actually led to an escalation of their difficulties. It was an inevitable historical irony that the desire to withdraw from state-sanctioned persecution ultimately led to the Saints' greatest confrontation with the American constitutional order.

## Brigham Young and the State of Deseret

Like the Jehovah's Witnesses' experience in the shift in leadership from Charles Taze Russell to Joseph Rutherford, the Mormon shift from Joseph Smith to Brigham Young signaled a reorganization of strategies regarding the American constitutional order. Unlike Rutherford, Young had no legal training and no serious personal experience with the legal order. Like Rutherford, though, he was a consummate organization man, succeeding much as Rutherford did in bureaucratizing the prophetic message of his institutional predecessor. The ability to do that, combined with Smith's earlier plans for a temporal kingdom and the realities of the continuing persecution of the Saints, set the stage for the confrontation that was to define this community for the rest of the nineteenth century.

By the late 1840s, the institutions established by Joseph Smith in Ohio, Missouri, and Illinois had been transferred en masse to Utah, where they grew, relatively unimpeded by non-Mormon state governments. These institutions were secular as well as religious, and they covered the entirety of life in the Great Basin. Initially at the center was the Council of Fifty, the political unit created in Illinois as a shadow government for the new society that was to be ushered in during the millennial era. Intended originally as a worldly governing body, not merely an organ of the LDS Church, the council had the freedom into the 1860s to exercise considerable political power in the territory as the engine behind all Mormon governmental institutions.[14] Through the council Brigham Young was able to establish what Joseph Smith had only dreamed of, a completely integrated society in which the leadership of the Mormon community oversaw theological and ritualistic operations as well as temporal, day-to-day activities. Although there were some difficulties, none of them resembled the conflicts left behind in Ohio, Missouri, and Illinois, and for the most part the temporal kingdom functioned completely and (initially) without impediment within the territory.[15]

Of course, the growth of an independent political and economic entity in the American interior was viewed with growing caution and suspicion by the American constitutional order, and the relationship between the Mormon settlement in the Great Basin and the federal government grew increasingly tense. The community had had obvious difficulties with various state governments from the early 1830s to the mid-1840s, but there was little direct conflict with the federal government during that period. Indeed, the Mormon leadership continued to express optimism toward the federal system, provided they could control specific aspects of it. The Saints had moved out of Illinois and headed for an area of the continent still technically under Mexican control at least in part to reestablish their temporal kingdom without the interference of local non-Mormon governments or jealous citizens. Although Mormon literature suggests that the move was made for theological reasons, there is little question that the Church's anticipation of America's impending expansion was also involved.[16] The Mormons removed themselves to the Great Basin to avoid recurrent interference with non-Mormon (and thus, it seemed, anti-Mormon) state governments. Thus they could await the eschatological moment when they would be able to enforce the high ideals of the U.S. Constitution in the manner suggested by their own interpretations. The Church's alternative understanding of that document was one of the issues at the heart of the Mormon confrontation with the constitutional order, a confrontation that would not come to its fullest expression until the Mormons were clearly under federal jurisdiction and the federal government was ready to address the challenge.

Too far removed to be considered an immediate physical threat—and benefiting from the distraction caused by other major political battles of the day—the Mormon community in the Great Basin was relatively free, for a time, to develop its own understanding of power and authority on the fringes of the constitutional order. That delay of direct confrontation bought the community time and peace that translated into political self-confidence. Soon after Young had settled his community in the Great Basin and the structures of the temporal kingdom were established, efforts toward the formation of the State of Deseret were begun.[17] The combination of the desire to control their own fate with the Mormons' belief in the inspired nature of the U.S. Constitution left them—after the Great Basin came under federal control—favoring independent statehood under Mormon control but also fully expecting the collapse of the Union that had corrupted its own founding documents.[18] At least, when they were in control of their own state, the Mormons could control those issues that had caused so many problems in Ohio, Missouri, and Illinois. The federal government had been no help but had not really posed an immediate threat. So long as Mormon autonomy could be maintained on the state level and adherence to the principles of the Constitution could be maintained on the national level, the Saints saw no harm in using the federal system to safeguard their own interests. As instructions provided to California LDS Church leader Amasa Lyman stated (referring to states' rights debates raging at the time and the role Utah statehood played in that debate), "[W]hile government is using us to save the nation, we are using them to save ourselves."[19]

The Mormons clearly understood the arena in which they operated. On the other side of the power equation, the federal government did not initially view the issue of Mormon statehood as having anything to do with Mormon justifications. Thus, positions favoring or opposing plans for statehood rested on larger national issues. Historian Glen Leonard suggests that on the issue of statehood, the federal government may have articulated a position that, for entirely different reasons, supported Mormon designs. He notes that President Zachary Taylor supported skipping the usual process of creating territories of the new Mexican acquisition in favor of creating a large state of California, which would have included present-day Nevada and Utah. Such a maneuver, Taylor hoped, would avoid a heated congressional debate over the issue of slavery, an issue that threatened to destroy the Union.[20] Such a plan would not necessarily thwart Mormon desires, since the constitution of the resulting state would contain a separation clause permitting the Mormons to create a Mormon state from this larger version of California at the appointed time.

In any event, dissimilar motivations dominated the national debate over Mormon statehood from 1848 until the end of the Civil War. As far as the federal government was concerned, the debate focused on the issues of slavery, the maintenance of the Union, and the balance between free and slave states required for admission into the Union. For the Mormons, however, the debate was about the right to practice religion free of non-Mormon state interference.

As a result, though a significant amount of energy was spent on appealing to the federal government to accept Deseret as an autonomous Mormon state within the federal structure, an equal amount of energy was expended scrutinizing the appeals in terms of their larger political ramifications. As early as 1849, members of the LDS community met to create a constitution for the State of Deseret and sent Dr. John M. Bernhisel as a messenger to Congress requesting admission into the Union. Declares historian Richard Poll, "The rejection of Deseret's bid for statehood was an aspect of the contest for sectional advantage [between Northern and Southern states], rather than a judgment upon any of the qualifications of the residents of the Great Basin."[21] The following year the entire area was organized as a federal territory, an action seen by the Mormons as an insult that denied their desires for local autonomy in favor of federal administration of the territory. Nevertheless, with the defeat of the "Wilmot Proviso" (which would have prohibited slavery in territory ceded from Mexico), antislavery members of Congress lost interest in Utah, and those supporting the notion of local political control—including President Millard Fillmore—were able to secure Brigham Young as territorial governor.[22]

Again in 1856 Mormons met to draft a constitution for the State of Deseret, but the timing of the resulting request for statehood was decidedly bad. Since 1854 the debate over the role of slavery and the impending collapse of the Missouri Compromise was focusing Washington's attention on the issue of states' rights, also known as "popular sovereignty." This notion was championed by Democratic Illinois senator Stephen Douglas and favored by Southern slave states as a check on federal (antislavery) forces.[23] Fearing a Southern advantage by giving new territories the option of permitting slavery, dominant antislavery forces rejected the idea of admitting Utah into the Union as potentially both a slave and a polygamy state. That same year, possibly in response to opposition over popular sovereignty, President Franklin Pierce failed to reappoint Brigham Young as territorial governor, and non-Mormons were sent to fill a number of governmental positions. Before the year was out, the second draft of a constitution for the State of Deseret was thus also rejected.

Mormon reaction to this imposition of federally appointed leadership coincided with rampant rumor-mongering in Washington by non-Mormon officials back from the territory, and President Buchanan had the justification he needed to react strongly against the Mormons: he sent Young's replacement under armed escort. With such a show of force, he also undoubtedly hoped to prove that Democrats did not support plural marriage. The resulting standoff between federal troops and the Mormon militia proved to be more a test of wills than an outright assault, although the fact remains that both sides were prepared to face each other in combat.[24] Because of President Buchanan's loss of will—and the sectional problems continuing between Northern and Southern states—the Mormons were able to maintain de facto if not de jure control of the territory, and future standoffs that might threaten armed conflict were avoided.

The Civil War produced confidence among the Mormons that Joseph Smith's prophecies of the ultimate demise of non-Mormon America had been correct. This served as justification for yet a third effort at constitution drafting in 1862—based on the anticipation that the Union would fall and that the Mormons would be the only group able to safeguard the ideals embodied in the U.S. Constitution. On paper and through minimal political ritual, the State of Deseret operated more as a Mormon government-in-waiting and less as an expectant state of the Union. Again Brigham Young was elected governor.[25] The Civil War did not turn out as anticipated, though, and by 1872 this incarnation of Mormon governmental authority was abandoned. A fourth state constitution, this one including a greater voice for non-Mormons, was drafted by the territorial legislature, again following the previous designs to join the Union. This effort was also rejected by Congress.

By this time the Civil War was over: slavery had been defeated and the Union saved. The mid-1870s saw sectional competition muted and the notion of popular sovereignty well on its way to becoming a dead letter. The attention of the national government could now be turned more directly to the other perceived threat to its authority and use of power. Compared to the legal and political war that was about to be waged against the church by the American constitutional order, the armed skirmishes of the 1850s would appear as nothing.

## The Saints' Legal Battles Begin (1875–1887)

Like the legal battles of the Jehovah's Witnesses, those of the Latter-day Saints did not begin with the familiar barrage of litigation but with formative experiences traced to an early period in the life its founder, Joseph Smith. Tried as a young man for fraudulent divining (a misdemeanor in New York in the 1820s), Smith later faced more serious challenges by both state and federal institutions. However, it was not until the majority of the Saints had left all state jurisdictions in 1846 and ventured into federally controlled territory that the relationship between Mormons and the federal government became notoriously litigious.[26]

The repeated attempts by Mormon leadership to get the State of Deseret admitted into the Union had failed consistently either because of sectional competition between the Northern and Southern states over the issue of states' rights or, once that dispute was settled, because of congressional fear regarding the seemingly monolithic political control exercised by the LDS Church over the territory in direct competition with the American constitutional order.[27] The eventual resolution of the first issue, which occurred when Southern advocates of popular sovereignty left Congress to join the Confederacy, had permitted the passage of the first federal anti-Mormon legislation, the Morrill Act of 1862, which outlawed polygamy. But the second factor impeding Mormon political designs, the perception of competition from the Mormon Kingdom of God experienced by the American constitutional order, could not be addressed until well after the Civil War.

Although the Mormon doctrine of plural marriage was not acknowledged publicly by LDS Church leadership until 1852—after the Mormon community was free from state persecution—it had hardly been a secret practice in Ohio, Missouri, and Illinois.[28] Regardless of the date assigned to the foundation of the practice, though, there is no mistaking the fact that, from the establishment of the Utah Territory in 1850 until the Morrill Act was signed into law in 1862, polygamy was not a federal crime. It would be unreasonable to suggest that this fact reflected acceptance of the practice of plural marriage, yet it does seem that the 1862 act was as much an official assertion of congressional authority as it was the legislation of morality. Mormon historians Leonard Arrington and Davis Bitton point out that even though plural marriage was practiced on a limited basis within the Mormon community and required permission from the highest authorities, there were no men in positions of high authority within the LDS Church who were monogamists. This meant that the federal government's attacks on plural marriage were not simply attacks against that institution, but, as legal historian Edwin Firmage puts it, effectively "served to paralyze Mormon society by removing its leadership." In addition to addressing the issue of polygamy, the Morrill Act also dealt a blow to LDS Church authority, annulling its corporate charter and prohibiting real estate holdings over fifty thousand dollars. Even with these draconian measures, the act functioned mostly as a symbolic expression of the dynamics of power and still permitted Mormon-staffed courts to adjudicate violations. Containing no real mechanisms for enforcement, the measure went largely unenforced until the 1870s.[29]

The impetus for federal action against polygamy came from an unexpected quarter, a damages suit heard before the U.S. Supreme Court in which one party alleged that grand and petit jurors had been improperly removed from service. The resulting 1871 decision in *Clinton v. Englebrecht* declared that the lower territorial courts in Utah, though overseeing the same jurisdiction as the federal courts, were not free to disregard territorial jury requirements, a practice performed to exclude Mormons from polygamy cases.[30] Congress reacted by passing the Poland Act of 1874, which determined jury size and selection procedures, granted U.S. marshals and U.S. attorneys jurisdiction in the territorial courts in criminal cases, and determined the jurisdiction and procedure of the territorial court system as it related to the federal courts. In other words, the Poland Act ensured that federal officials would enforce the Morrill Act in federal courts before acceptable juries.

The following year, still confident in the ability of the Supreme Court to uphold the Constitution and correct the errors of an increasingly hostile Congress, the LDS Church leadership worked with the U.S. attorney to develop a test case. Polygamist George Reynolds, an assistant to Brigham Young, was selected to challenge the constitutionality of the Morrill and Poland Acts. Originally acquitted on technical grounds, Reynolds was eventually found guilty of polygamy and appealed. The Supreme Court rendered a decision in 1879, declaring that, although religious belief was an unlimited right, religious actions could be controlled by law. After providing a short history of the meaning of religion with regard to the First Amendment, the Court, calling the practice of plural marriage "odious" and an "offense against society," upheld the Morrill Act as a constitutional safeguard by society against religious anarchy. In a statement justifying the denial of Reynolds's claim that he had the right to a religion-based exemption from the legislation even if it had been ruled constitutional, the Court clearly articulated the power of the American constitutional order: "To permit this [exemption] would be to make the professed doctrines of religious belief superior to the law of the land, and in effect to permit every citizen to become a law unto himself. Government could exist only in name under such circumstances."[31] By affirming the government's position on antipolygamy legislation, the Supreme Court removed the issue from judicial jurisdiction and placed it squarely under congressional jurisdiction, leaving Congress to scrutinize the behavior of all Mormons closely and to legislate against them as it saw fit.[32] From this moment, the Court played only a confirming role, and Mormon confidence in support from any of the federal institutions decreased dramatically. The full confrontation with the American constitutional order was now engaged.

Two years later, in response to the federal government's ongoing battle to prosecute polygamists, the Supreme Court clarified the issue of spousal testimony raised in *Reynolds*. In *Miles v. United States*, the Court ruled that an alleged second wife could not be forced to testify against her husband if the first marriage had not been established by a trial court. The Court ruled that in such cases of doubt, the second wife was to be considered prima facie an incompetent witness and could be required to testify only if the first marriage was not in dispute. Although apparently ruling for the Mormons, the Supreme Court noted clearly that the matter was not one of first liberties, and with simple congressional action taken to change the law, it could (and would) rule otherwise in the future. "If both wives are excluded from testifying to the first marriage, as we think they should be according to the existing rules of evidence, testimony sufficient to convict in a prosecution for polygamy in the Territory of Utah is hardly attainable. But this is not a consideration by which we can be influenced. We must administer the law as we find it. The remedy is with Congress, by enacting such a change in the law of evidence in the Territory of Utah as to make both wives witnesses on indictments for bigamy."[33]

Congress took the hint and by 1882 had passed the Edmunds Act, sponsored by Vermont senator George Edmunds to amend the Morrill Act. Primarily a response to the Court's ruling in *Miles*, it was also aimed at reining in LDS Church authority and removing

Mormon polygamist George Q. Cannon as territorial delegate to Congress. Notes historian Edward Lyman, quoting the sponsor, the bill was not "seeking so much to put down polygamy as to break down the 'Mormon' system of theocracy," which Edmunds thought was unconstitutional and thus a greater threat to the American people than unusual marriage arrangements.[34] The act repeated the Morrill Act's provisions, which declared polygamy a felony punishable by a prison term of up to five years and a fine of five hundred dollars, but also made the much more easily proven violation of cohabitation a misdemeanor punishable by a prison term of up to six months and a three-hundred-dollar fine. Those practicing or sympathetic to plural marriage were excluded from jury service, and those participating in plural marriage were disfranchised, vacating any elected office filled by such a person. Those who were willing to renounce the Mormon church could be granted amnesty by the president of the United States, and polygamous issue (children) who had been born before January 1, 1883, were declared legitimate for inheritance purposes. Finally, the act vacated the offices of persons responsible for elections and the registration of voters in the territory and replaced them with a board appointed by the president and approved by the Senate.

This congressional control over the Mormons—a result of *Reynolds* and fully expressed after the passage of the Edmunds Act— was continually confirmed by the Supreme Court. In 1885 and 1886 the Court delivered six decisions permitting congressional restrictions by refusing to extend constitutional protection to the Mormons.[35] In *Murphy v. Ramsey,* it ruled that the disfranchisement provisions of the Edmunds Act were well within congressional jurisdiction, not only because of the relationship between Congress and the territories, but also because of the "wholesome and necessary" value to society of the "holy estate of matrimony" between one man and one woman. The Supreme Court's actions removed even further the possibility of constitutional protection for the Mormons accused of polygamy and guaranteed only congressional oversight of their actions. The theory of ultimate congressional authority in these matters, and thus the Mormon community's Gordian knot, was best articulated by the Court in *Murphy:*

The people of the United States, as sovereign owners of the National Territories, have supreme power over them and their inhabitants. . . . But in ordaining government for the Territories, and the people who inhabit them, all the discretion which belongs to legislative power is vested in Congress. . . . The personal and civil rights of the inhabitants of the Territories are secured to them, as to other citizens, by the principles of constitutional liberty which restrain all the agencies of government, State and National; *their political rights are franchises which they hold as privileges in the legislative discretion of the Congress of the United States.*[36]

Of course, had the Mormons won their cause for statehood, they would not have been subject to "all the discretion which belongs to legislative power . . . vested in Congress," but instead would have enjoyed their full democratic rights as state citizens.

Within a month of the passage of the Edmunds Act, the territorial legislature in Utah had called for a constitutional convention to draft what would be the fifth effort to be admitted to the Union. This attempt suffered the same fate as the previous four—largely because it did not address the two most pressing congressional concerns, Mormon hegemony and plural marriage. Mormon legal battles raged in the Supreme Court, and the control of the federal government continued to grow. With pressure increasing from the legislative and executive branches, and the judicial branch serving less to defend the principles of the Constitution and more to confirm legislative action, Mormon belligerence toward the constitutional order grew measurably. As cohabitation defendant Rudger Clawson put it simply: "I very much regret that the laws of my country should come in conflict with the laws of God; but whenever they do, I shall invariably choose the latter. If I did not so express myself, I should feel unworthy of the cause I represent."[37] The official statement from the LDS Church leadership was much more direct and was framed as more than simply a dilemma over conscience. Church president John Taylor reacted to the now total assault of the American constitutional order by requesting that all monogamous church officials either take a second wife or resign, symbolically throwing down the gauntlet in the face of federal challenges. As historians Arrington and Bitton note, with the passage of the Edmunds Act, "[t]he final grounds of the confrontation were fixed."[38]

## The Saints' Legal Battles Conclude (1887–1907)

The year 1887 can be understood as the end of the first stage of legal confrontations between the Mormons and the American constitutional order and the beginning of the second. During that year Mormon president John Taylor died and an interregnum period began that would ultimately see the Mormon community through to both the conclusion of confrontations with the federal government and the admission of Utah as the forty-fifth state. More significantly, 1887 was also the year of the passage of the most stringent legislation used to attack LDS Church leadership in the Utah Territory. In March Congress passed the Edmunds-Tucker Act, a measure that added to the burden of the Edmunds Act by attacking what lay at the center of the conflict between the Mormon community and the constitutional order—the authority and consolidation of power enjoyed by the LDS Church itself.[39] In addition to addressing various sexual improprieties, the act (repeating previous legislation) liquidated Church assets in excess of fifty thousand dollars, with the proceeds to be used to fund non-Mormon schools in the territory. It also annulled the charter of the Perpetual Emigrating Fund Company, the organization that had borne responsibility for helping foreign-born Mormons migrate to the Utah Territory. The act disfranchised women in the territory (who had been given the vote in the 1870s) and annulled the charter of the Mormon militia (the Nauvoo Legion).

With the adoption of the Edmunds-Tucker Act, pressure on the LDS leadership increased dramatically.[40] Denied all significant rights and fearing arrest, John Taylor and other Mormon leaders who practiced plural marriage were forced into hiding. The LDS Church leadership, making one last attempt to forestall the complete dissolution of the Mormon community, called a sixth constitutional convention in late June 1887, to address the restrictions required by the act. Recognizing the importance of compromise on the issue of plural marriage in the statehood debate, the convention adopted an article reflecting language directly from Article 4, section 4, of the U.S. Constitution. "Bigamy and polygamy being considered incompatible with a republican form of government," announced the article, "each of them is hereby forbidden and declared a misdemeanor." But this state constitutional provision was not understood to dissolve current plural marriages, nor was it understood to prohibit the practice of men cohabiting with women with whom they had religious unions that had not been solemnized by the state. As significant as the compromise may have seemed to the Mormon community, it was not acceptable to Congress, and the sixth attempt at a state constitution was rejected. The promise of statehood rested on proof that the Mormon leadership considered plural marriage not only illegal in the state but also unacceptable as Mormon behavior.

For the two years after John Taylor died "underground" on July 26, 1887, the LDS Church was without a clear president. During that period, while the Church leadership struggled with the demands of the federal government over the issue of polygamy and Church control over Utah politics, the federal government increased its pressure. The Council of the Twelve, under Wilford Woodruff's leadership and serving in its capacity for the vacant First Presidency, worked persistently on these issues. By 1890 Woodruff emerged as the president of the LDS Church, roughly at the same time the U.S. Supreme Court was upholding some of the most devastating legislation to affect his community. The Court's decision in *Davis v. Beason* solidified its position that the specific issue of polygamy and the more general matter of government-Mormon relations were under the jurisdiction of the now thoroughly non-Mormon state and territorial courts and were not, in most circumstances, an issue for the federal court system. The Court affirmed an Idaho statute that denied the vote to any person "who is a member of any order, organization or association which teaches, advises, counsels, or encourages its members or devotees or any other persons to commit the crime of bigamy or polygamy, or any other crime as defined by law, either as a rite or ceremony of such order, organization, or association."[41] Understanding its responsibilities in the matter to be very limited, the Supreme Court, after a lengthy diatribe against the Mormon practice of plural marriage, declared that the only issue to be decided was Idaho's authority to create such restrictions. Despite the appellant's arguments that such restrictions violated Article 6 and the First and Fourteenth Amendments of the U.S. Constitution, the Court decided that such authority was properly vested in the state and that Samuel Davis was properly denied his franchise.[42] As a result of this decision, members of the House and Senate introduced legislation that would accomplish on the national level what Idaho had done on the state level.[43]

Three months later, the Court announced a ruling in its most sweeping expression of authority over the very functioning of the LDS Church. In *Late Corporation of the Church of Jesus Christ of Latter-day Saints v. United States,* the high court ruled that, as the ultimate source of all territory, and thus of all control over its use, the U.S. Congress was well within its authority both in requiring the LDS Church to stop advocating the practice of polygamy and in seizing its property when it did not do so. Noting that the Morrill and Edmunds-Tucker Acts had legally disincorporated the LDS Church and provided for the dissolution of its real estate holdings, the Court ruled that the Mormons had forfeited their rights by disobeying rightful authority. A companion case that was incorporated into this decision *(Romney v. United States)* argued that the property should rightfully revert to the membership for whom the LDS Church functioned. This logic was rejected by the Court.

Finally, by late August Woodruff received confirmation that the federal government would in fact confiscate Mormon temples, the centerpieces of Mormon ceremonial ritual and the symbol of church authority. Legal historian Ken Driggs argues that the combination of these events "forced Mormon leaders to realize that no compromise was possible. They had to elect between loyalty to their unique social, political, and economic customs and their very survival." Klaus Hansen concludes with considerably more irony that by 1890 "it was apparent that the inland empire of the kingdom of God was no match for the American empire."[44] The cost of maintaining the practice of plural marriage and with it increasing government persecution proved to be too great. Realizing that concession on this issue meant that he might salvage the remainder of the LDS Church leadership's authority, Woodruff announced the result of his prayers for guidance. Advising fellow Latter-day Saints "to refrain from contracting any marriage forbidden by the law of the land," Woodruff publicly announced a new direction for his community.[45]

Considerable debate continues over whether the manifesto was motivated by religious revelation or political expediency. Klaus Hansen, representing the latter opinion, describes Woodruff as having "caved in so obviously to pressures of the United States government that his insistence that he had indeed acted under revelation has always seemed somewhat suspect to all but the most credulous among the faithful." Historian D. Michael Quinn observes that the community vote to sustain the manifesto, taken on October 6, 1890, was called to satisfy the U.S. secretary of the interior that the declaration was now official church policy. Edward Lyman notes that Woodruff did not intend by his pronouncement "'to please the world,' but with laws enforced and upheld by a nation of sixty-five million people, reality must prevail." However, the decision to change course was a momentous occasion and not an act to be read totally as one of political expediency. Woodruff, choosing between sacrifice and annihilation, secured the future of his community by conceding temporal authority to the American constitutional order. As Thomas Alexander assesses: "Since the church had to be on the earth to greet Christ at His second coming, the abandonment of virtually everything but the church organization was possible. . . . Thus, far from abandoning the millennial hope, Woodruff's manifesto served as a reaffirmation of his basic conviction."[46]

Regardless of the motives behind the manifesto, the pronouncement served as a powerfully symbolic capitulation to the American constitutional order. Even if it is understood as modification rather than renunciation, it provided the Mormons a means to salvage their theological particularities as they recognized the ultimate authority of the constitutional order. Alexander observes that the manifesto initiated a sea change in Mormon millennial expectations: with it the Mormons no longer looked for "the destruction of nearly all gentiles and of the United States government." He concludes that

[u]ntil 1890, however, the belief in the imminence of the second coming, the destruction of worldly governments including the United States, and the need for all Saints to flee to Zion continued to play a central role in Mormon revolutionary premillennialism. With the manifesto and the succeeding accommodation, friendly relations with the gentile community and the nation developed, and the sense of immediacy of the millennium abated. . . . In essence, what Woodruff had accomplished with the manifesto was an expedient compromise with the United States government which bought the time the church needed to fulfill its millennial expectations.[47]

Of course, the LDS Church leadership apparently knew that the confrontation with the American constitutional order had not had to do merely with the issue of plural marriage but had in fact focused on the use and expression of authority. Mormon authority to determine interpretations and practices was at least as great a threat to the constitutional order as the actual interpretations and practices had been. Thus, shortly after the announcement of the manifesto, the LDS Church leadership, recognizing that the instruments of Mormon political solidarity had been partially responsible for exacerbating relationships with the non-Mormon community, began to dismantle their institutions of temporal authority. By May 1891 the Church leadership was suggesting affiliation with recognized national political parties, and church attorney Franklin Richards, acting in his capacity as its chair, dissolved the Mormon-dominated People's Party.[48] The final objections to Mormon political authority had been removed.

The response to the pronouncement did seem to confirm the value of submitting to the constitutional order. By late 1890 the Supreme Court had reversed its support for the use of wives as witnesses against their husbands in cases alleging polygamy, a position that had been suggested in *Miles* ten years earlier and had been enacted in legislation by Congress in the form of the Edmunds-Tucker Act. The high court also reversed the Supreme Court of the Territory of Utah, which had ruled that the child of a polygamous union was illegitimate and thus could not inherit his father's estate.[49] In 1893 Congress passed a joint resolution returning property to the LDS Church, an act that was judicially reciprocated by the Court's reversal of its 1890 decision dissolving the LDS corporation.[50] The Court heard several more cases involving the issue of inheritance over the next few years,[51] but since its role of providing constitutional sanction to the actions of the legislative and executive branches in their relations with the Mormon community had outlived its need, the Court's work was now, for the most part, complete. In 1893 President Benjamin Harrison announced a general amnesty for those imprisoned for cohabitation on the condition that they would, in the future, obey the laws of the United States.[52] In 1894 Congress passed legislation creating the State of Utah, and President Grover Cleveland offered a general amnesty similar to Harrison's.[53] By November debate began on the new Utah constitution—its seventh and final attempt—and language that forever prohibited plural marriage was included in the final draft. On January 4, 1896, President Grover Cleveland issued the formal proclamation making Utah the forty-fifth state in the Union.[54]

Of course, the pronouncement of the Woodruff Manifesto and Utah's subsequent admission into the Union did not signal the complete reintegration of Mormon society into the mainstream of the American constitutional order. Suspicion still ran high among federal legislators that the LDS Church clandestinely accepted polygamy and cohabitation even though the state constitution prohibited it. The year after the manifesto was announced, Congress, in the Alien Labor Immigration Act, expanded the list of prohibited immigrants to include polygamists. And according to historian D. Michael Quinn, the suspicion was well grounded—though many Mormon leaders interpreted the law and the manifesto to prohibit new contracts of plural marriage, and not to dissolve family obligations (including cohabitation) that had been made before 1890, there is also significant evidence of the continuation of the practice of plural marriage into the twentieth century.[55]

Lingering suspicions finally reached a peak with the election of Brigham Henry Roberts to the House of Representatives on November 8, 1898. Roberts, a convicted (though perhaps unrepentant) cohabitator, won the right to represent Utah in Congress, beating his closest opponent by more than 8.5 percentage points.[56] However, non-Mormon opposition, which had been relatively moderate in Utah before the election, became overwhelmingly vocal nationwide after the vote, and petitions allegedly containing over seven million signatures flooded the House of Representatives from around the country, demanding that Congress refuse to seat Roberts.[57] Among the issues of concern was the matter of his cohabitation (to which he had pleaded guilty in 1889 and for which he had served four months in prison). No less significant was his connection to the First Council of the Seventy, the Mormon missionary administration, which critics claimed would make him a biased, and therefore improper, representative of "Mormondom" in Congress. Part of their fear was based on the fact that in two previous election cycles, Roberts had been one of several Mormons in positions of authority to be censured by Mormon leadership for not consulting with them first about their plans to run for political office.[58] As a result of the second incident, Roberts—who had a history of disagreement with church leadership—signed a "political manifesto" that indicated his willingness to obtain church permission for any future political endeavors. In any event, members of Congress were certainly willing to listen to these concerns, in part because of the history of Mormon relations with the constitutional order, but also because Roberts, a Democrat, now faced a majority Republican House. It became clear early in the debate that the matter centered not on whether to seat Roberts but on whether to deny him a seat or seat him first and then expel him. In January 1900 Roberts was denied his seat by a vote of 268 to 50, with 36 not voting.[59]

Suspicion over the authority of the LDS Church did not end with Roberts's defeat, and thus neither did the Mormon confrontation with the constitutional order. In 1904 Reed Smoot, a member of the Council of the Twelve Apostles (the second highest governing body in the LDS Church), was elected to represent Utah in the U.S. Senate. A nonpolygamist, Smoot was challenged after his election on the basis of his official ties to the Mormon hierarchy and thus the degree of his loyalty to the American constitutional order. During the ensuing investigation, although it became clear that Smoot himself was perfectly eligible for service in the Senate, it also became clear that his status hinged on the question of how the Senate perceived Mormons and the LDS Church. Smoot and the LDS Church leadership recognized this when, early in the investigation, opposition leaders were given broad power to call witnesses. The first witness called to testify before the Senate Privileges and Elections Committee was the president of the LDS Church, Joseph F. Smith. Smoot asserted, "I do hope I will be successful in retaining my seat, for if I am, I am very sure that in a short time the country will take it as a vindication of the Church, because the fight has been made entirely on the Church, but if I loose [sic] the public will take it as a condemnation of the Church."[60] The three-year investigation resulted in a committee vote recommending against Smoot. Nonetheless, as in the Roberts case several years earlier in the House, part of the final committee vote focused on whether to deny Smoot his seat or to seat him and then expel him.[61] With the legitimacy of his election put to a vote on the Senate floor, Smoot finally emerged victorious, and official questions concerning his status as a member were removed. But the episode had served notice to the LDS Church leadership that their status was still in question. Historian Jan Shipps observes that "[t]he fact that the investigation failed to unseat the apostle proved to be unimportant; it still accomplished its purpose by persuading the most important leaders of the church that the old order had indeed passed away, and so cleared the way for a fusion of the Mormon-Gentile establishments in the Great Basin Kingdom." President Joseph F. Smith announced what became known as the "second" manifesto in April 1904, indicating that the LDS Church, which had advised against new plural marriages after the Woodruff Manifesto of 1890, would no longer tolerate them—nor unlawful cohabitation—at all. Smith declared that those continuing to participate in such a state would be excommunicated. As legal historian Ken Driggs writes, "This time the Church meant business."[62] Apparently the Smith declaration satisfied national critics of Mormonism. Although there was some opposition to Smoot's reelection—most notably from fellow Mormon Brigham H. Roberts—the issue of his relationship to the church died with the filing of the Senate committee's report, and Smoot went on to serve a total of thirty years in the Senate.[63]

During those thirty years, the LDS Church leadership shifted its political role from being involved kingmakers to acting as leaders of an involved interest group. The dissolution of the People's Party left the Mormons divided between the national Democratic and Republican parties, and as a result all of the day's national—and thus non-Mormon—political issues were brought to the state level.[64] Party politics in Utah began to look much like politics elsewhere in the country, even including a Republican machine known as the "federal bunch," controlled by Smoot. Indeed, it had been Smoot's understanding of party politics that saved him after the negative Senate committee vote. Because he was willing to promise pro-Roosevelt delegates to the 1906 Republican convention, the president supported him when the Senate committee report reached the Senate floor. Over time, debates over such issues as Prohibition, World War I, and the League of Nations seized the attention of the Mormon community. It is worth noting that, despite the Mormon text known as the Word of Wisdom, Smoot and LDS President Joseph F. Smith opposed Prohibition. They feared that Mormon support of it would alienate non-Mormons, potentially leading to further persecution based on claims of improper Mormon political control of the state.[65] Utah had become so integrated politically by 1916 that its first non-Mormon governor was Simon Bamberger, a Jewish businessman of German descent. According to historian Thomas Alexander, "the church had moved in the direction of taking a political stance similar to that of most other religious groups. That is, the Latter-day Saints became more like a pressure group dealing in what they perceived to be the best interest of the community but declining to operate an exclusive political system." Smoot biographer Milton Merrill puts the issue more dramatically: "The country and the Church were at peace. . . . The Church supported the government, the government supported the Church."[66]

## Mormons Join the Constitutional Order

The shift that occurred between Brigham Roberts's and Reed Smoot's attempts to be seated in the House and the Senate, respectively, was indicative of the changes during that period in the relationship of the Mormon community and the constitutional order. Roberts, a firm believer in Mormon theology and a practicing "cohabitator," was also something of a free spirit so far as Mormon leadership and politics were concerned. Reed Smoot, about whom there was no question of marital status, was the self-styled representative of the church and its interests in the Senate—the proverbial "company man"—and never denied his close affiliation and loyalty to Mormon leadership. Yet, in his ability to integrate his loyalty to the church with his loyalty to the Senate—as well as in his political savvy and his willingness to compromise—the finest expression of the power of the American constitutional order can be seen. Although there is no doubt that many people wanted (and some may still want) to convert the Mormons to a brand of mainstream Protestantism, so far as the constitutional order was concerned the goal of the encounter was to integrate the Mormon community into the system. This meant that the Mormons had to accept the authority of the constitutional order to determine values. Much in the way Jewish Supreme Court Justice Louis Brandeis later declared Zionism to be the best expression of American democratic ideals,[67] Smoot's prominent participation in the Senate signaled the complete integration of Mormon and constitutional ideals.

Indeed, by the beginning of World War II, the Mormon community was beginning to show all of the signs of joining the mainstream. The LDS Church leadership was even assisting in the prosecution of Mormon fundamentalists who denied its authority and continued the practice of plural marriage. Correspondingly, in 1946 and 1947, when three such cases came before the U.S. Supreme Court, the response of the constitutional order was noticeably more restrained.[68] The last of these, *Musser v. Utah*, the Supreme Court remanded to the Utah Supreme Court to clarify the status of advocating—as compared to practicing—polygamy.[69]

This procedural decision to return to the state—an overwhelmingly Mormon state—the question of the legality of advocating polygamy significantly marks the integration of the Mormon community into the American constitutional order. The Supreme Court, confident in the legal system of the state of Utah, its comparability to those of the other states in the Union, and its compatibility with federal authority, was willing to let the citizens of that state determine an issue that earlier under the territorial agreement had been reserved for the federal government. The state mechanisms, controlled by Utah citizens who might be Mormon (rather than controlled by the LDS Church, which wanted its members to be treated as citizens), could now be judged to operate fully within the standards of the federal judicial system. And the LDS Church, seeking to distance itself from those who threatened the hard-fought victories resulting in that inclusion, was now part of the American constitutional order. Historian Klaus Hansen summarizes: "Perhaps no phenomenon establishes a former sect more firmly among mainline faiths than the fact that it spawns sects dedicated to its reform. Needless to say, Mormon leaders vigorously attempt to disassociate themselves from such movements."[70]

By the second half of this century, the Church of Jesus Christ of Latter-day Saints had taken on all of the characteristics of an established, mainstream religious community in the American constitutional order. The two decisions announced by the Court in the last ten years involving the LDS Church (or the practices of its members) have addressed employment practices and tax deductions—issues of concern to established communities, not to those trying to gain entrance into (or force the acceptance of) the establishment. As noted by political scientists Frank Way and Barbara Burt, a shift in the pattern of a community's litigation from "consequential" to nonconsequential issues indicates the difference between mainstream and nonmainstream religious communities.[71] The Mormons no longer have to litigate over basic religious tenets and practices—those have either ceased to be believed and practiced or have become acceptable to American society. Now simply one bureaucratized denomination among many, the LDS Church is left guarding its prerogatives and safeguarding the status and practices of its membership. As a symbol of its status within the American constitutional order, the Mormon community can boast of a number of its members who have attained high rank and authority within the American constitutional order.[72]

Based on its particular social and theological structures, the Church of Jesus Christ of Latter-day Saints set out to establish the Kingdom of God on earth. It was similar to the Kingdom of God being built by mainstream Christianity, yet different enough to pose a threat, and the Mormons faced a series of confrontations over their beliefs and their interpretation of national destiny. Thus they were chased into the American frontier. Once there, they encountered the raw power of the American constitutional order, unobstructed by any vestiges of restraint Mormons had known as citizens of specific (if hostile) states. Believing in a sacred role for America but not the role envisioned by the American constitutional order, the Mormons established their own competing order in the hopes of reconciliation or eventual supercession. The American constitutional order, led by the legislative branch, endorsed by the executive, and confirmed by the judiciary, felt threatened by an internal competitor. Justifying its actions by its citizens' reaction to a moral outrage, it increasingly squeezed the Mormon leadership until Mormons could no longer survive without choosing between political annihilation and recognition of the order's ultimate authority.

Unlike the Jehovah's Witnesses, the Mormons could not make the case that their particularistic sources of authority were parallel to those of the American constitutional order. They could therefore not work out a separate peace and live lives congruent with the order. By basing their claims on temporal, territorial foundations, the Mormon community touched the nerve of power maintained by the federal government, and from that point forward its fate was determined. It is significant that one organization to break from the LDS Church—the Reorganized Church of Jesus Christ of Latter Day Saints (RLDS)—which stayed in the Midwest, did not accept Brigham Young's authority after the death of Joseph Smith and also rejected the practice of plural marriage, encountered no significant difficulties with the federal government. The Utah Mormons, however, announced their claim to authority within the expanse of the American frontier and consequently drew the ire of the American constitutional order. In the ensuing confrontation, unable to translate such claims to satisfy the order, the Mormons were forced to concede its foundation. They were exposed to the awesome power of the federal government in protecting the constitutional order, and they were eventually brought into line with its demands.

Nevertheless, Mormon historians Leonard Arrington and Davis Bitton argue that although the standard interpretation of LDS history for the thirty years immediately following the Woodruff Manifesto is one of accommodation, it must also be understood that that was a period of adjustment in a way distinctive to Mormon (rather than non-Mormon) community standards. Attempting to balance their own values with those of the rest of American culture, the Saints worked hard to join the American scene and to be accepted, even offering their sons in the Spanish-American War. Arrington and Bitton note that the political accommodation was the "most complete" of all those made by the Church, and they conclude that this realm—as well as the social, economic, and educational realms—was "relinquished in order that the church could survive as an ecclesiastical institution with its own unique theology and religious practices."[73] In other words, the church accepted the formula for pluralism in the American constitutional order.

The history of the confrontation of the Mormons with the federal government provides us with a second model for religious minorities' encounters with the American constitutional order. We have seen an example of congruence with—and now one of conversion to—the dictates of its authority. But still another option remains in the encounter. In the previous cases, each community had the ability to negotiate with the dominant culture, though each worked out a different solution based on a variety of factors. What happens when a minority religious community does not share the cultural resources with which to negotiate the dilemma over conflicting authority? The outcome, unlike the intense period of litigation by Jehovah's Witnesses and unlike the political capitulation by the Mormons, is continuous conflict within the constitutional realm.

# 4

# Constitutional Conflict

*Native American Religious Traditions
and the Constitutional Order*

> However extravagant the pretension of
> converting the discovery of an inhabited country
> into conquest may appear; . . . if the property of
> the great mass of the community originates in
> it, it becomes the law of the land, and cannot be
> questioned. . . . However this restriction may be
> opposed to natural right, and to the usages of
> civilized nations, yet, if it be indispensable to
> that system under which the country has been
> settled, and be adapted to the actual condition of
> the two people, it may, perhaps, be supported by
> reason, and certainly cannot be rejected by
> Courts of justice.
>
> CHIEF JUSTICE JOHN MARSHALL

Up to this point this study has examined the confrontations of nonmainstream Protestant groups, and the discussion has suggested the possibility, if not the desire, to reconcile particularistic sources of authority with those of the American constitutional order. For example, the Jehovah's Witnesses were able to translate their claims both to reduce the threat of confrontation and to convince the order of the validity of those claims; the Church of Jesus Christ of

Latter-day Saints was able to become integrated into the order once it ceded its claims to rival political authority. Both communities possessed the ability to communicate with—and understand the demands of—the constitutional order. They simply worked out their respective confrontations differently.

Now comes the question of how a religious community not sharing a European and predominantly Christian orientation can hope to survive a confrontation with the American constitutional order. How can a community for whom the order's very terms and presuppositions are unfamiliar come to a resolution with its demands? Is the American constitutional order exclusively Christian? Or can it admit a plurality of cultures and traditions under its umbrella?

Once again we move back in time to a more complex account, and the reader may be struck by the contrast between the following discussion and the previous chapters. This difference is both important and revealing, and for a variety of reasons it is also necessary. First, unlike the Jehovah's Witnesses and the Mormons, traditional Native American religions are extraordinarily diverse and are not centralized; therefore, any discussion of the interaction between them and the constitutional order must be broad and general. Even though referring to Native Americans and traditional Native American religions as monolithic (as I do) is a violation of the diversity of these cultures, such a representation is important to my treatment.[1] For one thing, it reflects the fact that representatives of the constitutional order rarely understood Native American cultures as anything other than monolithic. It is partly because of that fact that there is no single character or institution around which to focus the narrative. With no single community leader, such as Hayden Covington of the Jehovah's Witnesses or Brigham Young of the Mormons, to represent this vast assortment of traditional Native American cultures, no biography around which to construct the account, the story line is a bit more difficult to follow.

Finally, the period of time during which the interaction with the federal government occurred is much greater, removing the likelihood that any one individual would play a significant and sustained role. It becomes necessary to look for more than a single catalyst or a single event in the investigation of the encounters between traditional Native American religions and the federal government, and the entirety of the relationship must be examined for clues to its significance. The previous chapters focused on engagements between the particular religious community and elements of the constitutional order, but we must now examine the entire system to identify the nature of the encounter.

The case involving traditional Native American religions is, at least as much as the previous two cases, set against the backdrop of political power negotiations. Indeed, given the attitude toward Native Americans that has been typical of the American constitutional order, it would appear initially that this struggle has been defined entirely by power concerns and has had little to do with religion. However, as the story of the relationship between Native Americans and the federal government unfolds, so too does its religious component. Against the background of the other two cases, it is possible to see the most difficult of encounters with the American constitutional order—constitutional conflict.

## Constitutional Order and the Conflict over Authority

By December of 1992, Nathan Jim, Jr., an Oregon member of the Yakima Indian Nation, had already served a prison term for violating the Eagle Protection Act and the Endangered Species Act. Yet in that month he was caught with the carcasses of several protected birds—including a bald eagle—in his truck. Though Jim argued that his actions were justified on religious grounds, in a plea bargain for probation in lieu of more prison time he promised to stop killing the protected birds. "I will obey your law," he told the federal district court judge.[2]

The media reported the events involving Nathan Jim in simple terms—the conflict's potential to serve as an early test of the Religious Freedom Restoration Act. Apparent in Jim's words, however, are the deeper levels of conflict inherent in the struggle between traditional Native American religions and the American constitutional order. His retort to the judge exposes the highest dilemma over authority in our society, and as Jim expressed it, there was no confusion or mingling of *his* sources of authority: "I will obey your law." Not *the* law, but *your* law. Jim did not accept the law as inherently applying to all, but admitted that, given his own legal situation, for the time being he would agree to abide by a law considered authoritative by others though not by him. Implied in his comment was an acknowledgment that the source of authority for his own actions was not co-opted by the legal authority threatening another prison term—he merely agreed not to act on beliefs he thought were justified. He promised that he would behave as the federal authorities demanded; but by recognizing the difference between the two sources of authority, he implied he would not compromise his own system of beliefs.

Nathan Jim's comments regarding the two sources of legal authority express the dilemma faced by communities that by choice or by circumstance may not be included in the pluralism envisioned by the Constitution. In 1852 the same sense of marginality and exclusion from the constitutional order was expressed by Frederick Douglass in his famous speech, "What to the Slave Is the Fourth of July?" Noting that the Constitution—the foundation upon which any appeal to maintain the Union had to be built—specifically gave less than full membership to the slaves, Douglass reached further back in history, to the ideals of human equality reflected in the Declaration of Independence, for greater inclusion of all peoples within the framework of the American constitutional order. As Milner Ball argues, Douglass's conclusion that "this Fourth [of] July is *yours*, not *mine*" was "a plea to make it his as well, a plea to render the story [of American origins] capable of embracing him."[3] In terms used earlier, he was seeking to locate his community within the myth of primal unity.

Rendering the story "capable of embracing" the Native Americans, and thereby locating them within that same myth, has been a much greater challenge, making their inclusion within the constitutional order much more difficult. Although the history of the Native American encounter with European Americans is in part analogous to that of African Americans, particularly in the arena of religion, structural differences have led to an apparently inherent conflict over authority between Native Americans and the constitutional order that was not present in the African American encounter. African American slaves, removed from the structures of their traditional religions throughout Africa, were compelled to adjust their religious beliefs by adopting slightly altered Christian meanings for their inherited religious behaviors. Native American communities were often placed in a similar situation, in the sense that disregarding traditional native religious behaviors in favor of Christianity was often the price of acceptance in American society.[4] Neither African American rights nor Native American rights were originally protected in the U.S. Constitution. Both communities experienced European culture through force and violence and found themselves in no position of advantage to negotiate an equilibrium. But whereas Africans were forcibly and violently brought to this continent, Native Americans were here when the Europeans arrived. They had developed intricate social structures and had governed their own affairs free of European intrusion. They did not have their social structures destroyed by transplantation across an ocean; they were not a diaspora searching to find meaning in new surroundings. Instead, they were an increasingly occupied people searching to retain meaning against overwhelming force. The introduction of a competing system of authority profoundly threatened the very structure of Native American society, and the integration of the two systems has continued to be a source of conflict.

For Native Americans, the continuing dilemma over the authority of the American constitutional order can be linked to the depth of the systemic conflict of the competing authorities. In part, this is because of the manner in which interaction between Native Americans and the American constitutional order has unfolded historically. But just as significantly, conflicts over the very *notions* of sovereignty and territoriality inevitably have led to continuing struggles over authority within the constitutional order. This struggle between Native American territorial claims and American political demands for sovereignty has been complicated by noncongruous understandings of such concepts expressed by Native Americans and the American legal system. The powerful meaning ascribed by Native Americans to the notion of community (tribal) sovereignty or sacred land, for example, is virtually unrecognizable in the American constitutional order because these terms are rarely used within a federalist context. The terminology of the American constitutional order, as we shall see, cannot account well for concepts whose reference is outside of the traditional structures of the federal government. This, combined with the evolving status of Native Americans in the United States, has put them in limbo with regard to American legal history. Consequently, Native American communities have resisted accepting the demands of the constitutional order—and have been largely unable to live independent of them—because of the direct nature of the conflict over authority and especially the symbolic and tangible role of land in that conflict. Even the idealistic rhetoric found in the Declaration of Independence, the very embodiment of the competing authority to which Douglass was able to appeal, has not been sufficient to secure religious equality. Although it required extraordinary sacrifices, Africans became African Americans through an appeal to universal equality. Native peoples on this continent have also been required to sacrifice much of their distinct and collective identities, but ironically, because they existed on this continent before European contact and therefore encountered the American constitutional order as an intruder rather than an enslaver, they have not had access to the same principles to which Frederick Douglass and others could appeal. And whereas slavery almost required African Americans to adopt the concepts of the American constitutional order, the encounter experience of Native Americans seemed to prevent it. Thus, because of the conflicts over group identities and the sources of authority for Native Americans and the constitutional order, the First Amendment guarantee of religious freedom continues to be a confounding ideal. Religious freedom is not yet fully realized by the Native American members of the American constitutional order.

## The Beginning of the Occupation

It is probably no understatement to suggest that the relationship between the federal government and the various Native American communities has been troubled from the very beginning of U.S. history. The predominantly British culture on the Atlantic seaboard, which developed in a world of competing colonial powers, treated the indigenous peoples they encountered on this continent with caution born not out of respect for the sovereignty of tribal authority, but out of concern for the alliances these peoples might form with the other colonial powers. As Henry Bowden points out in his history of Native American missionary contact, although all of the colonial powers expressed a strong arrogance toward the indigenous peoples in the Americas, the English may have been the worst offenders and "the least concerned to preserve any aspect of native civilization."[5] Of more importance than the humanity of the native peoples were concerns about how the various tribes could be used as buffers against the competition. Indeed, most of the settlers seemed less interested in integrating the Native Americans into their own religious worldview and more interested in removing them from areas deemed desirable.

Little was changed with the establishment of the United States as an independent nation. The federal government approached the indigenous peoples as instruments of foreign policy, and engagement with the tribes in the form of missionary work was promoted as an element of control in pacifying them, or—in the more common parlance of the period—in "civilizing" them. "The new nation," writes church historian Pierce Beaver, "inherited from the colonial era, and particularly from the New England colonies, a common assumption that the Indian missions were the proper concern of the state and were beneficial to the welfare of the state."[6] With the missionaries working to contain the indigenous non-European peoples, the federal government could protect its citizenry from the threat of French, British, or Spanish expansionist policies.

The official attitude shifted considerably once the European colonial powers were eliminated as a threat. By the early nineteenth century, with competition from France and England effectively out of the way in the Midwest, the federal government was freed of its external national security concerns and could operate with greater self-confidence with regard to territorial expansion. "As long as the Indians were pawns in the larger chess game, they received a modicum of respect," summarizes Bowden, but once the threat of outside alliances disappeared, "they lost that small advantage and became simply obstacles in the path of American pioneers."[7] Native Americans as a group became less of an external threat and more of an internal nuisance. By the end of the War of 1812, interactions with the various tribes focused on public policy concerns, not international relations.

Significantly, none of those public policy concerns focused on the interests of Native Americans since, from the standpoint of the government, Native Americans were not considered part of the government's constituency. Article 1 of the new Constitution excluded "Indians not taxed" from the apportionment of representation and empowered Congress to regulate commerce with the tribes in the same manner it would with foreign nations—through the Senate's ratification debates over a treaty negotiated and signed by the president and the third party.[8] Even when Article 1 was amended by the Fourteenth Amendment in 1868, Native Americans were still excluded from apportionment formulas.[9] In addition, though the threat of collaboration with international forces was reduced significantly, oversight for matters concerning Native Americans was assigned to the secretary of war, who in 1824 created the Bureau of Indian Affairs. Only with the establishment of the Department of the Interior in 1849 did oversight of Native American issues transfer out of the War Department's jurisdiction.[10]

The tribes were not completely uninformed about their ambiguous standing in the new nation. On July 4, 1827, the Cherokee tribe in Georgia adopted a tribal constitution that itself was an adaptation of the federal Constitution. The state of Georgia, perceiving a threat to its state sovereignty, responded by extending state jurisdiction to the Cherokee territory and then incorporating the tribe's territory into the state. After being blocked by Georgia from suing in state court, the Cherokee tribe filed under the provisions of Article 3, section 2 of the U.S. Constitution, which permits foreign nations to bring legal actions to the Supreme Court. The resulting suit brought by the tribe, *Cherokee Nation v. Georgia,* was dismissed by the Court in 1831 on the grounds that, since the Cherokee tribe was not a foreign nation, the issue was not within the Court's jurisdiction.[11]

Although the Court lacked jurisdiction, the justices took the opportunity to discuss at some length the nature of the relationship of Native Americans with the constitutional order. "The relation of the Indians to the United States is marked by peculiar and cardinal distinctions which exist no where else," observed Chief Justice John Marshall, writing for the majority. Native Americans should be understood as "domestic dependent nations," he concluded, since "they occupy a territory to which we assert a title independent of their will. . . . Their relation to the United States resembles that of a ward to his guardian." Justice William Johnson, dissenting from the Court's decision, argued that the mere fact that the federal government interacted with the tribes through the mechanism of treaty indicated that they were considered foreign nations as understood by the Constitution. "And if, as here decided, a separate and distinct jurisdiction or government is the test by which to decide whether a nation be foreign or not; I am unable to perceive any sound and substantial reason why the Cherokee nation should not be so considered."[12]

The following year, the Supreme Court saw the logic of Justice Johnson's dissenting opinion in *Cherokee Nation v. Georgia* when it was again faced with a suit involving Native American standing in the constitutional order. This suit also involved the Cherokee tribe in Georgia, but this time the case, *Worcester v. Georgia,* was brought by the Congregationalist American Board of Commissioners for Foreign Missions on behalf of one of its missionaries, Samuel Worcester, who had defied a Georgia statute and entered the Cherokee territory without state authorization.[13] Justice Marshall, recognizing the futility of a land grant from a king in Europe over territory that was not his to give, as well as the constitutional reality of the treaty mechanism mentioned by Justice Johnson the previous year, nullified Georgia law over the Cherokee territory. He went on to identify the tribe as equal in status to any foreign nation. However, populist President Andrew Jackson, fearing that enforcing the Supreme Court's ruling would exacerbate separatist sentiment in the South, condemned the ruling, refused to enforce it, and suggested that Justice Marshall enforce it himself. Meanwhile, Christian missionaries chose to "sacrifice the Cherokees to save the Union" by counseling the tribe to settle the suit and relocate in the West.[14] The ruling left the status of Native American communities in an ambiguous position within the realm of political theory. Functionally, though, it was clear that they were subject to the will of the American constitutional order.

Outside the Supreme Court, the country's territorial expansion continued to affect the status of Native Americans in the constitutional order. Their increasing absence from life in the East tended to soften their image among the settled, who responded nostalgically with feelings of love that translated into remorse for their earlier behavior of hostility toward Native Americans. This remorse, combined with a sense of moral and religious duty, led non–Native Americans to conclude that the only act of restitution available was to give them that which was so valuable to European Americans: the Gospel. The government agreed with the "gift" to be given to Native Americans but not necessarily for the same reasons; the increased missionary zeal continued to serve public policy goals and was therefore not only supported but actively pursued. Thus, for the better part of the nineteenth century, the federal government and the various churches worked in cooperation for the "elevation of the Indians." In fact, by providing institutional and financial support, the federal government was able to make such missionary work more appealing to groups that might ordinarily have preferred more attractive assignments overseas. Both the government and the missionary societies were able to benefit from the arrangement; the government secured political as well as military advantage by supporting the missionaries, and the missionary societies gained at least an imagined stake in the welfare of the nation.

The concern shared by the political authorities and the missionary societies did not specifically include respect for the personhood of Native Americans or the dignity of Native American culture. In fact, in a manner reminiscent of some of the political battles of the modern period, the availability of federal money encouraged competition for government financial support rather than enthusiasm for the stated goal of the funding. Assesses Beaver, "Neither the Protestant nor the Roman Catholic missionaries and officials were really concerned about the Indian's right to maintain and defend his own religion, and they were fighting more for freedom of action by the missionary agencies."[15] The competition grew more fierce when, in an expression of virulent anti-Catholicism, the American Protective Association published a letter revealing the disproportionately high amount of money Catholic missionary societies were receiving from the federal government as part of President Ulysses Grant's "Peace Policy."

By the end of the nineteenth century, as the Protestant cultural monopoly began to weaken, the role of the missionary societies in negotiating the relationship between Native Americans and the federal government began to disappear. Religion ceased to be a prime element in the relationship between the federal government and the Native Americans; as concern over Native Americans diminished, so did concern for their spiritual well-being. In 1871, in a rider to the Indian Appropriation, the House of Representatives effectively put an end to whatever "foreign" or independent position tribes might have had until then by ending the treaty process unilaterally. Although this unorthodox violation of constitutional protocol may have been an assertion of authority on the part of the House over the Senate, it is also true that the move represented the conclusion that Native Americans no longer posed even the slightest threat to American expansionist aims and were a domestic rather than an international concern.[16] Coast to coast, Native Americans found themselves within American borders, and the frontier, to be declared closed by historian Frederick Jackson Turner only five years later, ceased to be either a place of refuge for Native Americans or the outer boundary of civilization for the expansionist Americans.

With Congress's recategorization of relations with Native Americans from an international to a domestic issue, the government was now in a position to make even greater (though possibly more subtle) demands for membership in the constitutional order. Congress insisted that Native Americans had to be successfully integrated into the American constitutional order. To accomplish this goal, Native Americans had to be remade as recognizable constituents—individual citizens cognizant of the federal government's supreme position of authority. The government would no longer accept collective representation outside the framework of the federalist structure. Significantly, this meant that Native American participation in the constitutional order would have to be carried out by individuals— at the cost of the different tribal sovereignties. Now there was no place in the federal structure of authority for tribal authorities competing with the states.[17] In simpler terms, Native Americans would be encouraged to work the land and even own it, but the federal government, through the principle of eminent domain, would possess the ultimate title, and no one else could stake any superior claim.

Actions symbolic of this altered stance toward Native American authority again came in the guise of good intentions. The General Allotment Act of 1887 (also known as the Dawes Act) was intended to provide individual ownership of tribal land to the Native Americans who had lived on that land. As Native American legal scholars Vine Deloria, Jr., and Clifford Lytle argue, members of Congress and American culture as a whole seemed to believe that "private property . . . had mystical magical qualities about it that led people directly to a 'civilized state.'" The program that emerged from the Dawes Act was disastrous, however, and led to an eventual diminution of Native American land holdings that was finally halted in 1934. Before that, in 1919, American citizenship was awarded to Native American veterans of World War I; and then in 1924, by the Indian Citizenship Act, it was granted to all Native Americans born within the United States. In 1968 the Indian Civil Rights Act extended to Native Americans who lived on reservations under tribal jurisdiction most of the rights other Americans had secured nearly two hundred years earlier, including the First Amendment right to the free exercise of religion. All of these programs of good intent for Native Americans came at great cost; individual property ownership removed the authority of the different communities from the land (and in many cases also removed the Native Americans from it as well), and citizenship reinforced the individuality of identity and ignored or minimized the communal authorities asserted by separate tribes. Even the highly praised Indian Civil Rights Act, argues Milner Ball, "diminish[ed] the power of tribal government" by asserting federal protection over internal tribal relationships and "threaten[ed] to remake tribal courts in the image of the federal judiciary."[18]

By the second half of this century, Native American status as defined by the federal government was, for good or ill, more clearly established. In the 1955 case of *Tee-Hit-Ton Indians v. United States,* the Supreme Court articulated the federal government's position on the unilateral incorporation of Native American reservations, noting that "the savage tribes of this continent were deprived of their ancestral ranges by force and that, even when the Indians ceded millions of acres by treaty in return for blankets, food and trinkets, it was not a sale but the conquerors' will that deprived them of their land." The historic process of incorporation was symbolically concluded in 1978 when the Court, quoting from a nineteenth-century decision, observed in the case of *Oliphant v. Suquamish Indian Tribe,* "Indian reservations are 'a part of the territory of the United States.' Indian tribes 'hold and occupy [the reservations] with the assent of the United States, and under their authority.'"[19] Although expressed as dicta in both decisions, these comments clearly reflected the Court's evaluation of the relationship between Native Americans and the federal government; the federal government as possessor of ultimate authority dominated the rhetoric. The emphasis in Justice Marshall's original phrase "domestic dependent nations" was placed on *domestic dependent* rather than on *nations.*

Thus, by the last quarter of the twentieth century, the Supreme Court unilaterally completed the goal of the Declaration of Independence by asserting that all were indeed created equal. In the name of that equality, however, any distinction to be found in Native American culture was in danger of eradication. The U.S. Constitution had originally distinguished between individual Native Americans and those who maintained their connection with their tribe ("Indians not taxed"), but the Court now leveled the field by making tribal communities simply collections of individual Native Americans who happened to live on federal property. Members of Native American tribes, once feared for their ability to influence international relations, had become ordinary citizens in the eyes of the law: they had been given citizenship, they were taxed, and they were given opportunities to own and farm land. Granted individual membership in the constitutional order without asking for it, Native Americans could now do virtually everything that all other citizens could, with one significant exception. They could not express themselves through their distinctive collective identities—since those identities inherently involved expressions of territorial sovereignty over land now controlled by the same Constitution that served them as individuals.[20]

## Native American Religions Encounter the Constitutional Order

The precarious position of the Native American community within the constitutional order only exacerbated the position of Native American religious traditions within the framework of the First Amendment. Because citizenship was not conferred upon Native Americans until late in American history, the practitioners of various Native American religious traditions could not, until that time, appeal to the constitutional order for protection. And as we have seen, even when relief was sought through the court system, Christian (predominantly Protestant) presuppositions about the American legal system and its concomitant conceptions of authority and territoriality severely disadvantaged Native Americans. Constitutional scholar Edward Gaffney points out that the legacy of biblical imagery is both a strong and a necessary element in the construction of identity in the American constitutional order: "Biblical traditions cannot be eliminated from the way that America tells her tale . . . without a significant loss of cultural identity and purpose."[21]

This relationship between Christian conceptions and its operation has characterized American society since colonists first came ashore from Europe. The connection deeply affected how settlers interacted with the new peoples they encountered. Ventures such as John Eliot's "praying Indian" villages in seventeenth-century Massachusetts, organized on a model derived from the book of Exodus, seemed perfectly logical to Europeans familiar with the passage. That was not, of course, a particularly familiar model for native peoples on this continent.[22] Often seen by European Americans as not religions at all, the various religious traditions of the Native Americans were easily overlooked. Because of the significant differences between European American and Native American religious concepts, dialogue between the two worlds was virtually meaningless, and respect for Native American religious traditions on the part of the European settlers was virtually nonexistent. Native American human agency was generally ignored, as European Americans assumed Native Americans to be merely part of the Christian "cosmic drama"; they were either used by God to aid the European Americans toward salvation or used by Satan to confound those efforts.

Ironically, it was not until the year that incorporation of tribal reservations was completed by unilateral Supreme Court fiat (in *Oliphant v. Suquamish Indian Tribe* [1978]) that Congress passed the American Indian Religious Freedom Act (AIRFA). This nonbinding resolution, which recognized the extension of the free exercise clause to traditional Native American religions, urged federal agencies that interacted with Native Americans to be respectful of their religions. But the act was written without corresponding penalties, making it essentially meaningless. If AIRFA was to have any strength, its tenets would have to be tested in the courts.

As a result of the historic evolution of rights traced above, no Native American free exercise claim was addressed by the Supreme

Court until January 1986. Since most Native Americans had not been declared citizens until after World War I and had not been specifically protected by the Bill of Rights until 1968, it is not surprising that the federal courts did not recognize their free exercise claims until the 1970s. In the lower federal courts Native Americans have been predominantly unsuccessful. In *Sequoyah v. Tennessee Valley Authority* (1980) and *Badoni v. Higginson* (1980), two different federal circuit courts ruled that flooding (by the damming of nearby rivers) of different sites deemed sacred by members of the Cherokee and Navajo communities did not violate their respective free exercise rights. Three years later, in *Fools Crow v. Gullet* (1983), another federal circuit court ruled that public use of park land in South Dakota did not violate the free exercise rights of members of the Lakota and Tsistsistas communities. That same year, the federal circuit court for the District of Columbia ruled that the construction of a ski resort in the San Francisco Peaks region of Arizona did not violate the free exercise rights of the Hopi and Navajo communities. These two communities considered the mountains to be the home of their deities and believed that the mountains themselves were also deities. Such losses at the circuit level have had a strong negative impact on litigation and have left the practice of traditional Native American religions "more hampered and threatened than is the practice of any other traditional religion in this country," according to Robert Michaelsen. It is not a coincidence, he continues, that "the most significant losses have occurred in connection with access to sacred site claims."[23]

Nevertheless, there have been victories for Native Americans claiming that governmental rules for land use are an infringement on their free exercise rights. In *United States v. Means* (1985), a district court affirmed Lakota claims that the Park Service's denial of "special use" permits violated their free exercise rights over land use. Three years later, however, a circuit court reversed this ruling. In *Northwest Indian Cemetery Protective Association v. Peterson* (1983), a district court affirmed claims that the construction of a logging road would violate Karuk, Yurok, and Tolowa free exercise rights over land use. Though a circuit court rejected part of the district court's ruling in 1986, it affirmed that court's decision regarding free exercise claims.

This last decision (now identified by the party replacing Peterson in the suit, Richard Lyng) was the first land-use dispute brought by Native Americans to reach the U.S. Supreme Court, and it clearly demonstrates the disadvantageous position of traditional Native American religions in federal courts. The members of the tribes represented in the case argued that the proposed logging road would desecrate the sacred meaning of an area known as "the high country," which included the three highest peaks in the region. They understood this rather remote area to be a place where they could communicate with their Creator and therefore a place of unmatched religious significance.[24] In an amicus brief filed in conjunction with the National Congress of American Indians, the Association on American Indian Affairs, and the tribes affected by the case, Steven Moore of the Native American Rights Fund argued that one significant difference between "world" religions and "tribal group" religions was that the former were commemorative whereas the latter were continuing. This meant that most European American religious communities sacralized events commemorated from their past, in contrast with Native American religious communities, which sacralized events that were continuously revealed to them. European American communities could commemorate events anywhere, but Native American communities had to remain in contact with the location where instructions were continually received from the transcendent sources of authority.[25] Since the "high country" represented a place where ongoing revelations were received, no other place could be substituted. It was sacred by the very nature of the ongoing communication, rather than because of the commemoration of an event in the past, and construction on it, through it, or even around it would destroy the integrity of the location.

Prior to the *Lyng* decision (known informally as the "G-O Road" decision, since the logging road would connect the towns of Gasquet and Orleans), the closest the Supreme Court had come to a sacred site dispute was the 1890 decision in *Late Corporation of the Church of Jesus Christ of Latter-day Saints v. United States,* discussed in chapter 3. This judicial action was hardly a cause for optimism for Native Americans; it had resulted in the disfranchisement of the Mormon community and the wholesale dismantling of church real estate holdings in the Utah Territory. In *Lyng* the Court followed the precedent established in the Mormon decision but also relied heavily on the holding in *Bowen v. Roy,* which suggested that the federal government had the authority to determine its operational needs, even at the cost of occasionally offending religious sensibilities. Overcoming objections on religious grounds raised by the Cemetery Protective Association, the Court determined that there existed a "compelling interest" to build a road through lands deemed sacred by a number of tribes in northern California, and it effectively reversed the decisions of the two lower courts.[26]

This case, like the other, lower court cases involving Native American claims over land for religious free exercise purposes, does not pit the traditional Native American religions against specific government "interests," but instead pits them against the most general of governmental interests, its own authority. According to the brief submitted to the Supreme Court on behalf of the Cemetery Protective Association, any decision involving conflicting claims over land use must address two questions. First, do the Native Americans demonstrate that "the land in question is central and indispensable to the exercise of their religion and that the proposed governmental operations will interfere with that exercise?" Second, does the government demonstrate that "its operations serve a compelling interest?" The combination of factors, including Native Americans' and European Americans' cultural differences and the necessary balance a court must strike given these two questions, places a high burden on Native American religious traditions. And since the courts have been unsympathetic to Native American religious free exercise claims, it is inevitable that they would decide most cases in favor of the governmental interests, regardless of how "compelling" they might be. It is in the government's interest to control its territory, and Native American challenges to that control, in the shape of religious claims, usually are not successful. As Michaelsen summarizes: "Governmental interests have been generally well treated in Native American sacred site cases. Indeed, as the Circuit Court of the District of Columbia commented in one case, some courts have even implied that 'The Free Exercise Clause can never supersede the government's ownership rights and duties of public management.' On the contrary, that court continued in a statement that is both obvious and necessary: 'The government must manage its lands in accordance with the Constitution.'"[27]

## Common Land as Uncommon Symbol

"The government must manage its lands in accordance with the Constitution." This powerfully symbolic statement, written in a circuit court opinion in 1983, makes painfully obvious the level of conflict over the meaning of land and its role in the power struggle between Native Americans and the American constitutional order. When the dispute over the authority of the Constitution involves religious issues, the conflict over simple land management and authority becomes a theological clash of monumental proportions. This is where the clash occurs between what it means to be a practitioner of traditional Native American religions and what it means to be a citizen of the American constitutional order. Whereas debate over the use of various sacraments or rituals may continue between the dominant religious community and various minority communities, it is the difference over the meaning of land that presents the most perplexing dilemmas in the confrontation between Native American religious communities and the dominant culture. Ultimately, as the LDS Church learned, the issue in the confrontation with the American constitutional order is authority over the land. However, unlike the Mormons, who started with familiar theological underpinnings, or the Jehovah's Witnesses, who were able to find a common language to express their needs, the various Native American religious communities did not have basic theological orientations that were familiar to the dominant culture. Native American legal scholar Vine Deloria, Jr., characterizes the difference in orientations in terms of the relative importance attached to space or time: "American Indians hold their lands—places—as having the highest possible meaning, and all their statements are made with this reference point in mind. Immigrants review the movement of their ancestors across the continent as a steady progression of basically good events and experiences, thereby placing history—time—in the best possible light." In other words, because Christianity (the predominant religion of the European American settlers) focuses on redemption through the grace of God, it views this world as a temporary stage on which human actions are played out over time in preparation for elevation to another, higher stage. Traditional Native American religions, in contrast, generally picture the land as part of what is essentially sacred, so that "all aspects of life take on religious significance and religion and culture are intimately connected."[28] Christianity occupies space while it anticipates the passage of time; Native American religious traditions occupy time while orienting themselves to space.

This difference is most clearly manifest within the constitutional order in the reactions of the mainstream religious community to the two most significant decisions handed down by the Supreme Court in cases involving Native American religious freedom. After the *Lyng* decision, in which Native American sacred site land claims were refused in favor of the construction of a logging road, there was hardly any reaction from the organized religious community.[29] But there was an uproar when the Court upheld a state's prohibition of the ritual use of peyote in *Employment Division v. Smith.* The Court ruled that the sacramental use of a substance designated as illegal by the Oregon legislature did not enjoy constitutional protection simply because of religious meaning attached to it. Scores of politically organized religious groups banded together (many for the first time) to ask for a rehearing from the Supreme Court.[30] When that failed, they organized and lobbied for legislative redress in the form of the Religious Freedom Restoration Act, which they helped write. What accounted for these quite different responses? Significantly, many observers thought that the Court's decision in *Smith* could mean sweeping changes in constitutional jurisprudence

that potentially could affect the status of non–Native American religious communities. In other words, the non–Native American
religious communities did not feel threatened by the Court's decision in a sacred land decision based on a principle that was unlikely
ever to affect them. They did, however, feel threatened by the
Court's decision in a case involving ritual, a category more easily
accessible to Western religious traditions and one that is used by
them to mark the passage of time.

Western culture generally assumes that land is a commodity that
can easily be exchanged. This assumption stands in stark contrast
to many traditional Native American religious beliefs that posit a
custodial or partnership approach. Ball argues, quoting Standing
Bear, that the entire idea of wilderness—in the European American
vision of it as wild and dangerous—is the creation of a society that
has become alienated from nature. By contrast, Native American
attitudes toward land were "characteristic of a gift economy"; Native Americans saw land in terms of its interdependence with a
community, not as a commodity. Such an attitude toward land is
virtually unrecognizable in European American culture, except in
the case of the Mormons. Even in that community the attachment
is based on a biblical construction of property rather than on the
interrelationship between individual, land, and community. Once
the LDS Church leadership conceded temporal authority to the
constitutional order, it could—like the Jehovah's Witnesses—accept
the occupation of the federal government until, literally, the end of
time. Many traditional Native American communities, though—
the Cheyenne and Sioux (Black Hills) and the Taos Pueblo (Blue Lake
and neighboring mountains), for example—recognize certain lands
as sacred. The Navajo believe not only that the San Francisco Peaks
are the home of their gods, but that the peaks themselves are also a
deity in a sacred cosmos.[31] Traditional Native American religions,
centered as they are on space and not on the passage of time, could
not so easily reinterpret their relationship to account for the occupation of the American constitutional order. This contrast in attitudes provides a powerful explanation for the conflicts between the
two cultures and suggests a reason both for the inability to reach a

meaningful understanding about the religious significance of land and for the incidence of Native American millenarian responses after contact with European American cultures was established.

Such different levels of meaning have made cross-cultural dialogue difficult. Of greater significance, however, this conflict over meanings of space and time helps to preserve the dispute over authority between Native Americans and the constitutional order. As missionary societies were attempting to convert Native Americans to Christianity during the nineteenth and early twentieth centuries, the federal government was trying to make them into "good citizens." There can be no question that the former goal well served the latter for several reasons. First, it is unlikely that the framers of the Constitution wrote the First Amendment to include religious traditions that did not have a Protestant worldview. This assumption, articulated by early Supreme Court Justice Joseph Story in his multivolume work *Commentaries on the Constitution of the United States,* suggests a close connection between the two categories of communion and citizenship, at least early in American history.[32] Second, although the preamble of the Constitution clearly rests its authority on a communal category ("We, the people"), it actually expresses rights in terms of the individual.[33] As already seen, the individualistic understanding of rights proved to be a serious and continuing challenge to the structure and authority of Native American communities. It ensured, as well, the dominance of the constitutional order in their stead. Third, the parallelism between the symbolic voice of authority for Protestant Christianity and the symbolic voice of authority for the American constitutional order masked the *actual* source of authority of the latter, namely territorial sovereignty. The Word made flesh, the light of the world who is the Savior in Christian theology, is for the American constitutional order a word made on parchment, a light to the nations that promises freedom but is grounded upon power and control. With mainstream Christian theology placing its emphasis on the world to come, the American constitutional order could assert its authority over the world that was, specifically all the territory under its control. Since the focus of traditional Native American religions was on the land, this masking obscured the full ramifications of the federal government's challenge to Native American land claims, especially when they reached religious dimensions. Because citizenship was symbolically defined by a written contract (the U.S. Constitution), the foundation of the federal government's authority over territory did not conflict with underlying Protestant belief but actually complemented it in the life of the citizen. But because the source of authority rested on the federal government's ability to control territory (or maintain sovereignty), Native American claims of sovereignty over land, whether religiously based or not, threatened the very foundation of the constitutional order's authority.

From the earliest days of cultural interaction, the intellectual foundations through which European Americans could have understood Native American religious traditions were meager; the inclusion of Native Americans as a quasi-independent unit in the constitutional order probably never had much of a chance. Indeed, early on, European Americans' appropriation of traditionally recognized title to land had little to do with the presence of Native Americans. In 1629 John Winthrop declared that possession of land in the Massachusetts Bay Colony would be determined by the doctrine of *vacuum domicillum;* ownership meant improvement (as in buildings or farming), not mere occupancy (as in transient living or hunting patterns), and improvement meant European culture. In the absence of such improvements, the entire colonial period was governed by the doctrine of discovery, in which any aboriginal claims to the land were virtually ignored. Nearly one hundred sixty years later, as Milner Ball points out, the Constitution would be declared "the supreme law of the land," thereby shifting authority away from those political units that could participate democratically (as defined by the rest of the document for individual citizens and the states) to a geographic region encompassing all peoples and institutions, both willing and not.[34] For the federal government and the dominant European heritage it represented, land was a possession, a tool in the business of this world, and subject to God's command to "have dominion over" it until the end of time. The federal government, as representative of the dominant culture and imbued with its own transcending authority, subsumed under its command the right to control all property for the time being and for the benefit (salvation, even) of its citizenry. The doctrine of Manifest Destiny and its implicit theological presuppositions governed the attitude toward land expressed by the American constitutional order.[35]

## The Constitutional Order Meets Native American Religions

Because of the extraordinary differences between their cultures, as we have seen, Native American conceptions of religion and law were virtually unrecognizable to European settlers, colonists, and pioneers (and vice versa). Even when European Americans comprehended Native American religion and law, they did so in their own cultural terms, and so described Native American elements as inferior and uncivilized. Estimated one Christian missionary, "The two great hindrances to progress were the Indian religion and the absence of law."[36]

Native American religions and legal systems have functioned successfully in the frameworks of their various cultures for centuries, of course. However, a heavy burden has been placed on traditional Native American religions by the tenuous position of Native American religious claims in American jurisprudence and the consequent need to combat the constitutional order's extension of its authority to Native American territorial claims. Because of the negative, mythic image of "Indian" in American society, writes Robert Michaelsen, "if Indians do not conform to the majority image of them as a vanishing race which embraces a quaint but clearly other-worldly religion, then their keen interest in land must be understood in the earthbound terms of the majority view."[37]

As if taking a lesson from the Jehovah's Witnesses, scholars have suggested several strategies for translating Native American religious concepts of land into the "earthbound terms of the majority view," thereby securing more reliable guarantees for religious free exercise. Such methods as the use of analogy or metaphor have been considered, with some degree of success. Robert Michaelsen uses examples including the dirt in a medicine man's pouch as analogous to a land title, or the Native American Church, which chose to incorporate as a church in order to make its religious identity more readily understandable.[38] Yet the issue of reconciling Native American religious traditions with European American constructs of law may not be so simple as explanation by analogy or narrative. Deep differences exist between the very communal structures of Native American religious traditions and the deeply individualistic pattern of rights recognized and celebrated in the American constitutional order. Even the need to translate religious differences may have a profoundly adverse effect on traditional Native American patterns of religious authority by subordinating the particularistic religious authority to that of the Constitution and the pluralistic society it represents.[39] But if the root of the conflict itself is based in competing conceptions of authority in time and space, Native American religious expression may have little alternative to continuous struggle with the American constitutional order over land claims. Not simply a matter of rights or toleration, the real issue is who has the right to define a particular space and who has sovereignty over that space at any given time.

Ultimately, this problem of competing notions of authority underscores the dilemma of constitutional authority in the realm of religious free exercise. For traditional Native American religious expression, the concept of authority comes from the very structure of religious and social categories and cannot be aligned with American constitutional authority merely by a slight adjustment. Recent decisions suggest that the courts have made individualism the overwhelming paradigm in the conferral of religious rights, as they have in other areas of rights, but we must recognize the danger that this trend poses. The threat is acute for Native American religions, especially as it is incorporated into the basic conflict over land. The power of Christian American cultural dominance, with its potential for accepting temporal governments as caretakers of the realm until the final act of the cosmic drama, simply overwhelms traditional Native American religious communities, denying them the wherewithal to create a separate peace as the Jehovah's Witnesses have, or to reconfigure their structures of authority as the Mormons did.

Traditional Native American religious communities thus have a dilemma of greater proportions than either the Jehovah's Witnesses or the Mormons had. All minorities facing acculturation into the dominant culture find their community identity threatened when individual members are integrated into the American constitutional order. However, the tense relationship between Native Americans and the federal government and the subsequent struggle over territorial authority make the Native American case so much more difficult that Native American religious traditions have experienced continuous conflict with the American constitutional order. Representing as they do nations subsumed but not really integrated into the order, Native Americans continue to face limitations on religious claims that are perceived to conflict with the expression of authority vested in the federal structure. Because of marked differences in worldview orientation, they do not readily have at their disposal the means to translate their claims into concepts acceptable to the constitutional order. And even if they did, the nature of the claims is such that they strike at the foundations of the authority guarded by the American constitutional order, since Native Americans cannot accept delayed appropriation of the territory in exchange for salvation, as their Christian neighbors do. In a very real sense, they are damned if they do and damned if they don't.

The recognition of culture-based religious distinctions presents a challenge to American political rhetoric—although Americans say "all men are created equal," rights based on a collective identity have fared less well than rights founded on individual identities. In the past the courts occasionally have conferred religious identity and rights on the basis of community designation. For instance, as recently as World War I, membership in specific "Peace Churches" served as sufficient reason for automatic dismissal from military service. More recently, identification as a member of the Amish community permitted removal of children from public school before the state-mandated age.[40] Yet these solutions were crafted for thoroughly European American biblical traditions. It would seem that the foundation for authority in the American constitutional order—vested in the possession and the control of land—is threatened by the religious expressions of traditional Native American religions whose concepts of land challenge that authority. Ultimately, for traditional Native American religions, the legitimacy of the constitutional order might depend on how the two are integrated.

Native religions are not merely a unique example from American history. They are also harbingers of the challenge the American constitutional order will encounter as it faces the integration of larger non-Western communities that do not share the framers' biblical presuppositions and are not able to benefit from the complementary nature of Christian theology and political territoriality. Although the conflict over land may make the Native American struggle distinctive, it suggests that greater flexibility will be required if more diverse religious traditions not based on Christian millennial presuppositions are to be included in the constitutional order. Milner Ball points out, as Frederick Douglass argued in the 1850s, that the elements of this flexibility already exist in the nature of constitutional authority: "The Declaration's second sentence tacitly recognizes that, in a democratic society, even self-evident truth requires mediation, dialogue, consent. Had the truths recited by Jefferson been self-evident in the sense that they were politically monologic, i.e., irresistibly compelling, he would simply have announced them rather than prefacing them with the formula 'We hold.' This introduction is a grammatical acknowledgment that truth, equality, and rights require agreement in the republic. They are matters of opinion exchanged and held."[41]

Furthermore, notions of authority, sovereignty, and political participation are not necessarily constructed on a single intellectual foundation. In the case of Nathan Jim, as well as in the broader historical development of the relationship of Native American religious traditions and the American constitutional order, there are clear differences over how authority is determined, and by whom and under what circumstances. Native traditions, centered (at least in part) on the cultural orientation toward land, cannot but conflict with the American constitutional order's orientation toward the same land. Not so easily integrated into American cultural Christianity's symbolic emphasis on another world (and its relationship to the Constitution as symbolic of the federal government's dependence on this-world territoriality), Native American religious traditions expose the very real and tangible conflict that lies at the heart of the American constitutional order. The strength behind the Constitution is grounded in the control of the land, and any challenge to that control can be met with indirect, but powerful, resistance. Nathan Jim may not see the legal system of the American constitution order as his law, but he has understood the power it holds over him and has agreed to abide by it. So, too, in many ways, have Native American religious traditions agreed to abide by the American constitutional order. Unlike the Mormons, who were able to sacrifice community authority to preserve community identity, Native American religious traditions have had to either sacrifice both—linked as they are—or face continuous conflict.

# Constitutional Questions

## *The Future of Religious Minorities in the American Constitutional Order*

> We hold these truths to be self-evident.
> *Declaration of Independence*

The irony of "We hold these truths to be self-evident" should by now be clear. This statement stands as an ironic testament to the conflicts surrounding religious freedom in the American constitutional order. Who is the "we" of the statement, and which "truths" are held to be self-evident? It has become increasingly apparent that whatever truths are held by whichever group, they are not held by all, they may be truths to one community and not another, and they are certainly *not* self-evident. The history of minority religious communities and their encounters with the American constitutional order make this abundantly clear. The statement is an ideal; it signals a connection to Rousseau's myth of primal unity (described in the introduction) but ignores the reality of American pluralism. There may be no clear "we," and even if there is, the individuals making up that group do not necessarily hold the same "truths."

So what can be understood from the variety of encounters minority religious traditions have had with the American constitutional order? What is the larger significance of constitutional congruences, conversions, and conflicts, and how helpful are they as interpretive tools to help us understand the nature of religious pluralism in American society? There are several conclusions to be drawn from the case studies developed here. How close did each minority community seem to be to Protestant Christianity? How much of a factor has religious difference continued to be in the American constitutional order? And how much did the religious minority threaten the central tenets of the constitutional order, regardless of the constitutional order's seemingly increasing tolerance of religious difference? Only after we have addressed these questions and determined their value can we focus on what I argue is the central issue today for interpreting conflicts between religious minority communities and the American constitutional order: the difference between the ideological orientation of those communities and the constitutional order itself.

## Religious Proximity to Protestant Christianity

One of the first general conclusions from the three case studies is that the degree to which each of the three religious communities differs from general Protestant Christianity (or is perceived to differ by the dominant culture) *seems* to have an impact on the type of encounter that the particular community will experience. The pattern suggests that the closer a religious community is perceived to be to Protestant Christianity, the greater its likelihood of a "draw" with the American constitutional order. (The only "winners" in a political debate are the ones who get to establish the rules, so the best a nonmajority religious community can hope for is to be granted the right to retain its own sources of transcendent authority: a draw.) How have the respective communities' doctrines related to mainstream Protestant Christianity, and how have those relationships influenced their history of encounter with the American constitutional order?

There is no doubt that each of the communities examined has been perceived as markedly different from mainstream Protestant Christianity (whatever that term might mean at any given moment). But it is also clear that the ways in which the three minority religious communities diverge from that amorphous mainstream are different. For example, the Jehovah's Witnesses (an outgrowth of conservative, protofundamentalist forces that had given life to the Millerite movement and would later produce both Seventh-day Adventism and American Fundamentalism) were at their origin the closest of the three to the dominant Protestant culture. This might seem ironic, given their self-segregation from that culture and the disdain in which they were held in their early years. Yet one must consider that, their own idiosyncratic ideologies notwithstanding, the Jehovah's Witnesses began as a literalist, dispensationalist, millennialist Bible study group that (like other Protestant movements) did not encourage its original members to disaffiliate from their denominational institutions. Over the course of time the leadership introduced interpretations of the Christian Scriptures that were unorthodox in terms of traditional Protestant Christianity. But, in a very broad sense, the Jehovah's Witnesses began as a collection of Protestants who eventually emerged as a separate denomination—in the same way that many other Protestant groups have done in American history.

The members of the Church of Jesus Christ of Latter-day Saints can also trace their roots to many of the currents in American religious history. A product of the religious ferment of the "burned-over district" as well as the Protestant primitivist movements from which early members had converted, the LDS Church can be considered the perfect product of the religious influences of the era. As D. Michael Quinn so masterfully demonstrates, however, there were also strong elements of folk tradition and belief that became part of Mormon theology. One can trace many different religious influences in Mormon theology, including Swedenborgianism, Roman Catholicism, and possibly even Islam. But to argue that outside influences alone take Mormonism out of the mainstream is misleading. Were the Mormons simply idiosyncratic while operating within the traditional Protestant canon like the Jehovah's Witnesses, it is likely that they would not have been perceived as such outsiders. However, with the revelation of the Book of Mormon, the doctrine of continuous revelation through the living Prophet and head of the church, and the introduction of the Doctrine and Covenants, Mormonism distinguished itself as more than simply another Protestant denomination. Jan Shipps's work examining the development of Mormonism concludes that early Mormonism, like early Christianity, is best understood as a schismatic movement that became a distinct tradition operating within its own idiom. It is not without some irony that one of the largest non-Utah Mormon groups, the Reorganized Church of Jesus Christ of Latter Day Saints (RLDS), rejected the leadership of Brigham Young, rejected the doctrine of plural marriage, increasingly expressed itself in a mode more familiar to the primitivist Christian Church movement, and experienced significantly less conflict with its non-Mormon neighbors. By committing themselves to the westward journey under the leadership of Brigham Young, the (soon-to-be) Utah Mormons symbolically followed the path of the apostle Paul, who sought to move his religious tradition away from its original foundations, rather than that of James, who argued for maintaining a closer connection to the original religious foundation, and trekked their way into a new religious paradigm.[1]

By contrast, traditional Native American religions, having no historical Christian foundation until the contact period, were seen as the farthest from the dominant Protestant Christian culture—if recognized as religious traditions at all. Although there might have been concepts and ideals that these religious groups had in common with Protestant Christianity, they have traditionally been understood by most to be historically and culturally distinct, and the ways they express their religions have been divergent. Robert Michaelsen notes: "While a superficial view might see all religions as being alike or even similar, history has shown that there is really not much common ground or common language between the major religious traditions of American culture and Indian traditions."[2] It is therefore not surprising that Native Americans trying to explain their religious sensibilities to a primarily Protestant American constitutional order would experience both extraordinary difficulty and a strong desire to utilize symbols and concepts more familiar to that order. Hence, for example, peyotists struggled to organize the Native American Church and use familiar metaphors when describing its operation and beliefs surrounding the role of peyote. But for the traditional Native American religions, there has been less ability to employ symbols familiar to the dominant culture, and the opportunities for developing cross-cultural understanding by identifying similarities are fewer by far. As a result, traditional Native American religions have suffered at the hands of the constitutional order, if they have been recognized at all.

The perception of distance from the dominant Protestant cultural mainstream is significant, both for those in the dominant culture and for those in the religious minority. It is perfectly reasonable to expect that a dominant culture will have less difficulty accepting perceived deviance if it is moderately presented or if it vaguely resembles the reality the dominant culture understands to be authentic. But even in those cases the process of acceptance is not rapid. When we remember that the first non-Protestant president was not elected until 1960 and that the first non-Protestant Supreme Court majority was not formed until 1996, it is not unreasonable to assume that non-Protestants would experience some difficulty expressing themselves politically and would not find a sympathetic ear once they did.[3] This is particularly important when considering litigation before the U.S. Supreme Court; the first Roman Catholic justice was appointed in the 1840s and the first Jewish justice in the second decade of this century, but there has never been a member of the Court who was a Jehovah's Witness, a Mormon, or a Native American.[4]

Of course, the Jehovah's Witnesses' experience with the American constitutional order has less to do with actual coreligionists in positions of constitutional authority than with their ability to translate successfully their ideas of their particularistic sources of transcending authority to those who do not share them. Mormons were unable to do this—quite possibly because the leap required of the symbol systems was too great—and thus eventually responded to increasing political pressure. However, they later provided evidence of accepting and being accepted by the constitutional order by elevating coreligionists to positions of authority in it. Native Americans generally have been unable to translate their notions of particularistic sources of transcending authority, and they, too, have suffered from the intellectual distance between their sources and those of the constitutional order. Like the Mormons, the Native American community has elevated members from its ranks to positions of authority in the constitutional order.[5] This has not brought with it a corresponding effect on issues of importance to traditional Native American religions, though, and in many ways the conflict between traditional Native American religious communities and the constitutional order is just as engaged today as it was fifty years ago. But as I noted in the examination of the Native American encounter with the American constitutional order, there is much more to it than the simple (if great) distance between European and Native American modes of religiosity. The encounter also involves power politics and the confrontation of the minority religious communities with the political, as well as the ideological, presuppositions of the American constitutional order.

## The Independence of the Constitutional Order

If this is the case, there must be another, deeper explanation for the variety of encounters between minority religious communities and the American constitutional order. Indeed, we need not rely on the case of traditional Native American religions to realize that the proximity to Protestant Christianity is not the only determining factor in the dilemma of conflicting authorities. The American Roman Catholic community and the American Jewish community—both historically related but doctrinally distinct from the dominant Protestant culture and both held in some disdain by it until the second half of this century—easily "converted" to the tenets of the American constitutional order without the same type of encounters experienced by the Jehovah's Witnesses, the Mormons, or the Native Americans. At greater distance from the Protestant dominant cultures, adherents of Islam, Buddhism, and Hinduism have left comparatively few traces of conflict before the Supreme Court, suggesting a high level of "conversion" to the model encouraged by the constitutional order.[6]

Ironically, the fact that significant numbers of Muslims, Buddhists, and Hindus have in fact encountered difficulties with the constitutional order in the form of immigration restrictions is suggestive of an ideological shift rather than a religious conflict. Historically these non-Jewish and non-Christian religionists, like the members of traditional Native American religious communities, could not even make claims for their religious freedoms until they could be included as citizens in the order—which, as we have seen, contained strong traces of religious identification embedded in its nationalist rhetoric and sensibilities. It is therefore understandable that as the American constitutional order has shifted away from its close identification with Protestant Christianity, immigration laws have expanded to include more non-Europeans, and thus more non-Protestants. This suggests that, though the perception of distance from mainstream symbols and concepts may serve to stigmatize minority religious communities in the eyes of the dominant culture, it does not satisfactorily explain the connection between the challenges made by the minority religious communities and the reactions they elicit from the American constitutional order. For that, we must take into account the constitutional order's increasing independence of specific Protestant identification.

From the time of the ratification of the Constitution and the adoption of the First Amendment to the beginning of World War I, Protestant Christianity enjoyed decreasing privilege in the justification of governmental policy.[7] As recalled earlier, Article 6 required allegiance to the Constitution and prohibited religious tests for federal governmental office, and the First Amendment required a specific (though constantly debated) distance between federal and religious institutions. Some states continued to maintain religious requirements for voting and for holding office, but these requirements faded throughout the nineteenth century. As historian Robert Handy forcefully argues, by the end of the nineteenth century

American legal and political culture was no longer exclusively identified with Protestant Christianity.[8]

Interestingly, the movement away from a particularly Protestant identity coincided with a growth in the self-confidence of the leadership in the federal government. It became clear over time that Native American relations with the American constitutional order were more a matter of foreign, strategic, and military policy than of religiosity (see chapter 4). Something as seemingly religious as President Grant's "Peace Policy" (which provided federal funding for religious groups working with—and often proselytizing—Native American populations) functioned primarily as a tool of the federal government to keep Native Americans under control. When it became apparent that the government no longer needed the participation of the various religious missionary societies (including, it should be noted, Roman Catholic ones), the funding was stopped. The success of the Union in the Civil War—quite possibly the "coming of age" of federal identity—and the subsequent defeat of states' rights proponents similarly affected Mormons in Utah. As the federal government consolidated its authority, secured its domain, and settled state and regional antagonisms, it was better able to forge an identity separate from (though still largely drawn from) the dominant culture. With the unilateral pronouncement from the House of Representatives in 1871 that Native Americans would be handled as a domestic rather than an international concern—and the Senate's silent acquiescence—the federal government asserted its authority over the entirety of the nation, "from sea to shining sea." By the 1890s the move to apply the Bill of Rights to state action through the Fourteenth Amendment (ratified in 1868) marked the beginning of total dominance of the federal government over the states—a declaration of independence for the American constitutional order. The fact that significant First Amendment religion litigation did not begin until after the federal government had completed this process suggests a strong connection between the two.

The minority religious communities examined here encountered the American constitutional order at different stages in its growth in confidence and independence, and that fact can help to explain further the differences in the federal government's responses. Native Americans were originally treated as buffers, allies, or enemies, depending on the insecure political arrangements in colonial America. In the early Republic, as the self-confidence of the constitutional order expanded to match the growing nation, both Native Americans and Utah Mormons were seen as threats, subject to either political domination or assimilation. The communities struggled with both, although it is likely that the Mormon community had more options than the traditional Native American religious communities. By the time the Jehovah's Witnesses' encounters began, the constitutional order was more secure in its expression of authority, more dominant, and better able to integrate its needs with the needs of religious minorities seeking protection. The nature of the Jehovah's Witnesses' demands, based largely on free speech rather than on religious challenges, insulated the transcending authority of the constitutional order and enabled it to provide for the demands without relinquishing any of its authority.

The resulting independence of the constitutional order has meant that, within certain parameters, minority religious communities have been given greater freedom to participate as equals in it. It is no longer necessary to identify with Protestant Christianity: any group that is willing to play by the rules (as established by the American constitutional order) can participate. Madison's prediction in *The Federalist* has proven to be fairly accurate, and although it seems that some religious communities still have greater access to political power than others, there is no doubt in the halls of Congress that minority religious communities can participate as well as dominant ones in the competition among the "multiplicity of interests." Therefore, in recent years most religious communities have established offices (staffed by legal experts and lobbyists) responsible for interacting with the federal government. The Jehovah's Witnesses, however, although they maintain a legal office in Patterson, New York, from which much legal activity emerges, maintain no regular lobbying office in Washington, D.C. Allen Hertzke observes in his exploration of organized religious operations in Washington that the tendencies to compromise overcome all who participate; Washington influences the religious operatives and the agendas of the communities they represent as much as (if not more than) the operatives (for their communities) affect Washington.[9] The willingness to play by the rules established by the American constitutional order necessarily means compromising, and the Jehovah's Witnesses, having staked out their position years ago, are unwilling to make that sacrifice. That is not to imply that the religious communities that do participate are corrupted, but it does indicate the strong influence of compromise in the political arena, compromise that ultimately favors the American constitutional order.

The arena in which this expanded political participation occurs is therefore defined less by its content and more by its processes of governance. In the modern pluralistic American society, religious communities agree to disagree. In that sense religious claims forfeit their ability to command adherence from nonbelievers; losing the monopoly on the physical instrumentalities of the legal system, the dominant religious culture must compete with all others for the symbolic instrumentality. Phillip Hammond argues that, although religion may be more central to the lives of its adherents, it has lost its hold as sovereign over society in general: "It must be appreciated . . . that the very freedom to invoke religious sanction for (unconventional?) behavior on the grounds of religion's centrality in persons' lives—and the frequency with which such claims *are* allowed—is the same 'freedom' that diminishes the sovereignty of religion. In fact it is the government that grants the license; believers (or church, etc.) may *claim* a prior right but may not automatically exercise it in the name of religion. And of course, the rest of us need not share their belief in their *prior* right."[10] This formula presupposes that pluralism has replaced Protestant Christianity as the ideology of the American constitutional order. However, though such an arrangement seems to provide advantage to no particular community, it actually provides extraordinary advantage to the constitutional order itself as the only institution empowered to administer (referee, if you will) this negotiated peace.

The results have been astounding. On the one hand, religious communities on the periphery of, or outside of, the dominant culture, have struggled with the forces at work to remold them into acceptable members of the constitutional order. Native American religious communities at first might have had to contend with the missionizing impulses of the early settlers, but their toughest battles have been fought not over their own souls but over what they asserted was their own land. Mormons sought escape from the horrors of mob violence in the Midwest for the tranquillity of the Great Basin, but their peace ended when they asserted authority over land governed by the federal government, held in trust for the American people. Jehovah's Witnesses never asserted any authority over a physical territory and were eventually permitted to live in peace under the protection of the transcending authority of the American constitutional order—even though the Jehovah's Witnesses did not recognize that authority.

Ironically, on the other hand, the shift of the American constitutional order away from its Protestant Christian foundations has resulted in an increasingly alienated conservative Christian community, seemingly nostalgic for what it now considers its lost control over the culture. Increasingly engaged politically, this community is participating in what James Hunter calls a "culture war" over the symbols and institutions that define what it means to be an American. Combating what they believe to be the increasingly immoral nature of contemporary American society because of secularization and an abandonment of Christian morality, members of this often diverse community have worked to reclaim the American constitutional order and "restore" the proper role of religion—predominantly Christianity—in American society. Representing a wide variety of concerns, this general movement has been engaged in issues that range from abortion and euthanasia to gay rights and creation science.[11] As the government has increasingly distanced itself from any specific religious position or identity, this community in particular has felt the loss of cultural authority and has found itself increasingly in conflict with the American constitutional order that it feels it once controlled.

## Threat to Territorial Sovereignty

If the degree of association with a dominant religious culture is not the determining key to understanding the variety of encounters of minority religious communities, the degree of association with the interests of the constitutional order itself seems to be. The key ingredient again and again appears to be a conflict over political and ideological authority, resulting in a challenge to the ultimate territorial rights asserted by the federal government. The Constitution's identification (in Article 6) as the "supreme law of the land," which functions as the backdrop in the drama of pluralism, is grounded not only in the ultimacy of the document (and the institutions for which it stands), but also in the very tangible, manageable, physical reality of land. As Native Americans learned after the land they claimed was sold back to them (or out from under them), and as Mormons learned in the compromise that nearly ended with the seizure of their temples, the American constitutional order maintains its transcending authority through its control of the land. All discussions of pluralism, tolerance, and religious liberty must take that into account.

For this reason, it seems clear that institutional challenges grounded in assertions over land have the least chance for a sympathetic hearing by the constitutional order. Individual challenges to territorial authority are easily dispatched, and individual authority has long been recognized as inferior to governmental authority; a man's home may be his castle, but he still has to pay property taxes on it if they are assessed or vacate it if he is required to do so. In contrast, organizations making ultimate claims of territorial authority (that is, beyond simple land ownership) have historically been perceived by the constitutional order as sincere challengers, and as supporters of the Montana Freemen and the Republic of Texas have found, the constitutional order tends to respond with direct (and sometimes violent) means to secure its authority.

In order to alleviate competition between itself and outside sources of transcending authority, the American constitutional order must assimilate the individual religious adherent in such a way that institutional loyalties are integrated—if not fully, at least with minimal discord. Certainly the individual's—but maybe even the community's—particularistic ideology must be aligned with the political ideology expressed by the constitutional order. The encounters examined in this volume suggest that the operation of the constitutional order is smoothest when those of its functions that are the most central (for example, the very right to control the land) are not challenged; that shows that the two ideologies function in concert. If they do not, if the central functions of the order are challenged, the competing system must be either realigned or destroyed. The Utah Mormons eventually took the former course; traditional Native American religions have resisted the latter. It is likely that the strong sense of communal affiliation among traditional Native American groups has been both the source of the various communities' ability to withstand the pressures of the American constitutional order and one of the reasons for the continuation of the conflict in the first place. In contrast, the moment the Mormon community accepted constitutional authority (as it was expressed by the constitutional order itself, *not* as it was interpreted by the Mormons), they were immediately and successfully integrated. And much like American Catholics and American Jews, they have struggled with the challenges brought about by the forces of assimilation and "Americanization" ever since.[12]

## The Future of New Movements in American Religion . . .

Because the encounter of law and religion is not a matter of simple rules of social interaction, because it involves more importantly the particularistic religious ideology of a minority community in conflict with the dominant culture, the result carries ideological and theological significance. In addition to the various factors already discussed—a perceived proximity to Protestant Christianity as the best chance for intercultural translation, the acceptance of pluralism as the password to participation in the constitutional order, and the absence of territorial claims that directly threaten the source of constitutional authority—we must consider this dimension of worldview orientation. We have seen that sharing Protestant symbols and concepts permits religious communities like the Jehovah's Witnesses to express their particularistic claims in a language understandable to the dominant culture. It is also now clear that acceptance of pluralism permits religious communities to participate as equals in electoral politics and that territorial claims like those of traditional Native American religious communities elicit the wrath of the constitutional order, which perceives the challenge as potentially devastating. But there is something that Jehovah's Witnesses and Mormons share that Native Americans do not, an element of their identity that helps to explain contemporary events and even to suggest a pattern for the future.

The difference is not based on Christian versus non-Christian theology but on a general worldview orientation in time and space. As I suggested in chapter 4, many of the legal difficulties regularly experienced by traditional Native American religious communities are the result of a distinct difference in orientations: traditional Native American religions are oriented primarily in space, whereas European religious traditions are oriented primarily in time. This difference in orientation suggests that traditional Native American religions will regularly conflict with the American constitutional order over claims to spatial authority because the American constitutional order relies on the temporal orientation of European religious traditions to maintain its authority. Religious traditions that accept (if only implicitly) the notion that the earthly realm is governed by an authority different from that which governs the heavenly realm are better able to accept governance by an institution that is increasingly less identified with any specific religious tradition. Those seeking salvation (in whatever form) somewhere else, or at some other time, are more likely to accept—even if they do not support—a polity that asserts its control in the here and now. They can wait it out, as it were.

This is a marked departure from the era of Protestant hegemony, when Protestant Christianity and American culture were virtually identical and millennial expectation included the government as a possible vehicle for salvationary transformation. In the present era, as the American constitutional order upholds pluralism with self-confidence and maintains an identity apart from Protestant Christianity, those most likely to face a dilemma over conflicting authorities are those communities that either cannot accept the formula of awaiting salvation or have come to understand the American constitutional order as damnable and the time for redemption as immediate. This explains why the future confrontations over the transcending authority of the American constitutional order are likely to come not necessarily from minority religious communities that have historically distant relations to Protestant Christianity, but from minority religious communities that do not accept the formula of delayed authority upon which the increasingly secular order is reliant.

As we can see in the evidence from a wide variety of minority religious traditions, conflict with American sectarian groups is less and less a source of conflict with the American constitutional order. As I described earlier in the situations involving the Jehovah's Witnesses and the Mormons, and as others have suggested about the Seventh-day Adventist community, the Christian Science community, the Muslim community, and the Buddhist community,[13] many of the issues leading to conflict for these communities have either been addressed and resolved or are no longer a source of conflict at the highest levels of the American constitutional order. With its shift from its Protestant Christian foundation, the order has become more able to accept limited forms of theological difference. Absent any competing claims of territorial authority (including the right to determine what is or is not legal in a specific space), the federal government is increasingly open to expanded religious pluralism. Minority religious communities may continue to experience religious restrictions, but the government is more willing to justify restrictions in general terms that do not rely on religious sensibilities for their logic.[14] Of course, as I noted earlier, the coincidence of religious sensibilities and political institutions removes the need to articulate restrictions in the rhetoric of religious offense. However, the constant accumulation of evidence indicates that although this might have been the case before the second half of this century, because of cultural changes—from changes in the forms of American religiosity to changes in basic immigration laws—it is less and less the case today.[15] And though immigrant communities from around the world may bring challenges for greater religious freedom to the federal court system, it seems less likely that they will reach the Supreme Court in a sustained manner as those involving Native Americans, Mormons, or Jehovah's Witnesses have done. These cases may occasionally obtain a full hearing, but the identity of the American constitutional order is now more clearly established, and the formula for pluralism is more firmly inscribed.

## . . . And the Possibility of Violence

It is those minority religious communities whose worldview orientation cannot accept a system in which a non-Protestant, increasingly pluralistic, increasingly self-confident American constitutional order maintains territorial authority that will experience increased conflict with the American constitutional order. Unlike the traditional Native American religions that might conflict with the constitutional order in the realm of space, these communities will increasingly conflict with the constitutional order in the realm of time—the present or the very near future.

Given the earlier statements about the increasing sense of alienation of the conservative Christian community, it is not terribly surprising—though it does seem historically ironic—that the greatest source of future conflict may come from a small but increasingly noticeable segment of the Christian spectrum, the ultraconservative Christian communities often identified as fundamentalists. This term presents more problems than it clarifies, and I must be sure to remove from this discussion of conflict the broad array of Christian fundamentalist groups in this country who may merely feel a sense of alienation from what they see as the increasingly secular constitutional order. Most of the groups usually included in this overly broad—and therefore confusing—designation have (to use terms consistent with our previous discussion) either converted to the pluralistic worldview required by the American constitution order or accepted a congruence with it. They express their dissatisfaction either by withdrawing from the general culture or by attempting to change it in the very idiom required by the order: the political process.

However, on the far edges of American Christian fundamentalism exist communities whose worldview or ideology will not permit them either to accept the terms of participation required by the constitutional order or to find a separate peace with it. Such communities fit the description provided by religion scholar Bruce Lawrence: "ideologues who look in from the margins." He notes that though they are as much a result of the modern world as the institution they detest, "[t]hey demur from the modernist vision of a homogeneous global community ruled by an enlightened, which is to say secular, elite." Nationalism itself is the object of contention, the kind of secular nationalism that replaces a religious (and, one assumes, transnational) polity or community. Lawrence concludes that nationalism and this particular type of fundamentalism "are incommensurate opposites: contradictories rather than contraries, both cannot occupy the same ideological space."[16]

The concept of competing ideologies—and thus the significance of this type of worldview in our discussion of the American constitutional order—is clarified if we replace "fundamentalism" with "religious nationalism," a term preferred by political sociologist Mark Juergensmeyer. This term more accurately characterizes communities that aggressively oppose the trend followed by the American constitutional order, that is, the movement of modern nation-states toward an increasingly secular identity.[17] "From their perspectives it is secular nationalism, and not religion, that has gone wrong. They see the Western models of nationhood—both democratic and socialist—as having failed, and they view religion as a hopeful alternative, a base for criticism and change." Juergensmeyer uses the term primarily to describe religio-political movements outside the United States; he even suggests that "[n]ot even the most pious Christians in America—even those who disdain everything about secular culture—would care to reject the humanistic tenets of secular nationalism."[18]

Examples of such a rejection of the American constitutional order and the democratic worldview that it represents, though rare, certainly do exist, however. One of the more prominent, the Christian Identity movement, mixes fundamentalist Christianity, religioracial superiority, and premillennial expectation to produce a powerful (if relatively small) force in contemporary America. It is Identity's worldview, though, that makes it a strong candidate for conflict with the American constitutional order; this community does not hope for what political scientist Jeffrey Kaplan calls a "supernatural rescue." "[T]he Christian Identity believer is secure only in his ability to persevere—to survive by the grace of God but also by virtue of his own wits and through recourse to his own stores of food and weapons." Given this subculture's sense of conflict with the American constitutional order, it is strangely fitting that the most violent segment of the Christian Identity world is known not only as the Bruders Schweigen (silent brotherhood) but also, more commonly, as the Order. Described as "an active terrorist movement," this subgroup within the larger Identity movement, according to Kaplan, is often seen as "an example of a millenarian revolutionary movement par excellence" that is willing to engage the federal government it considers satanic with confidence "in the power of God to assure ultimate victory."[19]

In addition to the "by our own hands" element of the premillennial expectation, the movement also combines biblical literalism and conspiracy theory to produce a theology of suspicion for the federal government. Christian Identity's doctrine teaches that in the Garden of Eden, the snake impregnated Eve, with the result that two races were produced: the "good Aryan stock" of Adam (represented by Abel), and a demonic stock (represented by Cain). As Kaplan describes it:

Cain, in Identity theology, was the progenitor of the Jews, as his subsequent matings with non-Adamites created a race genetically predisposed to carry on a timeless conspiracy against the Adamic line, a race that today has achieved almost complete control of the earth. (This observation explains the efficacy of the epithet ZOG or Zionist Occupation Government for the American body politic.) From this doctrine springs the self-image of the Identity believer as the righteous remnant doomed to suffer the persecution of the demonic Jew until the soon-coming return of the Lord at the head of the avenging host.[20]

The "Zionist Occupation Government," what I have been calling the American constitutional order, is thus not only suspect but also detestable, and its efforts toward religious pluralism are simply attempts to further corrupt true Christianity. For Identity believers, "American religious pluralism is decried as 'Judeo-Christianity,' in Identity terms a vile syncretism aimed at perverting true Christianity and, not incidentally, serving to keep the secret of the Jewish usurpation of the covenant hidden."[21]

Members of this community seem (not surprisingly) ideologically unable to accept the shift of the constitutional order away from its identification with Protestant Christianity. What members of the Identity community might believe to be a righteous desire to be excluded from the constitutional order is correspondingly seen by the order itself as a direct and often violent (if small-scale) challenge to its prerogative of territorial control. Kaplan notes without irony that "the primary form that violence takes in Identity is defensive." He defines "defensive violence" as "violence undertaken as a last resort to defend an enclave into which a single adherent or a group of believers have withdrawn to sever to the greatest degree possible contact with the dominant culture."[22] Of course, with the case studies on the Jehovah's Witnesses, Mormons, and Native Americans behind us, we can see that withdrawing "to sever to the greatest degree possible contact with the dominant culture" requires certain sacrifices, including an ability either to bring the constitutional order into an understanding with your worldview or to move toward a compromise with its worldview. Vehement ideological contradiction with the American constitutional order over authority and the exercise of power, along with the willingness to use force to defend the Identity positions, does not bode well for a peaceful resolution for members of the Identity movement who come into conflict with that order. Indeed, given the two worldviews involved, it seems that conflict is unavoidable, and any attempt on the part of the Identity to cut itself off from the dominant culture may be interpreted by the order as a challenge to its authority. Like the struggles of traditional Native American religions, such conflicts would not be necessary were their protagonists to recognize themselves in the American constitutional order. But of course, the failure to recognize seems inevitable when the worldviews contradict.

## The Constitutional Order, at Last

Grammatically analyzed, the clause "We hold these truths" refers to the truths that are about to be articulated: that all men are created equal and that all are endowed by their Creator with certain rights. However, caution must be exercised, for a "we" may imply a "they." It cannot be assumed that the "truths" that "we" hold are universal—*these* truths as opposed to *those* truths. In the American constitutional order, there is no doubt that religious freedom is an ideal—a truth—that is exalted and protected. But in promising to safeguard the religious freedom of all, our society must establish an arbiter to judge competing values. The American constitutional order, through the legal and cultural disestablishments of the last two centuries, serves such a role and represents the ideal, even if it does not always provide the actuality of religious freedom. As sociologist of religion Phillip Hammond asks, though (paraphrasing Emile Durkheim), "What governs the governor of a governed order?"[23] What principles control the American constitutional order if the order itself provides the principles of control?

In her book on the interpretation of religious freedom, Bette Novit Evans proposes that pluralism itself be the guiding principle that both supports and limits the power of what I have called the American constitutional order. Defining pluralism as an appreciation of "the multiple sources of meaning" and the provision of "space for individuals to make or find their own meanings, while still recognizing the need for social cohesion," Evans suggests that such a limitation would "oppose the accumulation of power in any institution and thus advocate both the fragmentation of governmental power and the existence of countervailing sources of power." In her opinion, "a pluralist approach to the free exercise of religion must give an account of the centrifugal forces of religious freedom, which nurtures and protects diversity, autonomy, meditation. . . . And, it must protect sufficient centripetal forces to foster social coherence and sustain the bonds of common citizenship."[24]

Evans works hard to reconcile the seeming contradiction between the two clauses of the First Amendment: the first, which by prohibiting congressional action "respecting an establishment of religion" seems to forbid any legislative action whatever, and the second, which by forbidding congressional action "prohibiting the free exercise thereof" suggests legislative action to permit a community the latitude it needs to exercise its religion freely. She suggests that the limits of religious freedom should not be understood to be the limits of toleration expressed by the dominant culture; they should rather be seen as the limits of a civil society's ability to maintain itself without fragmenting into camps and factions. Religious difference must not only be permitted, but must be understood as integral to the health of society. Nevertheless, though refusal to participate in the life of the polity because of a desire to be left alone is, for Evans, less than ideal, the desire to require all others to live by one community's standards is worse since it stifles rather than encourages religious pluralism.

This solution is not without its hazards: we must remember that the task of the American constitutional order is to provide religious freedom while preserving itself. Religious freedom and separation are acceptable if they are accomplished in the way the Jehovah's Witnesses did it but apparently not acceptable if attempted in the ways the Mormons and the Native Americans have tried. And of course, they may never be acceptable in the way members of the Christian Identity movement try. There are limits on religious freedom, limits of which we are constantly reminded by the constitutional order itself.

Furthermore, since the identity of the order is dependent on the identity of its participants, and that identity is constantly in flux, the nature and boundaries of such limits are constantly changing. Throughout its history, the American constitutional order has reflected the makeup and sensibilities of its citizenry; in the beginning that reflection was entirely dependent on the order's coincidence with Protestant Christianity, but the order shifted away from that identity and opened a constantly expanding arena of participation for other religious groups. Whereas this coincidence of identities once meant that non-Protestants were at a severe political (and thus, religious) disadvantage, the departure from Protestant cultural hegemony has meant that religious identity is less a determinant of conflict with the American constitutional order. And though this suggests greater possibilities of religious freedom for religious minorities in this country, it also—unavoidably—bodes ill for those communities whose worldviews cannot accommodate the ultimate authority of an increasingly non–religiously identified federal government. Those religious communities whose ideologies conform to—or do not threaten—the temporal and spatial ideology of the constitutional order will find the means to avoid continued conflict with it. Rousseau's theory—those who do not agree to go along with the dominant culture face permanent outsider status—can have serious repercussions in the conflict with the American constitutional order over ultimate authority.

# Notes

## Introduction

1. Carol Weisbrod, "Comment on Curry and Firmage Articles," *Journal of Law and Religion* 7, no. 2 (1989): 319.

2. Marc Galanter, *Law and Society in Modern India* (New York: Oxford University Press, 1989), 249, quoted in Winnifred Fallers Sullivan, *Paying the Words Extra: Religious Discourse in the Supreme Court of the United States* (Cambridge, Mass.: Harvard University Press, 1994), 42.

3. Joseph R. Gusfield, "Moral Passage: The Symbolic Process in Public Designations of Deviance," *Social Problems* 15, no. 2 (1967): 177, 185. See also Joseph R. Gusfield, *Symbolic Crusade* (Urbana: University of Illinois Press, 1963). Prohibition was enacted by legislation empowered under Amendment 18, section 2 of the U.S. Constitution (adopted 1919) and repealed by Amendment 21, section 1 (adopted 1933).

4. Alexander Hamilton, John Jay, and James Madison, *The Federalist: A Commentary on the Constitution of the United States* (1787; reprint, New York: Random House, 1937), no. 51, 339, 340.

5. Jean-Jacques Rousseau, *The Social Contract: Or, Principles of Political Right*, trans. Maurice Cranston (1762; reprint, New York: Penguin Books, 1968), 59.

6. Sullivan, *Paying the Words Extra*, 7.

7. Ibid., 42. Harold Berman, *The Interaction of Law and Religion* (Nashville: Abingdon Press, 1974), 24.

8. Clifford Geertz, "Religion as a Cultural System," in *The Interpretation of Cultures: Selected Essays by Clifford Geertz* (New York: Basic Books, 1973), 90. Phillip E. Hammond, "Conscience and the Establishment Clause: The Courts Remake the Sacred," *Journal for the Scientific Study of Religion* 35, no. 4 (1996): 356–67.

9. Sullivan, *Paying the Words Extra*, 20–21.

## 1 – American Religions and the Authority of Law

1. Bob Cohn and David A. Kaplan, "A Chicken on Every Altar?" *Newsweek*, November 9, 1992, 79.

2. Ibid. Jeff Rosen, "Blood Ritual," *New Republic*, November 2, 1992, 9.

3. *Church of Lukumi Babalu Aye v. City of Hialeah* (1989), 526–29 (see Primary Sources for full citations of all decisions referred to in the text and the notes). "Lawyers Hopeful after Arguments," *Report from the Capital* 47, no. 10 (1992): 9.

4. Richard N. Ostling, "Shedding Blood in Sacred Bowls," *Time*, October 19, 1992, 60; "Lawyers Hopeful," 9. Amicus brief for Americans United for Separation of Church and State, *Church of Lukumi Babalu Aye, Inc., and Ernesto Pichardo v. City of Hialeah* (no. 91-948), 1.

5. Cohn and Kaplan, "A Chicken on Every Altar?" 79. "More Than Animal Sacrifice at Stake," *Report from the Capital* 47, no. 10 (1992): 8. To the credit of the committee, the newsletter indicated that the same Americans were also concerned that "[i]f a city or state can ban an unpopular religious practice like animal sacrifice, government could ban a more widely accepted practice, such as communion or baptism."

6. Cohn and Kaplan, "A Chicken on Every Altar?" 79.

7. Rosen, "Blood Ritual," 9.

8. See Joseph Murphy, *Santeria: An African Religion in America* (Boston: Beacon Press, 1988). *Church of Lukumi Babalu Aye v. Hialeah* (1989), 526.

9. For discussions of the role of Christianity (in various forms) in state legislation, see Morton Borden, *Jews, Turks, and Infidels* (Chapel Hill: University of North Carolina Press, 1984); H. Frank Way, "Death of the Christian Nation: The Judiciary and Church-State Relations," *Journal of Church and State* 29, no. 3 (1987): 509–29; and John K. Wilson, "Religion under the State Constitutions, 1776–1800," *Journal of Church and State* 32, no. 4 (1990): 753–73. Stephen A. Marini, "Religion, Politics, and Ratification," in *Religion in a Revolutionary Age*, ed. Ronald Hoffman and Peter J. Albert (Charlottesville: University Press of Virginia, 1994), 191, 215–17.

10. Edwin S. Gaustad, *Religious Issues in American History* (New York: Harper and Row, 1968), 246. For a nearly duplicate analysis, see also James E. Wood, Jr., "New Religions and the First Amendment: 'The Law Knows No Heresy,'" in *Religion and the State: Essays in Honor of Leo Pfeffer*, ed. James E. Wood, Jr. (Waco, Tex.: Baylor University Press, 1985), 192.

11. Frank Way and Barbara Burt, "Religious Marginality and the Free Exercise Clause," *American Political Science Review* 77, no. 3 (1983): 656,

658. The difference between "consequential" and inconsequential may be understood, for example, as the difference between proselytizing and real estate zoning. The terminology may be subjective and therefore problematic, but the differentiation is essential.

12. *McGowan v. Maryland* (1961); *Braunfeld v. Brown* (1961); *Lynch v. Donnelly* (1984).

13. For a good discussion of the difference in the writing of the Virginia Statute for Religious Freedom, see William Lee Miller, *The First Liberty: Religion and the American Republic* (New York: Paragon House, 1988), 4–6. Ronald B. Flowers, *That Godless Court? Supreme Court Decisions on Church-State Relationships* (Louisville: Westminster John Knox Press, 1994), 24, 31–32.

14. Harry W. Jones, "Church-State Relations: Our Constitutional Heritage," in *Religion and Contemporary Society,* ed. Harold Stahmer (New York: Macmillan, 1963), 178 (emphasis added).

15. R. Laurence Moore, *Religious Outsiders and the Making of Americans* (New York: Oxford University Press, 1986), 208.

16. Alexis de Tocqueville, *Democracy in America* (1848; reprint, trans. George Lawrence, ed. J. P. Mayer, New York: Harper and Row, 1969), 289.

17. See Joseph Story, *Commentaries on the Constitution of the United States* (Cambridge, Mass.: Hilliard, Gray, and Co., 1833; reprint, New York: Da Capo, 1970), 722–31; *Reynolds v. United States* (1879). The Court moved from a belief-behavior distinction for a period from 1963 (*Sherbert v. Verner* [1963]) until 1990 (*Employment Division, Department of Human Resources of Oregon, et al. v. Smith et al.* [1990]). An effort to reverse recent jurisprudential trends (which would have the effect of again removing the distinction) was enacted as the Religious Freedom Restoration Act. However, on June 25, 1997, the Court struck it down as an improper encroachment on judicial authority to interpret the Constitution. See Linda Greenhouse, "High Court Voids a Law Expanding Religious Rights," *New York Times,* June 26, 1997, A1, C24.

18. For two different approaches to this dilemma by constitutional scholars, see Jesse H. Choper, "The Religion Clauses of the First Amendment: Reconciling the Conflict," *University of Pittsburgh Law Review* 41 (1980): 673–701; Leo Pfeffer, "Freedom and/or Separation: The Constitutional Dilemma of the First Amendment," *Minnesota Law Review* 64 (1980): 561–84. For an example of the Court's expression of the same problem, see *Committee for Public Education and Religious Liberty v. Nyquist* (1973), 788–89. Also see chapter 5.

19. See Harry S. Stout, "Rhetoric and Reality in the Early Republic: The Case of the Federalist Clergy," in *Religion and American Politics: From the Colonial Period to the 1980s*, ed. Mark A. Noll (New York: Oxford University Press, 1990), 62–76.

20. This slightly modified phrase is borrowed, with all due respect, from Peter L. Berger, *The Sacred Canopy: Elements of a Sociological Theory of Religion* (Garden City, N.Y.: Doubleday, 1969), 28.

21. Robert N. Bellah, "Civil Religion in America," *Daedalus* 96, no. 1 (1967): 8.

22. For an in-depth discussion of the religious meaning of the American Revolution, see Catherine L. Albanese, *Sons of the Fathers: The Civil Religion of the American Revolution* (Philadelphia: Temple University Press, 1976). Albanese notes that the Constitution was the "most cherished sacrament" of the religion of the republic (215). Milton M. Klein, "Mythologizing the U.S. Constitution," *Soundings* 78, no. 1 (1995): 173, 178, 181 (the quotation is from p. 178). Thomas C. Grey, "The Constitution as Scripture," *Stanford Law Review* 37, no. 1 (1984): 3, 17.

23. For an analysis of a Jewish reaction to American civil religion, see Jonathan D. Sarna, "Is Judaism Compatible with American Civil Religion? The Problem of Christmas and the 'National Faith,'" in *Religion and the Life of the Nation*, ed. Rowland A. Sherrill (Urbana: University of Illinois Press, 1990), 152–73. See Henry J. Abraham, *The Judicial Process: An Introductory Analysis of the Courts of the United States, England, and France*, 6th ed. (New York: Oxford University Press, 1993), 64. Abraham points out that of the 106 justices sitting on the Supreme Court (through the Bush Administration), only eight have identified themselves as Roman Catholic and only five as Jews (two more Jewish justices have joined the Court since the publication of Abraham's book). Sidney E. Mead, *The Nation with the Soul of a Church* (New York: Harper and Row, 1975), 99.

24. A refreshing and pragmatic approach to the drafting of the Constitution can be found in Edwin S. Gaustad, "Religious Tests, Constitutions, and 'Christian Nation,'" in *Religion in a Revolutionary Age*, ed. Ronald Hoffman and Peter J. Albert (Charlottesville: University Press of Virginia, 1994), 225; see also John F. Wilson, "Religion, Government, and Power in the New American Nation," in Noll, *Religion and American Politics*, 77–91.

25. Alexander Hamilton, John Jay, and James Madison, *The Federalist: A Commentary on the Constitution of the United States* (1787; reprint, New York: Random House, 1937), no. 81, 523.

26. See *United States v. Nixon* (1974).

27. *Brown v. Allen* (1953) (Justice Jackson, concurring).

28. John Brigham, *The Cult of the Court* (Philadelphia: Temple University Press, 1987), esp. 196–217. Albert J. Beveridge, *The Life of John Marshall* (Boston: Houghton Mifflin, 1919), 4:515 (emphasis in the original).

29. See G. Alan Tarr, *Judicial Impact and State Supreme Courts* (Lexington, Mass.: D. C. Heath, 1977); Kenneth M. Dolbeare and Phillip E. Hammond, *The School Prayer Decisions: From Court Policy to Local Practice* (Chicago: University of Chicago Press, 1971); and Alexander M. Bickel, *The Least Dangerous Branch: The Supreme Court at the Bar of Politics* (Indianapolis: Bobbs-Merrill, 1962).

30. Sanford Levinson, *Constitutional Faith* (Princeton, N.J.: Princeton University Press, 1988).

31. For an early and more cynical analysis of the "unwritten Constitution," see Christopher G. Tiedeman, *The Unwritten Constitution of the United States: A Philosophical Inquiry into the Fundamentals of American Constitutional Law* (New York: G. P. Putnam's Sons, 1890; reprint, Farmingdale, N.Y.: Dabor Social Science Publications, 1978).

32. A contemporary example of the unwritten Constitution is illustrated by contrasting the popular debate surrounding the meaning of "the right to bear arms" with the actual case law regarding the Second Amendment. Grey, "The Constitution as Scripture," 16 (emphasis in the original).

33. Thomas C. Grey, "Do We Have an Unwritten Constitution?" *Stanford Law Review* 27 (February 1975): 716.

34. See Grey, "Do We Have an Unwritten Constitution?" and Edward S. Corwin, *The "Higher Law" Background of American Constitutional Law* (Ithaca, N.Y.: Cornell University Press, 1955), 5. Miller, *The First Liberty*, 342; Grey, "The Constitution as Scripture," 3.

35. Mead, *The Nation with the Soul of a Church*, 51. Emile Durkheim, *The Elementary Forms of the Religious Life*, trans. Joseph Ward Swain (New York: Free Press, 1965), 432.

36. Jürgen Heideking, "The Federal Processions of 1788 and the Origins of American Civil Religion," *Soundings* 77, nos. 3–4 (1994): 367–87. Phillip E. Hammond, "Pluralism and Law in the Formation of American Civil Religion," in *Varieties of Civil Religion*, by Robert N. Bellah and Phillip E. Hammond (San Francisco: Harper and Row, 1980), 138–63. Grey, "The Constitution as Scripture," 22, 18 (emphasis in the original).

37. Grey, "The Constitution as Scripture," 18–19.

38. Jean-Jacques Rousseau, *The Social Contract: Or, Principles of Political Right* (1762; trans. Maurice Cranston, New York: Penguin Books, 1968), 153.

39. This can be easily illustrated in the language of the practical meaning of law: the state need not be concerned with why people stop at red lights, as long as they do so, even if doing so is mandated for religious reasons. Only when the actions conflict is the state concerned.

40. Way, "Death of the Christian Nation," 515–16.

41. I wish to thank Brian Wilson for suggesting the term *congruence*, thereby saving my alliterative scheme. On the Amish, see Donald B. Kraybill, ed., *The Amish and the State* (Baltimore: Johns Hopkins University Press, 1993). See chapter 2 of this volume for the "congruence" of the Jehovah's Witnesses community.

42. Phillip E. Hammond, *The Protestant Presence in Twentieth-Century America: Religion and Political Culture* (Albany: State University of New York Press, 1992), 18.

43. See John Courtney Murray, S.J., *We Hold These Truths: Catholic Reflections on the American Proposition* (New York: Sheed and Ward, 1960), for an interesting articulation of postconversion Catholic theology; see Jerold S. Auerbach, *Rabbis and Lawyers: The Journey from Torah to Constitution* (Bloomington: Indiana University Press, 1990), for a clear thesis on the Jewish "conversion." On the Mormon "conversion," see chapter 3 of this volume.

44. For a famous illustration, compare *Minersville School District v. Gobitis* (1940) and *West Virginia Board of Education v. Barnette* (1943).

45. Governor Charles Evan Hughes, *Addresses*, 2d ed. (New York: Putnam, 1916), 185, quoted in Abraham, *The Judicial Process*, 320. Lee Hockstader and Saundra Torry, "Two Giants of Law Look to High Court's Future," *Washington Post*, May 25, 1988, A15.

46. On Christian Fundamentalism, see Dallas A. Blanchard, *The Anti-Abortion Movement and the Rise of the Religious Right: From Polite to Fiery Protest* (New York: Twayne, 1994); on Christian Identity, see Michael Barkun, *Religion and the Racist Right: The Origins of the Christian Identity Movement* (Chapel Hill: University of North Carolina Press, 1994).

47. *Church of Lukumi Babalu Aye v. Hialeah* (1993). In a decision unanimous in result if not in reasoning, the Supreme Court overturned the two lower court decisions and ruled the city ordinances to be unconstitutional.

48. Mike Clary, "Florida's Caribbean Immigrants Are Putting Their Faith in Santeria," *Los Angeles Times*, August 9, 1995, A5. Clary reports that,

since the Supreme Court decision involving the Hialeah Santerian community, there has been a noticeable decrease in hostility from without and an increase in participation from within, resulting in a desire on the part of some of the Santerian community to certify the credentials of its growing leadership, a requirement unprecedented in this religious community.

## 2 – Constitutional Congruence

1. See R. Laurence Moore, *Religious Outsiders and the Making of Americans* (New York: Oxford University Press, 1986), passim.

2. Malcolm Bull, "The Seventh-Day Adventists: Heretics of American Civil Religion," *Sociological Analysis* 50, no. 2 (1989): 177, 184. Bull's use of the term "heretic" is based on George Zito's differentiation between heresy and apostasy. See George V. Zito, "Toward a Sociology of Heresy," *Sociological Analysis* 44, no. 2 (1983): 123–30.

3. Bull, "Seventh-Day Adventists," 185.

4. I have chosen to use the label "Jehovah's Witnesses" throughout this chapter to designate both the national/international organization and the individual membership. Historically, as the collection of members coalesced into an organization, several labels were applied to various corporate entities. Though the general public referred to them pejoratively as "Russellites," the membership identified itself as Bible Students. The formal business structure was incorporated as the Watch Tower Bible and Tract Society of Pennsylvania. Because of state laws concerning duplication of corporate names, the first two words were combined—"Watchtower"—when the organization became incorporated in New York. See *Defending and Legally Establishing the Good News* (Brooklyn, N.Y.: Watchtower Bible and Tract Society, 1950), 74. The name "Jehovah's Witnesses" was officially adopted at an annual convention in 1931. See "A New Name," *Watchtower*, October 1, 1931, 291. Articles in the *Watchtower* are unsigned. James Penton suggests that, though the organization started as a loose association of like-minded religionists, the selection of the name in 1931 played a significant role in molding the loose-knit association into a more centralized organization, justifying my conflation of the two meanings. See M. James Penton, *Apocalypse Delayed: The Story of Jehovah's Witnesses* (Toronto, Ontario: University of Toronto Press, 1985), 62. For consistency and clarity, I use the labels "the Jehovah's Witnesses" and "the Witnesses," constructions most often used in the secondary literature.

5. Ronald Lawson, "Sect-State Relations: Accounting for the Differing

Trajectories of Seventh-day Adventists and Jehovah's Witnesses," *Sociology of Religion* 56, no. 4 (1995): 374.

6. See *Jehovah's Witnesses: Proclaimers of God's Kingdom* (Brooklyn, N.Y.: Watchtower Bible and Tract Society of New York, 1993) (hereinafter *Proclaimers*), 59, 67. The exact nature of those experiences is the subject of some disagreement. While on the witness stand defending himself during his sedition trial, Rutherford indicated that he had been a state circuit court judge in Missouri for fourteen years. See "Rutherford Denies Guilt," *New York Times*, June 18, 1918, 5. One source indicates that the title "Judge" was merely honorific. See Leonard A. Stevens, *Salute! The Case of the Bible vs. the Flag* (New York: Coward, McCann, and Geoghegan, 1973), 26. Others place the title in quotation marks. See David Manwaring, *Render unto Caesar: The Flag Salute Controversy* (Chicago: University of Chicago Press, 1962), passim; Peter Irons, *The Courage of Their Convictions: Sixteen Americans Who Fought Their Way to the Supreme Court* (New York: Penguin Books, 1990), 17. Another source indicates that he may have had the right to the title. See John E. Mulder and Marvin Comisky, "Jehovah's Witnesses Mold Constitutional Law," *Bill of Rights Review* 2, no. 4 (1942): 264. Lastly, Penton describes him as a part-time and a substitute judge. See M. James Penton, "Jehovah's Witnesses and the Secular State: A Historical Analysis of Doctrine," *Journal of Church and State* 21, no. 1 (1979): 61; Penton, *Apocalypse Delayed*, 47. Though seeming to be a minor point, the disagreement sheds light on Rutherford's relationship to the legal community, which may have had a significant bearing on his later reactions to Jehovah's Witness litigation, as well as any reception he might have received from the legal community.

7. See Penton, *Apocalypse Delayed*, 79.

8. Ibid., 13–35. Arianism is the belief that Jesus was formed by God (though not in the manner of the rest of humanity) and is therefore finite and not coeternal; conditionalism is the belief that humans are not endowed with an immortal soul but gain immortality "on the condition" that it is received from God through belief in Jesus. See John Norman Davidson Kelly, *Early Christian Doctrines*, rev. ed. (New York: Harper and Row, 1978), 226–31. On conditionalism, see Penton, *Apocalypse Delayed*, 15–17, 190–91. On Arianism among the Jehovah's Witnesses, see "The Hebrew Prophets and the State," *Watchtower and Herald of Christ's Presence*, March 15, 1928, 93.

9. The reference is to Revelation 7:4.

10. R. L. Moore, *Religious Outsiders*, 137.

11. Penton, *Apocalypse Delayed*, 44–46. Martin E. Marty, *Modern American Religion*, vol. 1, *The Irony of It All, 1893–1919* (Chicago: University of Chicago Press, 1986), 315.

12. See Penton, *Apocalypse Delayed*, 55–56. The seven other members indicted were William E. Van Amburgh, treasurer of the association; Robert J. Martin, auditor of the association; Frederick H. Robinson, Rutherford's personal representative; Alexander Hugh Macmillan (spelled "McMillan" in news accounts), superintendent of Bethel Home, the organizational residence in Brooklyn; George H. Fisher and Clayton J. Woodworth, both of Scranton, Pennsylvania, and both part authors of *The Finished Mystery* and directors of the association; and Giovanni De Cecca, who directed Witness translation efforts for the Italian language. The indictments charged them with (1) willfully conspiring to cause insubordination, disloyalty, and refusal of duty in the military forces of the United States; (2) willfully conspiring to obstruct the recruiting and enlistment service of the United States; (3) willfully attempting to cause insubordination; and (4) willfully attempting to obstruct the recruiting and enlistment service of the United States. "Arrest Russellites on Sedition Charges," *New York Times*, May 9, 1918, 22; see also "Russellites Guilty of Hindering Draft," *New York Times*, June 21, 1918, 7. Several scholars suggest that the Espionage Act may have been written with the Jehovah's Witnesses in mind. See Gary Botting, *Fundamental Freedoms and Jehovah's Witnesses* (Calgary, Alberta: University of Calgary Press, 1993), 3; William Shepard McAninch, "A Catalyst for the Evolution of Constitutional Law: Jehovah's Witnesses in the Supreme Court," *University of Cincinnati Law Review* 55, no. 4 (1987): 1008–11. The actual arrests followed a raid on the Bethel housing complex in Brooklyn by the Army Intelligence Bureau, which resulted in the discovery a vast supply of copies of *The Finished Mystery*. Newspaper accounts described the book, saying that it "reeked with passages condemning war and referring to patriotism as a delusion which caused men to kill each other." The letter also played a pivotal role in the trial, and a question arose concerning its authenticity. William F. Hudgings, a witness for the defense and a secretary in the organization, was held for contempt of court when he refused to identify the letter—which bore the stamped signature of Rutherford—as having been written by him. "Ten Years for Russellite," *New York Times*, July 11, 1918, 7. The Supreme Court finally stepped in and ordered Hudgings discharged, citing an "excess of power" on the part of the trial

judge. *Ex parte Hudgings* (1919), 385. For a description of the letter, see "Letter to Russellite Favors Opposing War," *New York Times*, June 7, 1918, 13.

13. *Rutherford v. United States* (1919), 863–65 (Judge Manton, dissenting). "Rutherford Denies Guilt," *New York Times*, June 18, 1918, 5.

14. "Could Not Talk of Loan," *New York Times*, April 29, 1918, 11. "Would Let Sinners Fight," *New York Times*, June 13, 1918, 7. The question was answered by Clayton J. Woodworth, part author of *The Finished Mystery*. Judge Howe was on assignment to the Federal District of New York from Vermont.

15. "Freedom Is Not Unlimited," *New York Times*, June 22, 1918, 8.

16. "Twenty Years in Prison for Seven Russellites," *New York Times*, June 22, 1918, 18. The "facts and documents presented . . . by the Italian Government" were Italian copies of the same letter that had been sent to American servicemen by the Jehovah's Witnesses, and they were the reason Giovanni De Cecca was included among the indicted.

17. "Russellites Guilty of Hindering Draft," *New York Times*, June 21, 1918, 7. "Twenty Years in Prison for Seven Russellites," *New York Times*, June 22, 1918, 18. Giovanni De Cecca was not sentenced immediately, and was later sentenced to only ten years after the court decided that he had not taken a leadership role in the actions but was merely following directions. See "Ten Years for Russellite," *New York Times*, July 11, 1918, 7. Motions for bail were repeatedly rebuffed. Federal Circuit Judge Manton, who later filed the lone dissent in the Rutherford appeal, refused to set bail ("Russellites Must Stay in Jail," *New York Times*, July 2, 1918, 20), and Supreme Court justice Louis Brandeis referred the motion back to the Circuit Court. "Russellites to Seek Bail," *New York Times*, November 10, 1918, 17. William McAninch suggests that the release was the result not of the appeal, but of the fact that the war had concluded and the issue was now moot. See McAninch, "Catalyst," 1012, in which he cites a letter from Judge Howe to the U.S. attorney general on this point.

18. "Russellites Out of Prison," *New York Times*, March 27, 1919, 6. "Russellites to Leave Brooklyn," *New York Times*, August 25, 1918, sec. 2, p. 3; Penton, *Apocalypse Delayed*, 55. See also "Birth of the Nation," *Watchtower*, March 1, 1925, 71–73. (This official publication of the Jehovah's Witnesses has been published under slightly different names over the course of its history. For the purposes of simplicity, for the remainder of this chapter I shall refer to it only as the *Watchtower*.) *Rutherford v. United States*

(1919), 863. Judge Manton, who had denied one of the earlier motions for bail, wrote the dissenting opinion.

19. Lawson, "Sect-State Relations," 363.

20. Penton, "Jehovah's Witnesses and the Secular State," 56–61.

21. Ibid., 61; Penton, *Apocalypse Delayed*, 44–46; Gary Botting, *Fundamental Freedoms*, 15–18.

22. Penton, *Apocalypse Delayed*, 48–55. "Birth of the Nation," *Watchtower*, March 1, 1925, 72, 74.

23. "Declaration against Satan and for Jehovah," *Watchtower*, September 15, 1928, 278–79.

24. "Rulers for the People," *Watchtower*, September 15, 1928, 279, 282, 286.

25. "The Higher Powers (Part 1)," *Watchtower*, June 1, 1929, 163–69; "The Higher Powers (Part 2)," *Watchtower*, June 15, 1929, 179–85. See also Manwaring, *Render unto Caesar*, 25–26.

26. "The Higher Powers (Part 2)," *Watchtower*, June 15, 1929, 183, 184.

27. "Do Men Govern Themselves?" *Watchtower*, May 15, 1931, 155.

28. "War and Government," *Watchtower*, April 15, 1932, 126–27.

29. "Our Responsibility," *Watchtower*, February 15, 1936, 55.

30. "Neutrality," *Watchtower*, November 1, 1939, 323–33. Penton, providing a brief synopsis of the events leading up to this announcement, explains the bureaucratic restructuring as part of the continuing consolidation of power initiated by Rutherford. See Penton, *Apocalypse Delayed*, 62–64, 68–69.

31. "A Personal Message," *Watchtower*, September 1, 1936, 268. See also "To the Faithful in All the Earth," *Watchtower*, March 1, 1937, 77.

32. McAninch, "Catalyst," 1013. Ronald Lawson notes that 18,866 Jehovah's Witnesses were arrested in the United States between 1933 and 1951. See Lawson, "Sect-State Relations," 365. Mulder and Comisky observe that by 1939 there were more than thirty-eight thousand phonograph and transcription machines in use by the Jehovah's Witnesses. Mulder and Comisky, "Jehovah's Witnesses Mold Constitutional Law," 265. Manwaring, *Render unto Caesar*, 27. Merlin Owen Newton, *Armed with the Constitution: Jehovah's Witnesses in Alabama and the United States Supreme Court, 1939–1946* (Tuscaloosa: University of Alabama Press, 1995), 48. Until 1940, neither of the First Amendment religion clauses had been applied to state action. See *Permoli v. First Municipality of the City of New Orleans* (1845). However, since the late 1890s, other rights contained in the

first ten amendments to the U.S. Constitution had been applied to state action. See *Gitlow v. New York* (1925), esp. 666. The Jehovah's Witnesses were ultimately successful in arguing for the connection of the religious free exercise clause of the First Amendment to state action. See *Cantwell v. Connecticut* (1940). The no establishment clause of the First Amendment was not so interpreted until 1947, in a non–Jehovah's Witness case. See *Everson v. Board of Education* (1947). McAninch, "Catalyst," 1001.

33. There are several legal histories of specific Jehovah's Witness cases. For an exhaustive article on all of the Supreme Court cases brought by the Jehovah's Witnesses, see McAninch, "Catalyst"; on the flag saluting cases generally, see Manwaring, *Render unto Caesar*; on *Minersville School District v. Gobitis* (1940) and *West Virginia State Board of Education v. Barnette* (1943), see Stevens, *Salute!*; on *Gobitis* specifically, see Peter Irons, *The Courage of Their Convictions*. The earliest court records misspelled the name "Gobitis," an error followed by later courts. See *Proclaimers*, 685–86. For the purposes of consistency, I have used the more familiar (though incorrect) spelling when referring to court cases and documents. On *Jones v. Opelika* (1943) and *Marsh v. Alabama* (1946), see Newton, *Armed with the Constitution*. *Lovell v. City of Griffin* (1938), 444. The case involved broad and discretionary city restrictions on the right to distribute literature without a license.

34. See Manwaring, *Render unto Caesar*, 121. Manwaring notes that Moyle's previous work with other organizations sympathetic to the Jehovah's Witnesses (such as the American Civil Liberties Union) eventually came to an end when he was released (121). Stevens, *Salute!* 77. See also Respondent's Brief, *Minersville School District v. Gobitis* (no. 690), reprinted in *Landmark Briefs and Arguments of the Supreme Court of the United States: Constitutional Law*, ed. Philip B. Kurland and Gerhard Casper (Arlington, Va.: University Publications of America, 1975), 37:367–412. Manwaring suggests that Rutherford's influence was obvious in the *Gobitis* Circuit Court brief as well, noting that he "could hardly be satisfied with a religious argument cast otherwise than as an eternal verity." Manwaring, *Render unto Caesar*, 110. Convington's name does appear on the brief.

35. See Penton, *Apocalypse Delayed*, 80–83. Stevens, *Salute!* 78. Compare Appellant's Brief, *Lovell v. City of Griffin* (no. 391); Respondent's Brief, *Minersville School District v. Gobitis* (no. 690).

36. Stevens, *Salute!* 91-92. Stevens admits that no recording of the arguments existed, implying the secondhand nature of this account.

37. Manwaring, *Render unto Caesar*, 26.

38. Of the fifty-three cases identified as reaching the Supreme Court from 1940 to 1960, five resulted in per curiam decisions (three in favor, two against), and twenty-three were argued jointly to produce only seven decisions between them. The Jehovah's Witnesses won thirty-six of the fifty-three cases, almost 68 percent. In *Jones v. Opelika* (1943) and *Douglas v. City of Jeanette* (1943), the Court originally ruled against the Jehovah's Witnesses, but the first was later vacated and in the second an injunction was denied in order to permit a locality to come into compliance with another decision favorable to the Jehovah's Witnesses. For this reason both are here calculated as victories for Covington and the Jehovah's Witnesses. Covington did not participate in two of the 1940 decisions, *Cantwell v. Connecticut* and *Minersville School District v. Gobitis.* He did not receive a positive ruling until 1943, and from that year until 1960 he won nearly 74 percent of the cases he argued before the Supreme Court (thirty-five of forty-seven). He also argued cases before the lower circuit and district courts as well as in Canada.

39. Compare Respondent's Brief, *Minersville School District v. Gobitis* (no. 690); Appellees' Brief, *West Virginia State Board of Education v. Barnette* (no. 591), reprinted in Kurland and Casper, *Landmark Briefs and Arguments,* 40:39–150.

40. Newton, *Armed with the Constitution,* 133–34.

41. "First Defeat of Totalitarianism," *Watchtower,* May 1, 1940, 140. "Persecution," *Watchtower,* December 15, 1940, 371–78. A later article specifically addressing the Gobitis decision included an alternative pledge that would be acceptable to members of the Jehovah's Witnesses community. See "Obedience," *Watchtower,* February 15, 1941, 60. "Libel-Sedition Cases, Past and to Be Expected," *Watchtower,* March 1, 1947, 76. Since the Jehovah's Witnesses considered "religion" to be the opposite of true Christianity, the use of the term carried negative connotations. Members of the organization do not capitalize "witnesses" or use it with a definite pronoun, indicating that they are witnesses for God (Jehovah).

42. Of the 50 cases concluded, 11 did not result in full decisions (either because they were denied certiorari or were decided per curiam). The remaining 39 cases resulted in 24 decisions (21 of the 39 were argued and decided jointly, resulting in 6 separate decisions). As noted above, *Jones v. Opelika* (1943) and *Douglas v. City of Jeanette* (1943) have been calculated as victories for the Jehovah's Witnesses. *Defending and Legally Establishing,* 88. Hayden C. Covington, "The American Doctrine of Stare Decisis," *Texas Law Review* 24 (Fall 1946): 190–205.

43. Even in death, Rutherford could not escape conflict with the legal order—attempts to have his body buried at the organization's San Diego estate were denied by the Board of Health because the property was not zoned for cemetery use. See Mulder and Comisky, "Jehovah's Witnesses Mold Constitutional Law," 264–65. From the time Covington took over litigation duties until Rutherford's death, both names were listed on legal briefs submitted to the Supreme Court, though Covington most often was listed as lead counsel. After Rutherford's death, only Covington's name appeared on behalf of the Jehovah's Witnesses. Newton, *Armed with the Constitution*, 112.

44. Penton, *Apocalypse Delayed*, 139–40. Penton, "Jehovah's Witnesses and the Secular State," 67.

45. "Subjection to 'Superior Authorities,'" *Watchtower*, November 15, 1962, 683–85, 689, 690.

46. "The Benefits of Subjection to Authorities," *Watchtower*, November 15, 1962, 691. "Benefiting by Subjection to Authorities," *Watchtower*, December 1, 1962, 709. Penton, "Jehovah's Witnesses and the Secular State," 69.

47. See Brief for the Petitioner, *Thomas v. Review Board of the Indiana Employment Security Division* (no. 79-952). McAninch, "Catalyst," 1054. McAninch provides a detailed analysis of the litigation the Jehovah's Witnesses continue to pursue on the lower court levels (1059–72). R. Laurence Moore, *Selling God: American Religion in the Marketplace of Culture* (New York: Oxford University Press, 1994), 256.

48. Although it is recognized that many factors play a role in the outcome of a Supreme Court decision, there can be no doubt that, except in the case of plurality decisions, the arguments of the majority decisions represent (in part or in whole) the philosophy of more than half of the justices participating in the case. It is with this in mind that a decision can be said to be representative of the Court and thus provide rhetoric for comparison. No attempt is made here to downplay the role of dissenting opinions, but neither is any attempt made to incorporate them into the arguments of the majority, unsuccessfully argued as they have been.

49. For the purposes of this analysis, I have combined consideration of the rights of free speech and freedom of the press since all of the cases discussed below that raise freedom of the press issues also raise free speech concerns, even though not all of the free speech cases raise freedom of the press arguments. *Cantwell v. Connecticut* (1940), 307–11. *Minersville School District v. Gobitis* (1940), 597–98.

50. *Jamison v. Texas* (1943), 414. *Murdock v. Pennsylvania* (1943), 109.

51. *West Virginia State Board of Education v. Barnette* (1943), 634.

52. *Marsh v. Alabama* (1946), 508–9.

53. *Niemotko v. Maryland* (1951), 273–89. Justice Frankfurter cited every case involving the Jehovah's Witnesses that had resulted in a full decision except for *Minersville School District v. Gobitis* (1940), *Murdock v. Commonwealth of Pennsylvania* (1943), *Douglas v. City of Jeannette* (1943), *Taylor v. Mississippi* (1943), and *West Virginia State Board of Education v. Barnette* (1943). For obvious reasons, cases involving Jehovah's Witnesses as conscientious objectors were also not cited.

54. David Souter, then attorney general, participated on behalf of the state of New Hampshire.

55. The option to claim "conscientious objector" status is not a right defined constitutionally, but is instead a privilege granted by Congress.

56. *Draft Act of 1917*, Public Law 12, 65th Cong., 1st sess. (18 May 1917); *Selective Training and Service Act of 1940*, Public Law 783, 76th Cong., 3d sess. (16 September 1940). For a legal interpretation of the various draft statutes, see the Court's decision in *United States v. Seeger* (1965), esp. 169–73.

57. *Falbo v. United States* (1944), 557.

58. *Reynolds v. United States* (1879), in which the Court upheld federal legislation prohibiting polygamy over Mormon religious free exercise objections; *Sherbert v. Verner* (1963), in which the Court ruled that a Seventh-day Adventist was eligible for unemployment benefits after being improperly fired for refusing to work on Saturday, her sabbath; and *United States v. Seeger* (1965), in which the Court ruled that the congressional requirement of religious training for conscientious objector status did not require specific ministerial education.

59. See *Coleman v. City of Griffin* (1937), *Leoles v. Lander* (1937), *Hering v. State Board of Education* (1938), *Gabrielli v. Knickerbocker* (1939), *Johnson v. Deerfield* (1939), and *Prince v. Massachusetts* (1944).

60. For a detailed analysis of the legal history of the Jehovah's Witnesses in Canada, see Botting, *Fundamental Freedoms*, passim, 14–64. Hayden C. Covington, "The Dynamic American Bill of Rights," *Canadian Bar Review* 26, no. 4 (1948): 638–70; W. Glen How, "The Case for a Canadian Bill of Rights," *Canadian Bar Review* 26, no. 5 (1948): 759–96.

61. Covington, "American Bill of Rights," 670; *Edwards v. California* (1942), 182.

62. How, "Canadian Bill of Rights," 769, 781.

63. Edward F. Waite, "The Debt of Constitutional Law to Jehovah's Witnesses," *Minnesota Law Review* 28, no. 4 (1944): 215, 246.

64. *United States v. Ballard* (1944); *Sherbert v. Verner* (1963). Phillip B. Kurland, "The Right to Proselyte," in *Religion and the Law: Of Church and State and the Supreme Court,* by Kurland (Chicago: Aldine Publishing, 1962), 50.

65. Victor W. Rotnem and F. G. Folsom, Jr., "Recent Restrictions upon Religious Liberty," *American Political Science Review* 36, no. 6 (1942): 1057. Newton, *Armed with the Constitution,* 8.

66. Joseph R. McKinney, "Flag Day: 'It's Not What It Used to Be,'" *Religion and Public Education* 17, no. 2 (1990): 277. Legal realism advocated pragmatism rather than absolutism when determining legal doctrine (267–69).

67. William W. Van Alstyne, *First Amendment: Cases and Materials* (Westbury, N.Y.: Foundation Press, 1991), 22. A number of scholars have suggested that religious liberty is the "first freedom." See William Lee Miller, *The First Liberty: Religion and the American Republic* (New York: Paragon House Publishers, 1988). This position relies on the claim that religious freedom is philosophically prior to all of the other individual freedoms, since the entirety of the First Amendment was actually the third among the amendments sent to the states for ratification. The first two were not ratified at the time, though the second of the two was finally adopted as the Twenty-Seventh Amendment in 1992.

68. See Joseph Story, *Commentaries on the Constitution of the United States* (Cambridge, Mass.: Hilliard, Gray, and Co., 1833; reprint, Da Capo, 1970).

69. Barry A. Kosmin and Seymour P. Lachman, *One Nation under God: Religion in Contemporary American Society* (New York: Harmony Books, 1993), 15, 118. Mark A. Noll, *A History of Christianity in the United States and Canada* (Grand Rapids, Mich.: William B. Eerdmans, 1992), 465. The Presbyterian Church in America should not be confused with the Presbyterian Church, USA, the older denomination from which they split. From 1980 to 1988, membership in the older denomination actually dropped 13 percent.

70. Kosmin and Lachman, *One Nation under God,* 258–62, 205.

## 3 – Constitutional Conversion

1. Originally incorporated as the Church of Christ, the followers of Joseph Smith, Jr., changed the name of their church in 1834 to the Church of Latter-day Saints and, in 1838, to the Church of Jesus Christ of Latter-day Saints. Unlike the Jehovah's Witnesses, who adopted their organizational name by choice, members of the Church of Jesus Christ of Latter-day Saints have merely accepted the name Mormon from common usage. Writes historian Klaus Hansen of the name Mormon, "Originally, this name was used as a term of opprobrium and derision, to which the Saints took vigorous exception. Yet as conflict ceased, Mormons readily embraced a name that simply would not come unstuck." Klaus J. Hansen, *Mormonism and the American Experience* (Chicago: University of Chicago Press, 1981), 38. It is instructive to note that Hansen dates the acceptance of the name with the cessation of conflict—suggestively confirming the thesis of this chapter. In keeping with contemporary scholarship, I have chosen to use the organization's official name, its abbreviation (LDS), and its shortened version ("Church") when referring to institutional structures; the unofficial name "Mormon" as well as the designation "Saints" refers to individuals or groups of individuals outside the bureaucratic institutions.

2. Although the "Theocratic Government" noted in chapter 2 was intended as a new model of government after the final cosmic battle between good and evil, for reasons that will be made more clear by comparison with the Mormons, the Jehovah's Witnesses did not initiate a fully integrated political society as the Mormons did. The governmental functions of this institution were always millennial in a manner significantly different from the Mormon social institutions. More importantly as far as the constitutional order is concerned, the Jehovah's Witnesses never staked out a specific territory over which to claim absolute authority. They were therefore not the threat to the foundations of the American constitutional order that the Mormons were.

3. For a different interpretation of this confrontation, see Gordon C. Thomason, "The Manifesto Was a Victory!" *Dialogue* 6, no. 1 (1971): 37–45.

4. For the purposes of this chapter, I distinguish between plural marriage (the Mormon doctrine described in Doctrine and Covenants 132:1–20, 41–47) and polygamy (the allegation of a violation of state and federal law). Though this might seem to be a difference of semantics, the different labels indicate substantial differences in subjective political and theological orientation. Lawrence Foster, *Religion and Sexuality: Three American Com-*

*munal Experiments of the Nineteenth Century* (New York: Oxford University Press, 1981), 240–43.

5. Klaus J. Hansen, *Quest for Empire: The Political Kingdom of God and the Council of Fifty in Mormon History* (East Lansing: Michigan State University Press, 1967), 25.

6. H. Richard Niebuhr, *The Kingdom of God in America* (New York: Harper and Row, 1937; reprint, Middletown, Conn.: Wesleyan University Press, 1988). It is intriguing that there is no reference to Smith or to Mormonism in Niebuhr's work, since in an odd, parallel way it so nicely proves his thesis.

7. Doctrine and Covenants 101:74–80. There are also a number of indirect references to American chosenness throughout the Book of Mormon. See Reed D. Slack, "The Mormon Belief of an Inspired Constitution," *Journal of Church and State* 36, no. 1 (1994): 35–56. For a discussion of the doctrines of the Kingdom of God, see Hansen, *Quest for Empire*, esp. 3–44; James R. Clark, "The Kingdom of God, the Council of Fifty and the State of Deseret," *Utah Historical Quarterly* 26, no. 2 (1958): 131–48. For a general discussion of the Book of Mormon, see Thomas F. O'Dea, *The Mormons* (Chicago: University of Chicago Press, 1957), 22–40.

8. Edwin Brown Firmage and Richard Collin Mangrum, *Zion in the Courts: A Legal History of the Church of Jesus Christ of Latter-Day Saints, 1830–1900* (Urbana: University of Illinois Press, 1988), 67–68, 81.

9. For an excellent discussion of this period of Mormon history, see Kenneth H. Winn, *Exiles in the Land of Liberty: Mormons in America, 1830–1846* (Chapel Hill: University of North Carolina Press, 1989).

10. *LDS Journal History*, September 8, 1851, quoted in Dale L. Morgan, "The State of Deseret," *Utah Historical Quarterly* 8, nos. 2–4 (1940): 79.

11. Richard D. Poll, "Joseph Smith and the Presidency, 1844," *Dialogue* 3, no. 3 (1968): 17–18. A facsimile of Smith's political platform can be found in "General Smith's Views of the Powers and Policy of the Government of the United States," reprinted in *Dialogue* 3, no. 3 (1968): 28–34. James Arlington Bennett was originally nominated to serve as the vice-presidential candidate but was found to be ineligible because he was a naturalized citizen and not born in the United States. Sidney Rigdon eventually replaced him on the ticket. See Fawn M. Brodie, *No Man Knows My History: The Life of Joseph Smith, the Mormon Prophet*, 2d ed. (New York: Vintage Books, 1971), 363. See also Gwynn W. Barrett, "Dr. John M. Bernhisel: Mormon Elder in Congress," *Utah Historical Quarterly* 36, no. 2 (1968): 152. J. D.

Williams, "Separation of Church and State in Mormon Theory and Practice," *Journal of Church and State* 9, no. 2 (1967): 247. This article is a reprint of an earlier one that had appeared under the same title in *Dialogue* 1, no. 2 (1966): 30–54. See also Brodie, *No Man Knows My History*, 352–54, 362–63.

12. Firmage and Mangrum, *Zion in the Courts*, 83. Poll, "Joseph Smith and the Presidency," 19.

13. Hansen, *Mormonism and the American Experience*, 114.

14. Edward Leo Lyman, *Political Deliverance: The Mormon Quest for Utah Statehood* (Urbana: University of Illinois Press, 1986), 13. James Clark suggests that the council operated well into the 1870s. See Clark, "The Kingdom of God," passim.

15. An example of the high degree of interaction of the leadership of the LDS Church in secular activities is *Young v. Godbe*, a dispute that eventually made its way to the U.S. Supreme Court. Godbe, a shareholder in the Deseret Irrigation and Canal Company, brought suit against Brigham Young for repayment of his investment plus interest and damages. Though the issue facing the Court was one of evidentiary admissibility, the case is noteworthy for the testimony of one witness who declared that the Mormon business was "so mixed up with the church that he did not know the difference between them." See *Young v. Godbe* (1872), esp. 563.

16. For an in-depth analysis of the biblical imagery used in the conceptualization of the Great Basin and the migration to it, see R. H. Jackson, "The Mormon Experience: The Plains as Sinai, the Great Salt Lake as the Dead Sea, and the Great Basin as Desert-cum–Promised Land," *Journal of Historical Geography* 18, no. 1 (1992): esp. 52–58. See also Jan Shipps, *Mormonism: The Story of a New Religious Tradition* (Urbana: University of Illinois Press, 1985), 41–65. Dale Morgan refers to Mormon preparations for Mexican as well as U.S. control, but he also provides significant documentation to indicate that such indecision was short-lived. See Morgan, "The State of Deseret," 75, 82. R. H. Jackson indicates that Brigham Young had written a letter to President Polk advising him of the Mormon plans to relocate to the west. Jackson, "The Mormon Experience," 45. Although ratification of the Treaty of Guadeloupe-Hidalgo may have taken time, the results of the Mexican-American War were fairly clear by the end of the 1840s.

17. The word *Deseret* is traditionally translated as "honeybee," and though originally reputed to be of Hebrew origin, it can be traced only to

the Jaredites in the Book of Mormon (Ether 2:3). See Armand L. Mauss, "Assimilation and Ambivalence: The Mormon Reaction to Americanization," *Dialogue* 22, no. 1 (1989): 30.

18. Stanley S. Ivins, "A Constitution for Utah," *Utah Historical Quarterly* 25, no. 2 (1957): 96. Dale Morgan comments with interest on the fact that the first order of business was not "providing civil laws and institutions," but instead was solely the "organization of the state on the one hand and an effort toward influencing Congress on the other." Morgan, "The State of Deseret," 89. Unless otherwise noted, information regarding the State of Deseret and its constitutional drafting processes have been drawn from these two works.

19. *LDS Journal History,* September 6, 1849, quoted in Morgan, "The State of Deseret," 93.

20. Glen M. Leonard, "The Mormon Boundary Question in the 1849–50 Statehood Debates," *Journal of Mormon History* 18 (Spring 1992): 127–28. The U.S. Constitution grants Congress the authority "to dispose and make all needful rules and regulations respecting the territory," but a state need not go through such a process. See Article 4, section 2. Under the provisions of the Treaty of Guadeloupe-Hidalgo, the region later to become the Utah Territory was originally placed under the military control of the Department of California. See Angus E. Crane, "Millard Fillmore and the Mormons," *Journal of the West* 34, no. 1 (1995): 71.

21. In 1849 Almon W. Babbitt, who accompanied Bernhisel to Washington, was rejected as a Congressional delegate from the State of Deseret, and the two men returned to the territory. In 1851 Bernhisel was seated as a delegate from the Territory of Utah, and he served as its unofficial voice in Washington for ten of the next twelve years, finally retiring in 1863. See Barrett, "Dr. John M. Bernhisel," 158–59. Richard D. Poll, "The Mormon Question Enters National Politics, 1850–1856," *Utah Historical Quarterly* 25, no. 2 (1957): 117.

22. In many ways, off and on from 1850 until 1890, there existed two governments in the territory—the federally established government of the Utah Territory, and the institutions inaugurated by the Council of Fifty and maintained as the State of Deseret. Compare Morgan, "The State of Deseret," passim, and An Act to Establish a Territorial Government for Utah. See Poll, "The Mormon Question," 117; Crane, "Millard Fillmore," 73–74. Crane suggests that naming Young governor was an expression of Fillmore's support of democracy and Mormon autonomy, but there can be no doubt that, regardless of the sympathy the president might have had for their

plight, the Mormons were still dependent on the whims of the federal government. This became increasingly clear to the Mormons in the coming decades, and it explains—better than fondness for the American system—the continuous efforts for statehood.

23. Vern Bullough suggests that Douglas's early affiliation with Mormons in Illinois, combined with his championing of "popular sovereignty," swayed the state of Illinois and possibly the election toward the Republican, Abraham Lincoln, whose party had campaigned against slavery and polygamy since 1856. See Vern L. Bullough, "Polygamy: An Issue in the Election of 1860?" *Utah Historical Quarterly* 29, no. 2 (1961): 119–31.

24. The Republicans had included in their platform attacks on slavery and polygamy. The Democrats, representing significant portions of the South, had, by the absence of such rhetoric, seemed much more supportive of the Mormon plight. See Poll, "The Mormon Question," 131. Although there were episodes of armed conflict, the worst—the Mountain Meadows Massacre—was the tragic result of mistaken identity. By and large the Mormons executed a scorched-earth policy and never directly attacked federal troops, whose losses came primarily from disease and exposure. See Norman F. Furniss, *The Mormon Conflict, 1850–1859* (New Haven, Conn.: Yale University Press, 1960), esp. 45–95. See also Leonard J. Arrington and Davis Bitton, *The Mormon Experience: A History of the Latter-Day Saints*, 2d ed. (Urbana: University of Illinois Press, 1992), 166–70; Lyman, *Political Deliverance*, 9.

25. Officially dissolved on March 28, 1851, the legislature of the State of Deseret continued to function as a "ghost government" until the 1870s, and the name was the subject of debate until the 1880s.

26. For a discussion of the New York case, see Brodie, *No Man Knows My History*, 30–31. Brodie also includes a secondhand account of the trial (427–29). See also Arrington and Bitton, *The Mormon Experience*, 10–12. For a detailed discussion of Mormon interactions in Ohio, Missouri, and Illinois, see Winn, *Exiles in a Land of Liberty*, passim. Even though the Fourteenth Amendment had been adopted in 1868, the Bill of Rights was not applied to limit state action until the 1890s, and states were left with considerable freedom to control the behavior of their citizenry, even in matters of religion. On federal property, however (such as territories), residents would automatically be under the authority of congressional action.

27. Though the constitution for the State of Deseret mentions a supreme being only one time more than the U.S. Constitution, and nowhere specifies Mormon control, the first elections established a pattern of coinciding

authority. The names of those elected to the positions of governor, lieuten-
ant governor, chief justice of the state supreme court, and secretary of state
were virtually identical to the leadership of the LDS Church. See Morgan,
"The State of Deseret," 87–88, 156.

28. Evidence indicates that the practice actually predates the official
designation of 1843. See D. Michael Quinn, "LDS Church Authority and
New Plural Marriages, 1890–1904," *Dialogue* 18, no. 1 (1985): 23; Shipps,
*Mormonism*, 61. Historian Klaus Hansen indicates, however, that the scriptural passage justifying plural marriage (Doctrine and Covenants 132) was
not added by the LDS Church until 1876, not to suggest that the practice
did not exist prior to that date, but "in support of its claim that plural
marriage was part of Mormon scripture." See Hansen, *Mormonism and the
American Experience*, 233 n. 48.

29. Arrington and Bitton, *The Mormon Experience*, 204; Edwin B.
Firmage, "Free Exercise of Religion in Nineteenth Century America: The
Mormon Cases," *Journal of Law and Religion* 7, no. 2 (1989): 291. Legal
historian Ken Driggs suggests that the lack of action on the part of the federal government implies tacit approval of the practice rather than the drama
of sectional and national politics. Though this may be partially correct, it
seems more likely that the lack of prosecution was at least the result of
these and other factors, such as Mormon control of the territorial courts
and a misunderstanding of the effects and limitations of federal legislation.
See Ken Driggs, "The Prosecutions Begin: Defining Cohabitation in 1885,"
*Dialogue* 21, no. 1 (1988): 110.

30. Unless otherwise noted, the legal analysis utilized in this chapter
has been derived from Edwin Firmage's comprehensive article on Mormon
litigation, "Free Exercise of Religion," 281–313.

31. *Reynolds v. United States* (1879), 164–65, 167.

32. Compare this to the situation discussed in chapter 2. Because the
Supreme Court reserved for itself the realm of free speech rights, Jehovah's
Witnesses were able to use the Court to keep the legislative branch in check.
Because the Supreme Court ceded its constitutional authority to Congress
in the *Reynolds* decision, it provided merely an advisory role on the statu-
tory construction of congressional action.

33. *Miles v. United States* (1880), 315.

34. Lyman, *Political Deliverance*, 23. Lyman is quoting Cannon from
"Political Aspects of Mormonism," *Harper's Magazine*, January 1882, 285–88.

35. *Clawson v. United States* (1885); *Murphy v. Ramsey* (1885); *Clawson*

*v. United States* (1885); *Cannon v. United States* (1885), vacated (1886); and *Snow v. United States* (1886).

36. *Murphy v. Ramsey* (1885), 44–45 (emphasis added).

37. Joseph Fielding Smith, *Essentials in Church History* (Salt Lake City: Deseret News Press, 1922), 599, quoted in Thomason, "The Manifesto Was a Victory!" 40–41.

38. Quinn, "New Plural Marriages," 27. Arrington and Bitton, *The Mormon Experience,* 181.

39. The measure passed without Democratic president Grover Cleveland's signature, as per the U.S. Constitution, Article 1, section 7. Such passage requires a two-thirds majority for the measure to pass each chamber, a strong indication of the support this measure had. For a detailed discussion of the political climate surrounding the drafting and passage of the act, see Henry J. Wolfinger, "A Reexamination of the Woodruff Manifesto in the Light of Utah Constitutional History," *Utah Historical Quarterly* 39, no. 4 (1971): 328–49.

40. Mormon leadership lobbied for the introduction of an amendment that would delay the implementation of the act for six months while an acceptable state constitution was drafted. This amendment was never adopted, and the act became law without it. See Wolfinger, "A Reexamination," 336–38.

41. Quinn, "New Plural Marriages," 33. *Davis v. Beason* (1890), 347.

42. Brief for Appellant, *Davis v. Beason,* October 1889, no. 1261, esp. 12–53.

43. Edward Leo Lyman, "The Political Background of the Woodruff Manifesto," *Dialogue* 24, no. 3 (1991): 25–26.

44. Kenneth David Driggs, "The Mormon Church-State Confrontation in Nineteenth-Century America," *Journal of Church and State* 30, no. 2 (1988): 287. Hansen, *Mormonism and the American Experience,* 128–29. There were legal victories for the Mormon community at the height of the confrontation: *In re Snow* (1887), which ruled that continuous cohabitation did not count as multiple offenses and therefore could not result in multiple charges, and *Ex parte Nielsen* (1889), which ruled that the refusal to provide for a writ of habeas corpus in a case involving imprisonment for cohabitation was a violation of the prisoner's rights. However, as beneficial as these decisions were, they represent only a part of the total case load, and they are primarily procedural. See, for example, *Clayton v. Dickson* (1890).

45. The full text of the manifesto can be found in Doctrine and Covenants, Declaration 1.

46. Hansen, *Mormonism and the American Experience*, 199; Quinn, "New Plural Marriages," 47; Lyman, "The Woodruff Manifesto," 34. Thomas G. Alexander, "Wilford Woodruff and the Changing Nature of Mormon Religious Experience," *Church History* 45 (March, 1976): 68.

47. Alexander, "Wilford Woodruff," 68–69.

48. Thomas G. Alexander, *Mormonism in Transition: A History of the Latter-Day Saints, 1890–1930* (Urbana: University of Illinois Press, 1986), 7.

49. *Bassett v. United States* (1890); *Cope v. Cope* (1891).

50. *United States v. Late Corporation of the Church of Jesus Christ of Latter-day Saints* (1893).

51. *Chapman v. Handley* (1894); *France v. Connor* (1896).

52. R. Davis Bitton, "The B.H. Roberts Case of 1898–1900," *Utah Historical Quarterly* 25, no. 1 (1957): 41.

53. Grover Cleveland, "By the President of the United States of America: A Proclamation," September 25, 1894, reprinted in *A Compilation of the Messages and Papers of the Presidents*, ed. James D. Richardson (New York: Bureau of National Literature, 1917), 13:5942–43.

54. Grover Cleveland, "By the President of the United States of America: A Proclamation," January 4, 1896, reprinted in Richardson, *Messages and Papers of the Presidents*, 13:6120–21. For an in-depth account of this final constitutional convention, see Ivins, "A Constitution for Utah," esp. 100–116. By the time Utah was admitted to the Union, there was little question concerning its borders; most of the surrounding states (Nevada, Idaho, Wyoming, and Colorado) had already been admitted, and those that had not (New Mexico and Arizona, established as the Territory of New Mexico) had their borders set as part of the Compromise of 1850. See Leonard, "The Mormon Boundary Question," 134–36.

55. See Quinn, "New Plural Marriages," esp. 49–59, 62. Quinn notes that only 10 percent of the plural marriages performed after the manifesto were exploitations of legal loopholes; the rest were performed by—or with the consent or knowledge of—the LDS Church leadership. Kenneth Cannon notes that between 1890 and 1905, 61 percent of the General Authorities were illegally cohabiting. Kenneth L. Cannon, Jr., "Beyond the Manifesto: Polygamous Cohabitation among LDS General Authorities after 1890," *Utah Historical Quarterly* 46, no. 1 (1978): 30.

56. Bitton, "The B.H. Roberts Case," 35. Unless otherwise noted, infor-

mation regarding the Roberts congressional career have been derived from this source.

57. David Brudnoy even suggests that the anti-Roberts campaign drew "support and publicity" from William Randolph Hearst. "Of Sinners and Saints: Theodore Schroeder, Brigham Roberts, and Reed Smoot," *Journal of Church and State* 14, no. 2 (1972): 267.

58. Thomas Alexander argues that this had less to do with church permission and more to do with the shifting image of the Church in national politics. See Alexander, *Mormonism in Transition*, 9. Craig Mikkelsen notes that the unease stemmed from desires on the part of the Church to appear "accommodating." See D. Craig Mikkelsen, "The Politics of B.H. Roberts," *Dialogue* 9, no. 2 (1974): 26.

59. After signing the document, Roberts spent the next two years in missionary work abroad. When he returned to run for Congress in 1898, he sought and received Church president Lorenzo Snow's permission. Mikkelsen, "The Politics of B.H. Roberts," 34–35; Arrington and Bitton, *The Mormon Experience*, 247. Though seemingly an insignificant point, denying a seat to a Representative-elect merely requires a simple majority vote, whereas expelling a sitting representative requires a two-thirds majority vote. Roberts was able to serve his country in another capacity later, as a chaplain during World War I. See Alexander, *Mormonism in Transition*, 47. A nonpolygamous Mormon, W. H. King, was elected to the vacant seat. Brudnoy, "Of Sinners and Saints," 274.

60. For the most detailed account of this entire episode, see Milton R. Merrill, *Reed Smoot: Apostle in Politics* (Logan: Utah State University Press, 1990), esp. 11–99. Unless otherwise noted, information regarding the Smoot senatorial career has been derived from this source. Reed Smoot to Joseph F. Smith, January 8, 1906, quoted in Merrill, *Reed Smoot*, 70.

61. This debate turned out to be moot, since Smoot had been officially sworn in as senator from Utah on March 5, 1903.

62. Jan Shipps, "Utah Comes of Age Politically: A Study of the State's Politics in the Early Years of the Twentieth Century," *Utah Historical Quarterly* 35, no. 2 (1967): 95. Ken Driggs, "Twentieth-Century Polygamy and Fundamentalist Mormons in Southern Utah," *Dialogue* 24, no. 4 (1991): 45. D. Michael Quinn suggests that the significance of the second manifesto was not in ending the practice but in ending the tacit approval of it by the LDS Church leadership. See Quinn, "New Plural Marriages," 98–99, 103–5.

63. Mikkelsen, "The Politics of B.H. Roberts," 36. Milton R. Merrill,

"Reed Smoot, Apostle-Senator," *Utah Historical Quarterly* 28, no. 4 (1960): 343. Popular opposition in any senatorial election before 1913 would have been difficult to measure—all senators before that year were selected by their respective state legislatures. Compare Article 1, section 3 of the U.S. Constitution with Amendment 17. Smoot's first reelection, in 1908, might have been affected by a shift in the makeup of the Utah statehouse, though that indirect a response is difficult to measure since the Republican Party did well across the state. Smoot's first popular election—and probably his most difficult—was in 1914, when he was reelected by less than 3 percent of the total vote cast. According to Merrill, Smoot "didn't win, he survived." Merrill, *Reed Smoot*, 129. Actually, he "survived" in office until 1932. See also Alexander, *Mormonism in Transition*, 33, 42–59.

64. Mormon folklore describing Mormon leaders' splitting congregations evenly among the Republicans and Democrats does not seem to withstand scrutiny. The Church leadership was generally Republican until the administration of LDS president Heber Grant, and the Mormon laity were generally less responsive to the Church's political admonitions than to specific issues. See Alexander, *Mormonism in Transition*, 33.

65. Ibid., 28, 34, 52–53; Shipps, "Utah Comes of Age Politically," 99, 102–6. The Mormon restriction against alcohol known as the Word of Wisdom states in pertinent part: "That inasmuch as any man drinketh wine or strong drink among you, behold it is not good, neither meet in the sight of your Father, only in assembling yourselves together to offer up your sacraments before him." Doctrine and Covenants, 89:5.

66. For a general discussion of this period, see Alexander, *Mormonism in Transition*, esp. 16–59; Shipps, "Utah Comes of Age Politically," 91–111. Alexander, *Mormonism in Transition*, 35. Merrill, *Reed Smoot*, 97.

67. Historian Jerold Auerbach writes that Justice Brandeis, arguing for the integration of American and Zionist ideals, noted that "[t]o be good Americans, we must be better Jews, and to be better Jews, we must become Zionists." Jerold S. Auerbach, *Rabbis and Lawyers: The Journey from Torah to Constitution* (Bloomington: Indiana University Press, 1990), 128.

68. See Mario S. De Pillis, "Viewing Mormonism as Mainline," *Dialogue* 24, no. 4 (1991): 59–68. Driggs, "Twentieth-Century Polygamy," 46–50. *Chatwin v. United States* (1946); *Cleveland v. United States* (1946); *Musser v. Utah* (1948). For a discussion of the events surrounding these decisions, see Ken Driggs, "After the Manifesto: Modern Polygamy and Fundamentalist Mormons," *Journal of Church and State* 32, no. 2 (1990): 382–83.

69. Possibly as a result of the successes being enjoyed by the Jehovah's

Witnesses at approximately the same time, in its brief in support of Musser (and others), the American Civil Liberties Union argued on the basis of free religious speech rather than action. Brief of the American Civil Liberties Union as Amicus Curiae, *Musser v. United States*, no. 1188, esp. 4–6. Arguments were originally heard in November 1947, but the case was reargued in January 1948.

70. Hansen, *Mormonism and the American Experience*, 213.

71. The first decision, announced in 1987, granted the church the right to deny employment based on religious justifications; it was argued solely on "no establishment" grounds. See *Corporation of the Presiding Bishop of the Church of Jesus Christ of Latter-day Saints v. Amos* (1987). The second denied Mormon parents the right to claim as a charitable donation (and thus a tax deduction) money given to their sons who were fulfilling their religious obligation as missionaries. See *Davis v. United States* (1990). Frank Way and Barbara Burt, "Religious Marginality and the Free Exercise Clause," *American Political Science Review* 77, no. 3 (1983): 658.

72. Such luminaries include former LDS Church president Ezra Taft Benson (secretary of agriculture under Eisenhower); J. Reuben Clark (undersecretary of state and ambassador to Mexico); James Fletcher (head of the National Aeronautics and Space Administration under Nixon, Ford, Carter, and Reagan, though not continuously); and George Romney (secretary of housing and urban development under Nixon). See Armand L. Mauss and Philip L. Barlow, "Church, Sect, and Scripture: The Protestant Bible and Mormon Sectarian Retrenchment," *Sociological Analysis* 52, no. 4 (1991): 401. In addition there have been numerous Mormon members of the House and the Senate (including Idaho representative Jake Garn, the first sitting member of Congress to travel in space). There have as yet been no Mormon Supreme Court justices, though it is significant that, with the elevation of Sen. Orrin Hatch to the chairmanship of the Senate Judiciary Committee, a Mormon is now in a position of extraordinary power over the confirmation process of any judicial nominee.

73. Arrington and Bitton, *The Mormon Experience*, 251–52, 261. See D. Michael Quinn, "The Mormon Church and the Spanish-American War: An End to Selective Pacifism," *Dialogue* 17, no. 4 (1984): 11–30. Charles Wilson discusses the parallel symbolic use of World War I by Confederate society as a means of "rejoining" American culture. Charles Reagan Wilson, *Baptized in Blood: The Religion of the Lost Cause, 1865–1920* (Athens: University of Georgia Press, 1980), esp. 161–82.

## 4 – Constitutional Conflict

1. For the purposes of this chapter, I have conflated Native American and European American religious traditions into general categories in much the same way, though I recognize their vast internal differences. With reference to the appropriateness of this convention for Native American religious traditions, Native American historian of religions Joel Martin notes that

> rather than focus upon their commonalities, pre-contact Native Americans must have been most conscious of the plethora of highly diverse religious, linguistic, political, social, and cultural forms that divided them into a great number of ethnic groups. . . . The situation changed dramatically when these diverse peoples were collectively misnamed "Indians" and then reconstructed as colonized subjects within a world-system dominated by European nation-states. Though ethnic differences did not diminish, and intertribal conflicts did not cease, very deep and widespread cultural and religious commonalities could not help but become more apparent.

Joel W. Martin, "Before and Beyond the Sioux Ghost Dance: Native American Prophetic Movements and the Study of Religion," *Journal of the American Academy of Religion* 49, no. 4 (1991): 691–92. See also Catherine L. Albanese, *America: Religions and Religion* (Belmont, Calif.: Wadsworth, 1981), 19–38.

2. Marc Peyser, with Sonya Zalubowski, "Between a Wing and a Prayer," *Newsweek*, September 19, 1994, 58. *Newsweek*, the source of this information, apparently misspelled the name of the tribe of which Mr. Jim is a member. I have used the generally accepted spelling rather than "Yakama" as reported.

3. Frederick Douglass, "What to the Slave Is the Fourth of July? An Address Delivered in Rochester, New York, on 5 July 1852," in *The Frederick Douglass Papers, Series 1: Speeches, Debates, and Interviews,* ed. John W. Blassingame (New Haven, Conn.: Yale University Press, 1982), 2:359, quoted in Milner S. Ball, "Stories of Origin and Constitutional Possibilities," *Michigan Law Review* 87, no. 8 (1989): 2282–83, 2283 (emphasis in the original).

4. See Albert J. Raboteau, *Slave Religion: The "Invisible Institution" in the Antebellum South* (New York: Oxford University Press, 1978), esp. 87–92. See Joel W. Martin, *Sacred Revolt: The Muskogees' Struggle for a New World* (Boston: Beacon Press, 1991), esp. 87–113.

5. Henry Warner Bowden, *American Indians and Christian Missions:*

*Studies in Cultural Conflict* (Chicago: University of Chicago Press, 1981), 113. By comparison, the French Jesuits were more readily accepted by the Native Americans, because of their "favorable attitude" toward the religion of the peoples with whom they worked (78).

6. R. Pierce Beaver, *Church, State and the American Indian: Two and a Half Centuries of Partnership in Missions between Protestant Churches and Government* (St. Louis: Concordia Publishing House, 1966), 53–54. Unless otherwise noted, the information regarding early governmental relations with Native Americans is drawn from this source, as well as two corresponding sources by R. Pierce Beaver, "Church, State, and the Indians: Indians Missions in the New Nation," *Journal of Church and State* 4, no. 1 (1962): 11–30; and "The Churches and President Grant's Peace Policy," *Journal of Church and State* 4, no. 2 (1962): 174–90.

7. Bowden, *American Indians and Christian Missions*, 163.

8. In a structural ambiguity of federalism contained in section 8, the Constitution also provides for the same delegation of authority to Congress when regulating commerce "among the several states." This inclusion confuses whatever parallelism might be asserted to exist between "foreign nations" and "Indian tribes." Chief Justice John Marshall addresses this issue in *Cherokee Nation v. Georgia* (1831), 18–19—taxed Indians were generally those who lived as individuals in urban settings, off the reservation and outside of tribal territory.

9. Article 1, section 2, which this portion of the amendment replaced, specified that slaves be counted as three-fifths of a person for the purposes of the apportionment of representation, a compromise that did not anticipate the independent status of Native Americans but merely addressed the marginal status of African American slaves and their role in preserving the Union, north and south. Amendment 14 did not address the status of Native Americans established in Article 1.

10. Beaver, *Church, State, and the American Indian*, 63.

11. For a history of the suit, see William G. McLoughlin, *Cherokee Renascence in the New Republic* (Princeton, N.J.: Princeton University Press, 1986), 388–447. For an analysis of the resulting majority and dissenting opinions, see Vine Deloria, Jr., and Clifford M. Lytle, *American Indians, American Justice* (Austin: University of Texas Press, 1983), 29–32.

12. *Cherokee Nation v. Georgia* (1831), 16–17, 57.

13. McLoughlin, *Cherokee Renascence*, 443–44.

14. President Jackson allegedly exclaimed, "John Marshall has made his decision:—*now let him enforce it!*" Albert J. Beveridge, *The Life of John*

*Marshall* (Boston: Houghton Mifflin, 1919), 4:515 (emphasis in the original). McLoughlin, *Cherokee Renascence*, 446.

15. Beaver, *Church, State, and the American Indian*, 157.

16. Under the structures of the Constitution and the doctrine of the separation of powers, the House of Representatives retains general primary responsibility over domestic affairs through its budgetary process, and the Senate retains primary responsibility for international affairs through the treaty process.

17. Ralph Lerner argues that the Native American political units may actually have been better treated than the Spanish and French political units the new American nation encountered as it expanded. There was never any question of incorporating the French or Spanish as separate political entities with equal rights in the American system, but an effort was attempted for the Native Americans, feeble though it might have been. See Ralph Lerner, "Reds and Whites: Rights and Wrongs," in *The Supreme Court Review, 1971*, ed. Philip B. Kurland (Chicago: University of Chicago Press, 1971), 202–4.

18. Deloria and Lytle, *American Indians*, 9–14. The policy of allotment was overturned by the passage of the Indian Reorganization Act, also known as the Wheeler-Howard Act. In recognition of the theocratic nature of some tribal governments, the Indian Civil Rights Act did not extend the prohibition against the establishment of religion to tribal authorities. In addition, the act did not extend Fifteenth Amendment rights, which guarantee voting rights regardless of race, for fear that this would limit the tribes' abilities to determine membership. Ball, "Stories of Origin," 2308. The federal government's extension protected *individual* Native Americans from actions taken by their *tribal* authority, meaning that Native Americans could now initiate causes of action in federal courts *against their own tribe* for the denial of basic rights. This brought protections available to Native Americans into line with those available to other citizens, who could turn to the Fourteenth Amendment (ratified in 1868 and eventually interpreted to extend Bill of Rights guarantees to cover state action) for protection.

19. *Tee-Hit-Ton Indians v. United States* (1955), 289–90. The Court denied compensation to a band of the Tlingit community in Alaska for the harvesting of lumber on property claimed by the Native Americans. *Oliphant v. Suquamish Indian Tribe* (1978), 208–9. The Court was quoting from *United States v. Rogers* (1846), 571–72, in which the Court denied a European American who had been adopted by a Native American community immunity from federal jurisdiction over the murder on a reserva-

tion of another European American who had also been adopted by a Native American community.

20. This is not to suggest that the individuality of Native Americans is a new category of existence. Although it is recognized that not all Native Americans live in geographic proximity to their tribal affiliation, or even necessarily retain such affiliation with respect to religion, there can be no argument that the federal government, since its inception, has distinguished Native Americans in their tribal groupings from those who lived their lives seemingly independent of tribal authority; see note 8. In addition, since specific rights as well as potential financial settlements have rested on the definition of who is or is not a member of a given Native American tribe, the very concept of affiliation has not escaped litigation. (See *Elk v. Wilkins* [1884], in which the Court denied citizenship—in the form of voting rights— to a Native American who provided no evidence of having paid taxes and thus still fell under the limitations of the Fourteenth Amendment; *Morton v. Mancari* [1973], in which the Supreme Court ruled the BIA hiring preference for Native Americans was politically rather than racially based and therefore not subject to employment restrictions; and *Santa Clara Pueblo v. Martinez* [1978], in which the Supreme Court ruled that the Indian Civil Rights Act did not require federal jurisdiction over all internal Native American disputes, in this case a dispute over tribal membership standards.) It is also a category of obvious distinction in some contemporary Native American scholarship, which notes the tribal affiliations for Native Americans but ignores parallel ethnic identifications for people of other non– Native American ethnicities. See John R. Wunder, *"Retained by The People": A History of American Indians and the Bill of Rights* (New York: Oxford University Press, 1994), 162.

21. Edward McGlynn Gaffney, Jr., "The Interaction of Biblical Religion and American Constitutional Law," in *The Bible in American Law, Politics, and Political Rhetoric,* ed. James Turner Johnson (Philadelphia: Fortress Press, 1985), 99.

22. Exodus 18:21 (King James Version) reads: "Moreover thou shalt provide out of all the people able men, such as fear God, men of truth, hating covetousness; and place such over them, to be rulers of thousands, and rulers of hundreds, rulers of fifties, and rulers of tens," thus providing for a hierarchical social structure of governance.

23. Robert S. Michaelsen, "American Indian Religious Freedom Litigation: Promise and Perils," *Journal of Law and Religion* 3, no. 1 (1985): 50, 53. In its first Native American religious freedom decision (*Bowen v. Roy*

[1986]), the Supreme Court ruled that a parent's religious objections could not overrule the government's need to maintain its internal accounting procedures, in this case by providing a child with a Social Security number.

24. Brief for the Indian Respondents in Opposition, On Petition for a Writ of Certiorari, *Richard E. Lyng, Secretary of Agriculture, et al. v. Northwest Indian Cemetery Protective Association et al.* (no. 86-1013), 2.

25. Brief of Amici Curiae, *Richard E. Lyng, Secretary of Agriculture et al. v. Northwest Indian Cemetery Protective Association et al.* (no. 86-1013), 9–11. Moore was citing the report issued in conjunction with the American Indian Religious Freedom Act.

26. For a detailed analysis of the decision, see Robert S. Michaelsen, "Is the Miner's Canary Silent? Implications of the Supreme Court's Denial of American Indian Free Exercise of Religion Claims," *Journal of Law and Religion* 6, no. 1 (1988): 97–114. The Supreme Court handed down another Native American religious freedom decision (*Employment Division, Department of Human Resources of the State of Oregon v. Smith* [1988]), in the same term as *Lyng*. However, in that decision the Court remanded the issue of a state's prohibition of sacramental peyote use for further consideration. This case returned to the Supreme Court two years later (*Employment Division, Department of Human Resources of Oregon, et al. v. Smith et al.* [1990]), and the state's prohibition was declared constitutional.

27. Brief for the Indian Respondents in Opposition, On Petition, *Lyng v. Northwest Indian Cemetery Protective Association*, 10–11. The "compelling interest" test was removed as a jurisprudential requirement in *Employment Division v. Smith* (1990), restored by Congress through the Religious Freedom Restoration Act, and removed again by the Supreme Court in 1997. Robert S. Michaelsen, "'We Also Have a Religion': The Free Exercise of Religion among Native Americans," *American Indian Quarterly* 7, no. 3 (1983): 132, quoting *Wilson v. Block, Hopi Indian Tribe v. Block,* and *Navajo Medicinemen's Association v. Block* (D.C. Cir. 1983).

28. Vine Deloria, Jr., *God is Red: A Native View of Religion*, 2d ed. (Golden, Colo.: Fulcrum Publishing, 1994), 62. Michaelsen, "'We Also Have a Religion,'" 112. In another work, Michaelsen suggests that the differences between traditional Native American religions and European American religions could best be understood utilizing categories developed by Robert Bellah to describe the various stages through which religion has evolved in human history. See Robert S. Michaelsen, "Sacred Land in America: What Is It? How Can It Be protected?" *Religion* 16 (July 1986): 249–68. Michaelsen

is referring to Robert N. Bellah, "Religious Evolution," *American Socio-logical Review* 29, no. 3 (1964): 358–74.

29. No non–Native American organizations were represented as signato-ries in the amici filed in the *Lyng* case. See Brief for the Indian Respondents, *Richard E. Lyng, Secretary of Agriculture, et al. v. Northwest Indian Cem-etery Protective Association et al.* (no. 86-1013), signed by representatives from California Indian Legal Services; and Brief of Amici Curiae, *Richard E. Lyng, Secretary of Agriculture, et al. v. Northwest Indian Cemetery Pro-tective Association et al.* (no. 86-1013), which included representatives from eight Native American tribes or associations.

30. Petition for Rehearing for the Native American Program, Oregon Legal Services, *Employment Division, Department of Human Resources of Oregon, et al. v. Smith et al.* (no. 88-1213). Representatives from nine-teen national political organizations (including the American Civil Liber-ties Union, the Christian Legal Society, the National Association of Evan-gelicals, the American Jewish Congress, the Lutheran Church–Missouri Synod, the Worldwide Church of God, People for the American Way, and the American Friends Service Committee) and forty-eight faculty members of various law schools signed the petition. The petition was denied.

31. Milner S. Ball, *Lying Down Together: Law, Metaphor, and Theology* (Madison: University of Wisconsin Press, 1985), 7. Michaelsen, "American Indian Religious Freedom Litigation," 60. For an interesting response to the magnified role of land within Native American scholarship, see Sam D. Gill, *Mother Earth: An American Story* (Chicago: University of Chicago Press, 1987).

32. For an early analysis of the relationship between Christianity and constitutional law, see Joseph Story, *Commentaries on the Constitution of the United States* (Cambridge, Mass.: Hilliard, Gray, and Co., 1833; re-print, New York: Da Capo, 1970). See also Morton Borden, *Jews, Turks, and Infidels* (Chapel Hill: University of North Carolina Press, 1984); H. Frank Way, "Death of the Christian Nation: The Judiciary and Church-State Re-lations" *Journal of Church and State* 29, no. 3 (1987): 509–29; and John K. Wilson, "Religion under the State Constitutions, 1776–1800," *Journal of Church and State* 32, no. 4 (1990): 753–73.

33. On this point, see Phillip E. Hammond, *With Liberty for All: Free-dom of Religion in the United States* (Louisville: Westminster John Knox Press, 1998), esp. chaps. 5–6.

34. See *United States v. Kagama* (1886), in which the Court ruled that

the murder of a Native American by a Native American was under the jurisdiction of the federal courts, overturning its own ruling in *Ex parte Crow Dog* (1883). Justice Miller provides an analysis of the doctrine of discovery and the U.S. attitude toward Native American protectorship (*United States v. Kagama*, 381–85). Ball, "Stories of Origin," 2305–6. Ball points out that an early draft of the Constitution's supremacy clause read that it would be "the supreme law of the several States." The change in wording indicated a radical shift in authority, since the first draft covered only those states participating in the Union, whereas the final version incorporated all land claimed by the Union—states, territories, possessions, and conquests. It also signified a shift in abstractions from authority over a polity to authority over space.

35. Genesis 1:26–30. This same attitude toward discovery can be seen in events within the last thirty years, such as in the planting of an American flag on the surface of the Moon.

36. Beaver, *Church, State, and the American Indian*, 196.

37. Michaelsen, "American Indian Religious Freedom Litigation," 64.

38. See Robert S. Michaelsen, "Dirt in the Court Room: Indian Land Claims and American Property Rights," in *American Sacred Space*, ed. David Chidester and Edward T. Linenthal (Bloomington: Indiana University Press, 1995), 43–45; Michaelsen, "American Indian Religious Freedom Litigation," 50, 62. However, he and other scholars have noted limitations to this approach. See Michaelsen, "American Indian Religious Freedom Litigation," 68; Ball, *Lying Down Together*, 22. Ball has suggested the use of metaphors that are more inclusive, such as a creation narrative for Americans that stresses the successive arrivals of different peoples (including Native Americans, African Americans, and new immigrant communities as well as the western European colonialists) rather than the conventional colonial narrative, which privileges one culture. See Ball, "Stories of Origin," 2311.

39. Michaelsen, "American Indian Religious Freedom Litigation," 73–74. Michaelsen suggests a more specific erosion of authority, namely the need to meet legal standards to participate in the system.

40. *Selective Draft Law Cases* (1918), 376. For an interesting discussion of the evolution of religion and the military draft, see *United States v. Seeger* (1965). *Wisconsin v. Yoder* (1972).

41. Ball, "Stories of Origin," 2293.

## 5 – Constitutional Questions

1. D. Michael Quinn, *Early Mormonism and the Magic World View* (Salt Lake City: Signature Books, 1987). Marianne Perciaccante, "The Mormon-Muslim Comparison," *Muslim World* 82, nos. 3–4 (1992): 296–314. Jan Shipps, *Mormonism: The Story of a New Religious Tradition* (Urbana: University of Illinois Press, 1985). Leonard J. Arrington and Davis Bitton, *The Mormon Experience: A History of the Latter-Day Saints*, 2d ed. (Urbana: University of Illinois Press, 1992), 91–93. It is also worth noting that the RLDS Church has experienced significantly less growth than the Utah-based community, suggesting the value of difference within a culture as an identity-forming category.

2. Robert S. Michaelsen, "American Indian Religious Freedom Litigation: Promise and Perils," *Journal of Law and Religion* 3, no. 1 (1985): 61.

3. Joan Biskupic, "Changing Faiths," *Washington Post National Weekly Edition*, August 12–18, 1996, 23. When Supreme Court justice Clarence Thomas reaffiliated with the Catholic church, the composition of the Court shifted to include three Roman Catholics (Scalia, Kennedy, and Thomas), two Jews (Ginsburg and Breyer) and four Protestants (Rehnquist, Stevens, O'Connor, and Souter)—or five non-Protestants and four Protestants. There has never been a non-Protestant majority in either chamber of Congress.

4. The closest to any of these groups might be Justice George Sutherland, who was born in England and raised in Mormon country, though not himself a Mormon. Justice Sutherland served from 1922 to 1938, a period in which there were no significant cases involving the LDS Church. See Henry Abraham, *The Judicial Process: An Introductory Analysis of the Courts of the United States, England, and France*, 6th ed. (New York: Oxford University Press, 1993), 376. See also Thomas G. Alexander, *Mormonism in Transition: A History of the Latter-Day Saints, 1890–1930* (Urbana: University of Illinois Press, 1986), 26.

5. One current member of the Native American community participating in the American constitutional order is Sen. Ben Nighthorse Campbell (R-Colo.). However, the issue is complicated by questions surrounding ethnicity and religion—Campbell does not identify a religious affiliation.

6. Most of the Catholic and Jewish involvement with the dominant culture occurred on the state level, before the First Amendment was applied to state as well as congressional action. For an analysis of Muslim interaction with the American legal system, see Kathleen M. Moore, *Al-Mughtaribun: American Law and the Transformation of Muslim Life in*

*the United States* (Albany: State University of New York Press, 1995). Moore notes that "the preponderance of Muslim settlers in the United States have approximated the accommodationist model" upon settling in this country (138).

7. For an interesting discussion of this shift, see William R. Hutchison, ed., *Between the Times: The Travail of the Protestant Establishment in America, 1900–1960* (New York: Cambridge University Press, 1989).

8. See H. Frank Way, "Death of the Christian Nation: The Judiciary and Church-State Relations," *Journal of Church and State* 29, no. 3 (1987): 509–29; John K. Wilson, "Religion under the State Constitutions, 1776–1800," *Journal of Church and State* 32, no. 4 (1990): 753–73. Robert T. Handy, *A Christian America: Protestant Hopes and Historical Realities*, 2d ed. (New York: Oxford University Press, 1984); Robert T. Handy, *Undermined Establishment: Church-State Relations in America, 1880–1920* (Princeton, N.J.: Princeton University Press, 1991).

9. For an analysis of organized religious community involvement in Supreme Court cases, see Gregg Ivers, "Organized Religion and the Supreme Court," *Journal of Church and State* 32, no. 4 (1990): 775–93. For an analysis of organized religious community involvement in Congress, see Allen D. Hertzke, *Representing God in Washington: The Role of Religious Lobbies in the American Polity* (Knoxville: University of Tennessee Press, 1988). Alexander Hamilton, John Jay, and James Madison, *The Federalist: A Commentary on the Constitution of the United States* (1787; reprint, New York: Random House, 1937), no. 51, 339–40. Evidence of the health of organized religious political participation can be found in the broad coalition organized in support of the Religious Freedom Restoration Act, which included the liberal Religious Action Center of the Union of American Hebrew Congregations (Reform Judaism), the considerably more conservative National Association of Evangelicals, and virtually everything in between. Hertzke, *Representing God in Washington*.

10. Phillip E. Hammond, *The Protestant Presence in Twentieth-Century America: Religion and Political Culture* (Albany: State University of New York Press, 1992), 14 (emphasis in the original).

11. James Davison Hunter, *Culture Wars: The Struggle to Define America* (New York: Basic Books, 1991). The literature on conservative Christianity is wide and varied. Of particular importance for my purposes are the discussions of the roots of alienation from the American mainstream felt by members of this community. Two of particular note are Randall Balmer, *Mine Eyes Have Seen the Glory: A Journey into the Evangelical Subcul-*

*ture in America* (New York: Oxford University Press, 1991); and George M. Marsden, *Fundamentalism and American Culture: The Shaping of Twentieth-Century Evangelicalism, 1870–1925* (New York: Oxford University Press, 1980).

12. See Armand L. Mauss, *The Angel and the Beehive: The Mormon Struggle with Assimilation* (Urbana: University of Illinois Press, 1994).

13. Ronald Lawson, "Seventh-Day Adventists and the U.S. Courts: Road Signs along the Route of a Denominationalizing Sect," *Journal of Church and State* 40, no. 3 (1998): 553–88; James T. Richardson and John Dewitt, "Christian Science Spiritual Healing, the Law, and Public Opinion," *Journal of Church and State* 34, no. 3 (1992): 549–61; Kathleen M. Moore, *Al-Mughtaribun;* Chloe Anne Breyer, "Religious Liberty in Law and Practice: Vietnamese Home Temples and the First Amendment," *Journal of Church and State* 35, no. 2 (1993): 367–401.

14. For an argument on the evolution of the religious liberty away from specifically Christian sensibilities, see Phillip E. Hammond, *With Liberty for All: Freedom of Religion in the United States* (Louisville: Westminster/John Knox Press, 1998). For a description of continued legal battles for new religious movements, see William C. Shepherd, *To Secure the Blessings of Liberty: American Constitutional Law and the New Religious Movements* (Chico, Calif.: Scholars Press, 1985). Indeed, as I noted at the very beginning of this discussion, the Supreme Court was unwilling to affirm restrictions on the Santerian community in Hialeah, Florida, in part because the same restrictions were not imposed on everyone else.

15. See Phillip E. Hammond, *Religion and Personal Autonomy: The Third Disestablishment in America* (Columbia: University of South Carolina Press, 1992); Wade Clark Roof, *A Generation of Seekers: The Spiritual Journeys of the Baby Boom Generation* (San Francisco: Harper San Francisco, 1993); Roger Finke and Rodney Stark, *The Churching of America, 1776–1990: Winners and Losers in Our Religious Economy* (New Brunswick, N.J.: Rutgers University Press, 1992); and J. Gordon Melton, "Another Look at New Religions," *Annals of the American Academy of Political and Social Science* 527 (May 1993): 97–112.

16. Bruce B. Lawrence, *Defenders of God: The Fundamentalist Revolt against the Modern Age* (New York: Harper and Row, 1989), 7, 83.

17. See Mark Juergensmeyer, *The New Cold War? Religious Nationalism Confronts the Secular State* (Berkeley: University of California Press, 1993), esp. 4–6.

18. Ibid., 2, 147.

19. Jeffrey Kaplan, *Radical Religion in America: Millenarian Movements from the Far Right to the Children of Noah* (Syracuse, N.Y.: Syracuse University Press, 1997), 4, 61.

20. Ibid., 47–48.

21. Ibid., 54.

22. Ibid., 57.

23. Phillip E. Hammond, *The Protestant Presence*, 121.

24. Bette Novit Evans, *Interpreting the Free Exercise of Religion: The Constitution and American Pluralism* (Chapel Hill: University of North Carolina Press, 1997), 230, 231.

# Primary Sources

## Court Documents

Amicus Brief for Americans United for Separation of Church and State. *Church of Lukumi Babalu Aye, Inc., and Ernesto Pichardo v. City of Hialeah.* No. 91-948.

Appellant's Brief. *Alma Lovell v. City of Griffin.* No. 391.

Appellee's Brief. *West Virginia State Board of Education v. Barnette.* No. 591.

Brief for Appellant. *Davis v. Beason.* No. 1261.

Brief for the Appellees. *United States v. Late Corporation of the Church of Jesus Christ of Latter-day Saints.* No. 887.

Brief for the Indian Respondents. *Richard E. Lyng, Secretary of Agriculture, et al. v. Northwest Indian Cemetery Protective Association et al.* No. 86-1013.

Brief for the Indian Respondents in Opposition, On Petition for a Writ of Certiorari. *Richard E. Lyng, Secretary of Agriculture, et al. v. Northwest Indian Cemetery Protective Association et al.* No. 86-1013.

Brief for the Petitioner. *Thomas v. Review Board of the Indiana Employment Security Division.* No. 79-952.

Brief of Amici Curiae. *Richard E. Lyng, Secretary of Agriculture, et al. v. Northwest Indian Cemetery Protective Association et al.* No. 86-1013.

Brief of the American Civil Liberties Union as Amicus Curiae. *Musser v. Utah.* No. 1188.

Petition for Rehearing for the Native American Program, Oregon Legal Services. *Employment Division, Department of Human Resources of Oregon, et al. v. Smith et al.* No. 88-1213.

Respondent's Brief. *Minersville School District v. Gobitis.* No. 690.

## Court Decisions

*Badoni v. Higginson*, 638 F.2d 172 (1980).

*Bassett v. United States*, 137 U.S. 496 (1890).

*Bates v. United States*, 348 U.S. 966 (1955).

*Bevins v. Prindable*, 39 F.Supp. 708; affirmed, 314 U.S. 575 (1941).

*Bowen v. Roy*, 476 U.S. 693 (1986).

*Braunfeld v. Brown*, 366 U.S. 599 (1961).

*Brown v. Allen*, 344 U.S. 443 (1953).

*Cannon v. United States*, 116 U.S. 55 (1885), vacated, 118 U.S. 355 (1886).

*Cantwell v. Connecticut*, 310 U.S. 296 (1940).

*Certain Real Estate Known as the Gardo House v. United States*, 163 U.S. 680 (1896).

*Chaplinsky v. New Hampshire*, 315 U.S. 568 (1942).

*Chapman v. Handley*, 151 U.S. 443 (1894).

*Chatwin v. United States*, 326 U.S. 455 (1946).

*Cherokee Nation v. Georgia*, 30 U.S. (5 Peters) 1 (1831).

*Church of Lukumi Babalu Aye, Inc., and Ernesto Pichardo v. City of Hialeah*, 723 F.Supp. 1467 (S.D. Fla. 1989); affirmed without judgment, 936 F.2d. 586 (1991); reversed, 508 U.S. 520 (1993).

*Clawson v. United States*, 113 U.S. 143 (1885).

*Clawson v. United States*, 114 U.S. 477 (1885).

*Clayton v. Dickson*, 132 U.S. 632 (1890).

*Cleveland v. United States*, 329 U.S. 14 (1946).

*Clinton v. Englebrecht*, 80 U.S. (13 Wall.) 434 (1871).

*Coleman v. City of Griffin*, 55 Ga. App. 423, 189 S.E. 427; dismissed, 302 U.S. 636 (1937).

*Committee for Public Education and Religious Liberty v. Nyquist*, 413 U.S. 756 (1973).

*Cope v. Cope*, 137 U.S. 682 (1891).

*Corporation of the Presiding Bishop of the Church of Jesus Christ of Latter-day Saints v. Amos*, 483 U.S. 327 (1987).

*Cox v. New Hampshire*, 312 U.S. 569 (1940).

*Cox v. United States*, 332 U.S. 442 (1947).

*Davis v. Beason*, 133 U.S. 333 (1890).

*Davis v. United States*, 495 U.S. 472 (1990).

*DeMoss v. United States*, 349 U.S. 918 (1955).

*Dickson v. United States*, 346 U.S. 389 (1953).

*Douglas v. City of Jeanette*, 319 U.S. 157 (1943).

*Edwards v. California*, 314 U.S. 160 (1942).

*Elk v. Wilkins*, 112 U.S. 98 (1884).

*Employment Division, Department of Human Resources of Oregon, et al. v. Smith et al.*, 494 U.S. 872 (1990); rehearing denied 496 U.S. 913 (1990).

*Employment Division, Department of Human Resources of the State of Oregon v. Smith*, 485 U.S. 660 (1988).

*Estep v. United States*, 327 U.S. 114 (1946).

*Everson v. Board of Education*, 330 U.S. 1 (1947).

*Ex parte Crow Dog*, 109 U.S. 557 (1883).

*Ex parte Hudgings*, 249 U.S. 378 (1919).

*Ex parte Nielsen*, 131 U.S. 176 (1889).

*Falbo v. United States*, 320 U.S. 549 (1944).

*Fletcher v. Peck*, 10 U.S. (6 Cranch) 87 (1810).

*Follette v. Town of McCormick*, 321 U.S. 573 (1944).

*Fools Crow v. Gullet*, 706 F.2d 856 (1983).

*Fowler v. Rhode Island*, 345 U.S. 67 (1953).

*France v. Connor*, 161 U.S. 65 (1896).

*Gabrielli v. Knickerbocker*, 12 Cal. 2d 85, 82 P.2d 391; dismissed, 306 U.S. 621 (1939).

*Gibson v. United States*, 329 U.S. 338 (1946).

*Gitlow v. New York*, 268 U.S. 652 (1925).

*Gonzales v. United States*, 348 U.S. 407 (1955).

*Gonzales v. United States*, 364 U.S. 59 (1960).

*Hannan v. City of Haverhill*, 120 F.2d 87; cert. denied, 314 U.S. 641 (1941).

*Hering v. State Board of Education*, 118 N.J.L. 566, 194 A. 177; dismissed, 303 U.S. 624 (1938).

*Hussock v. New York*, 23 N.Y.S. 2d 520; cert. denied, 312 U.S. 659 (1941).

*In re Snow*, 120 U.S. 274 (1887).

*Jamison v. Texas*, 318 U.S. 413 (1943).

*Jehovah's Witnesses v. King County Hospital*, 278 F.Supp. 488; affirmed, 390 U.S. 598; rehearing denied, 391 U.S. 961 (1968).

*Johnson v. Deerfield*, 25 F.Supp. 918; affirmed, 306 U.S. 621; rehearing denied, 307 U.S. 650 (1939).

*Johnson v. McIntosh*, 21 U.S. (8 Wheat.) 543 (1823).

*Jones v. Opelika*, 316 U.S. 584; vacated, 319 U.S. 103 (1943).

*Kovacs v. Cooper*, 336 U.S. 77 (1949).

*Largent v. Texas*, 318 U.S. 418 (1943).

*The Late Corporation of the Church of Jesus Christ of Latter-day Saints v. United States*, 136 U.S. 1 (1890), amended, 140 U.S. 665 (1891), reversed, 150 U.S. 145 (1893).

*Leiby v. City of Manchester*, 117 F.2d 661; cert. denied, 313 U.S. 562 (1941).

*Leoles v. Lander*, 184 Ga. 580, 192 S.E. 218; dismissed, 302 U.S. 656 (1937).

*Lone Wolf v. Hitchcock*, 187 U.S. 553 (1903).

*Lovell v. City of Griffin*, 303 U.S. 444 (1938).

*Lynch v. Donnelly*, 465 U.S. 668 (1984).

*Lyng v. Northwest Indian Cemetery Protective Association*, 485 U.S. 439 (1988).

*Marsh v. Alabama*, 326 U.S. 501 (1946).

*Martin v. City of Struthers*, 319 U.S. 141 (1943).

*McGowan v. Maryland*, 366 U.S. 420 (1961).

*Miles v. United States*, 103 U.S. (13 Otto) 304 (1880).

*Minersville School District v Gobitis*, 310 U.S. 586 (1940).

*Morton v. Mancari*, 417 U.S. 535 (1973).

*Murdock v. Commonwealth of Pennsylvania*, 319 U.S. 105 (1943).

*Murphy v. Ramsey*, 114 U.S. 15 (1885).

*Musser v. Utah*, 333 U.S. 95 (1948).

*Niemotko v. Maryland*, 340 U.S. 268 (1951).

*Northwest Indian Cemetery Protective Association v. Peterson*, 565 F.Supp. 586 (1983); affirmed in part, 795 F.2d 688 (1986); reversed, 485 U.S. 439 (1988).

*Oliphant v. Suquamish Indian Tribe*, 435 U.S. 191 (1978).

*Pascone v. Massachusetts*, 308 Mass. 591, 33 N.E. 2d 522; cert. denied, 314 U.S. 641 (1941).

*Permoli v. First Municipality of the City of New Orleans*, 44 U.S. (3 How.) 589 (1845).

*Poulos v. New Hampshire*, 345 U.S. 395 (1953).

*Prince v. Massachusetts*, 321 U.S. 158 (1944).

*Quick Bear v. Leupp*, 210 U.S. 50 (1908).

Reynolds v. United States, 98 U.S. (8 Otto) 145 (1878).

Rutherford v. United States, 258 F. 855 (1919).

Saia v. New York, 334 U.S. 558 (1948).

Santa Clara Pueblo v. Martinez, 436 U.S. 49 (1978).

Schneider v. New Jersey (Town of Irvington), 308 U.S. 147 (1939).

Selective Draft Law Cases, 245 U.S. 366 (1918).

Sequoyah v. Tennessee Valley Authority, 620 F.2d 1159 (1980).

Sherbert v. Verner, 374 U.S. 398 (1963).

Sicurella v. United States, 348 U.S. 385 (1955).

Simmons v. United States, 348 U.S. 397 (1955).

Simon v. United States, 348 U.S. 967 (1955).

Snow v. United States, 118 U.S. 346 (1886).

Stephens v. Cherokee Nation, 174 U.S. 445 (1899).

Sunal v. Large, 332 U.S. 174 (1947).

Taylor v. Mississippi, 319 U.S. 583 (1943).

Tee-Hit-Ton Indians v. United States, 348 U.S. 272 (1955).

Thomas v. Review Board of the Indiana Employment Security Division, 450 U.S. 707 (1981).

Trent v. Hunt, 39 F.Supp. 373; affirmed, 314 U.S. 573 (1941).

Tucker v. Texas, 326 U.S. 517 (1946).

United States v. Ballard, 322 U.S. 78 (1944).

United States v. Irwin, 127 U.S. 125 (1888).

United States v. Kagama, 118 U.S. 375 (1886).

United States v. The Late Corporation of the Church of Jesus Christ of Latter-day Saints, 150 U.S. 145 (1893).

United States v. Means, 627 F.Supp. 247 (1985); reversed, 585 F.2d 404 (1988).

United States v. Nixon, 417 U.S. 683 (1974).

United States v. Nugent, 346 U.S. 1 (1953).

United States v. Rogers, 45 U.S. (4 How.) 567 (1846).

United States v. Seeger, 380 U.S. 163 (1965).

West Virginia State Board of Education v. Barnette, 319 U.S. 624 (1943).

Wilson v. Block, 708 F.2d 735 (1983).

Wisconsin v. Yoder, 406 U.S. 205 (1972).

Witmer v. United States, 348 U.S. 375 (1955).

Wooley v. Maynard, 430 U.S. 705 (1977).

Worcester v. Georgia, 31 U.S. (6 Peters) 515 (1832).

Young v. Godbe, 82 U.S. (15 Wall.) 562 (1872).

## Statutes

*Alien Immigration Amendments*, Ch. 128, 36 Stat. 263, 61st Congress, 2d sess. (March 26, 1910).

*Alien Labor Immigration Act*, Ch. 551, 26 Stat. 1084, 51st Congress, 2d sess. (March 3, 1891).

*American Indian Religious Freedom Act*, U.S. *Code*, vol. 42, sec. 1996 (1994).

*An Act to Establish a Territorial Government for Utah*, Ch. 51, 9 Stat. 453, 31st Congress, 1st sess. (September 9, 1850).

*Anti-Polygamy* (Morrill) *Act*, Ch. 126, 12 Stat. 501, 37th Congress, 2d sess. (July 1, 1862).

*Draft Act of 1917*, Public Law 12, 65th Congress, 1st sess. (May 18, 1917), 76.

*Eagle Protection Act*, U.S. *Code*, vol. 16, sec. 668 (1994).

*Endangered Species Act*, U.S. *Code*, vol. 16, secs. 1531–43 (1994).

*Indian Appropriation*, Public Law 120, 41st Congress, 3d sess. (March 3, 1871), 566.

*Indian Citizenship Act*, Public Law 175, 68th Congress, 1st sess. (June 2, 1924), 253.

*Indian Civil Rights Act*, U.S. *Code*, vol. 25, secs. 1301–03 (1994).

*Indian General Allotment* (Dawes) *Act*, U.S. *Code*, vol. 25, secs. 331–58 (1994).

*Indian Reorganization* (Wheeler-Howard) *Act*, U.S. *Code*, vol. 25, sec. 461 (1994).

*Polygamy* (Edmunds) *Act*, Ch. 47, 22 Stat. 30, 47th Congress, 1st sess. (March 22, 1882).

*Polygamy* (Edmunds-Tucker) *Act*, Ch. 397, 24 Stat. 635, 49th Congress, 2d sess. (March 3, 1887).

*Religious Freedom Restoration Act*, U.S. *Code*, vol. 42, secs. 2000bb-2000bb4 (1994).

*Selective Training and Service Act of 1940*, Public Law 783, 76th Congress, 3d sess. (16 September 1940), 885.

*Utah Territorial Courts* (Poland) *Act*, Ch. 469, 18 Stat. (Part 3) 253, 43d Congress, 1st sess. (June 23, 1874).

# Index